Mike Rossiter is the author of a number of best-selling books on military history – *Ark Royal*, *Sink the Belgrano*, *Target Basra*, *I Sank the Bismarck* (which he co-authored with John Moffat) and *Bomber Flight Berlin*.

WE FOUGHT AT ARNHEM

MIKE ROSSITER

CORGI BOOKS

TRANSWORLD PUBLISHERS
61–63 Uxbridge Road, London W5 5SA
A Random House Group Company
www.transworldbooks.co.uk

WE FOUGHT AT ARNHEM
A CORGI BOOK: 9780552162333

First published in Great Britain
in 2011 by Bantam Press
an imprint of Transworld Publishers
Corgi edition published 2012

Addresses for Random House Group Ltd companies outside the UK
can be found at: www.randomhouse.co.uk
The Random House Group Ltd Reg. No. 954009

Penguin Random House is committed to a sustainable future for
our business, our readers and our planet. This book is made from
Forest Stewardship Council® certified paper.

MIX
Paper from
responsible sources
FSC® C018179

Printed and bound in Great Britain by Clays Ltd, Elcograf S.p.A.
Typeset in 12/15.5pt Times New Roman by Falcon Oast Graphic Art Ltd.

10

CONTENTS

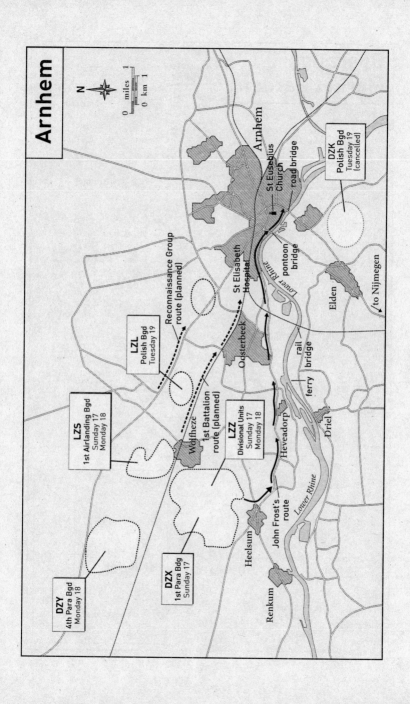

Arnhem

DZY
4th Para Bgd
Monday 18

DZX
1st Para Bdg
Sunday 17

LZS
1st Airlanding Bgd
Sunday 17
Monday 18

LZZ
Divisional Units
Sunday 17
Monday 18

LZL
Polish Bgd
Tuesday 19

Reconnaissance Group
route (planned)

1st Battalion
route (planned)

John Frost's
route

Renkum

Heelsum

Wolfheze

Heveadorp

Oosterbeek

St Elisabeth
Hospital

Driel

ferry

rail
bridge

Elden

Lower Rhine

Lower Rhine

St Eusebius
Church

road bridge

pontoon
bridge

Arnhem

DZK
Polish Bgd
Tuesday 19
[cancelled]

to Nijmegen

N

0   miles   1

0   km   1

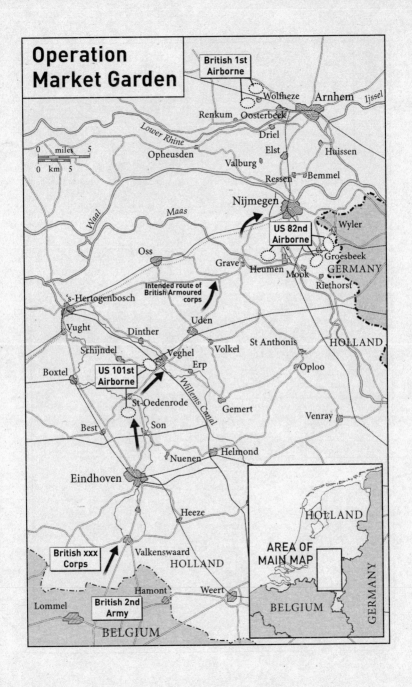

ACKNOWLEDGEMENTS

Clearly, I have a great many thanks to give to Ron Jordan, Tom Carpenter and Pat Gorman for their time and assistance in helping me with their stories. They put up with repeated questions by telephone and email, and lengthy and no doubt inconvenient visits without any complaint. They also gave me several maps and unpublished documents that I found extremely illuminating. They are truly remarkable people. Becks Skinner, at the Airborne Museum Archive in Duxford, helped me with some useful information, and Adam Harcourt-Webster's research was invaluable in helping to make sense of various accounts of the battle during a visit to Arnhem and Oosterbeek.

I would also like to thank my agent, Luigi Bonomi, and the staff at Transworld Publishers; in particular: editorial director Simon Thorogood, production editor Vivien Garrett and copy editor Brenda Updegraff, who transform my writing into something more logical and readable. The book wouldn't be complete without the work done by picture editor Sheila Lee and designer Philip Lord. All of them remain good humoured and unflappable in the face of indecision and missed deadlines. Finally, I must acknowledge the work of Madeline Toy, who does her best to ensure that the book gets before the public, and into your hands.

It isn't easy having a writer in the family. I would like to thank my wife Anne and my two sons Max and Alex for their forbearance while I wrote *We Fought At Arnhem*.

PREFACE

The battle for the rail and road bridges over the Rhine at Arnhem lasted for nine days, and almost 12,000 men took part in it. Each of these soldiers has his own unique story. Some of those stories are short, brutally ended when the men died in action. Others are well known, and have often been retold in the many books and films that have transformed what was officially known as Operation Market into a battle that has become synonymous with courage and fortitude.

This book tells just three of those stories, and they are of ordinary men who remain unknown beyond their immediate circle of friends and family. They all came from poor, working-class backgrounds, and they all, for a variety of reasons, volunteered to be airborne soldiers. Unknown as they are, their individual stories are still remarkable.

I first met Ron Jordan when I was working on the

search for the *Ark Royal*, and it is a matter of amazement to me that after serving in the navy he ended up at Arnhem. He introduced me to his mates, Pat Gorman, a young prizefighter before the war, and Tom Carpenter, a member of the Home Guard before he enlisted, both of them with gripping stories to tell.

Operation Market started to go wrong in the first few hours after the landings and it was a battle where, almost from the start, no one had a clear idea of the course of events. Even the most senior commanders were ignorant of what was happening to their men just a few miles away. Spread over a large area, the operation became disjointed and broken up, and the fighting, from 17 to 25 September 1944, took place in three separate locations. The three men who are the subjects of this book individually saw action in all the main parts of the battle – at the bridge itself, in the town of Arnhem and in the village of Oosterbeek. What is equally interesting, however, is what the three had experienced before the battle. None of the men at Arnhem arrived there without a history and a previous life. Like the three men in this book, most of them had grown up in a depression-hit country and had watched war approaching.

The men who fought in Arnhem had, like Ron and Pat, seen action in other theatres and other battles – even if, like Tom Carpenter, it was on the receiving end of the Battle of Britain and the Blitz. They were all volunteers, and they took pride in their training and their toughness. They had lived through the early years of the war when the situation looked hopeless, then at last had seen Britain's fortunes change. The landings on D-Day had been a success and it seemed to everyone that the German Army was in total retreat. Perhaps for the first time in five years of war it was possible to think of peace, for people realistically to see some light at the end of the tunnel.

Whatever the faults and mistakes made in the planning of Operation Market, it is important to understand the mood of optimism that existed in the summer of 1944, as well as the type of men who volunteered to take part in operations like the Arnhem landings. Tough, self-sufficient, they had no thought of defeat or surrender. But out of the 12,000 men who took part in the battle for Arnhem, 6,500 were taken prisoner, and I realized as I talked to the three airborne troops whose story I wanted to tell that their experiences as prisoners of war had been as important to them as the events of the battle itself. I take the view that it is artificial to describe a battle and the men taking part in it and imagine that there is a sudden, abrupt beginning and end. The people who landed at Arnhem did so not only with their own individual histories behind them, but for almost two thirds of them the battle continued after the last shots had been fired in Oosterbeek and they were marched, hands above their heads, towards imprisonment that lasted for another seven months. The stories of their time behind the wire are deeply moving, and are as revealing about their strength of character as are their recollections of parachute training or advancing towards the enemy.

Although this book is really the story of three men who fought in Arnhem, I hope that it will tell the reader some of the history of the airborne forces. It will also describe how Operation Market and the associated advance of the land forces to the bridges across the Rhine, Operation Garden, originated and how the combined plans unfolded.

Together, Operation Market Garden, as the joint operation was called, was considered a failure by many who took part in it and had to witness the destruction of a British airborne division. Any number of books have been written seeking to point the finger at the men who were responsible for the failure to capture the bridges at Arnhem and attempting to enumerate the reasons why the operation was doomed from the start. I do not intend this book to be one of them, but after I had started interviewing I found that one of my subjects, Tom Carpenter, had been witness to one of the early failures – failure to secure the railway bridge before moving on to the road bridge. I was not aware until then that there was a longstanding dispute about whose task it had been to capture the rail bridge.

The 9th Field Company, Tom Carpenter's unit, insist that they were instructed to secure it and that they were surprised by the arrival of a company from the 2nd Battalion who advanced on the German defenders with guns firing. If the rail bridge had been taken intact on that Sunday afternoon, it might have transformed the outcome of the battle. British forces would have had an alternative route to the road bridge, and the 1st Airborne Division would have been able to capture a greater part of Arnhem. But it is important to bear in mind the word 'might'. None of the other errors and problems that contributed to the failure of the operation would have disappeared. There are so many imponderables in war that nothing can be predicted with any certainty. It is a military truism that no plan survives contact with the enemy. So rather than pursue a pointless debate, I tell the story of the rail bridge as Tom described it to me, because this is fundamentally a book about the experiences of three men in the 1st Airborne Division.

Their story starts in peacetime, as they grew up facing a world that appeared to have little use for them. Political tensions rose in Europe, war started and they went into it, willingly more or less, driven by patriotism and young men's dreams of adventure. They volunteered for one of the toughest jobs in the armed services, fought hard and were taken prisoner. They survived experiences that almost nobody in the West has had to endure for a generation. They returned home into a different peace.

Field Marshal Montgomery, who fought for and instigated the disaster that was Operation Market, wrote, 'In years to come, it will be a great thing for a man to be able to say, "I fought at Arnhem".' This then is the story of three men who did just that.

1

THE UNBREAKABLE BOND

September 1944–September 2009

Pat Gorman lay flat, his mate Jonty Bright slightly to the side. Around him were other men, strangers from the 2nd Battalion, South Staffordshire Regiment, and a few from his own 11th Battalion, 4th Parachute Brigade. They were all pressed into what cover they could find, in hedges, the gutter of the cobbled road, crouched behind a bullet-chipped garden wall. A grey mist rose off the black surface of the Rhine to their right. Above Pat, smoke drifted in the air, and his nostrils were filled with the stink of cordite and burned wood and rubber. Ahead of him there was a flickering red light from blazing buildings around the bridge. That was the objective. That was where he and Jonty were headed. But they weren't in the desert, or the scrub of some heath, where they could duck and dive, find some cover and a flanking route. They could only go forward. Forward down a narrow street with buildings on either side. A street where German machine guns would be firing, at knee height, on lines already calculated and fixed.

The sky in the east was lightening and soon it would be time to move. From a few hundred yards ahead came the sharp rattle of the German machine guns and the single shots of rifles and Sten guns. To his right along the lower road by the river there were shouts and screams, and the flash of gunfire from the far bank. He eased the strap of his helmet and shifted the grip on his PIAT anti-tank weapon, a 3-foot-long tube, 8 inches in diameter, which was cumbersome and heavy. He had had nothing to drink since yesterday afternoon and his mouth was parched. Pat was scared, and he didn't have to ask how Jonty felt. But that was all right. He was used to it. Every time he stepped out of a plane he felt fear and faced it head on. Everyone did. He was in a foreign country, surrounded by enemy soldiers and frightened, but what else was he going to do but fight?

Ahead of him now there was more gunfire. He could hear the noise of engines and tank tracks on the cobbles, and the louder reverberating crack of a German 88mm gun. There were shouts from up ahead, urgent, 'PIAT gunner, where's a PIAT gunner?' A sergeant loomed out of the dark behind him. 'Go on, lads, move up, move up.' Pat got to his feet, shifted his pack and his awkward PIAT and ran up the hill at a crouch. Jonty was close behind with his pack of anti-tank rounds. The air seemed thick with flying metal. They passed a smashed overturned tram, bodies like bags of rubbish lying on the road and pavement. An area of scrub and trees shielded the road as it approached the crest of the hill, and they moved closer to it for cover. Bullets were zipping down the road, and now a mortar bomb exploded in the trees, whipping shrapnel and splinters through the air. Red tracer was spinning lazily towards them from the far bank. There were more bodies, and Pat and Jonty started crawling, keeping low on their elbows and toes, the hail of bullets seeming intense and impenetrable.

Pat looked for a tank on the skyline, a silhouette, anything that would reveal its presence. This was the bad part – not getting close, but rising up, putting the PIAT to his shoulder. That was when a Jerry would spot him and send a bullet his way, no longer random but aimed. But he couldn't see any sign of a Panzer or a self-propelled gun. They probably had to go further, to the brow of the hill, where he could already see crouched shapes and gun flashes against the sombre sky. The noise of battle was over-powering, the screams and shouts of soldiers mingling with the explosions of mortars and grenades, the rattle of Sten guns and machine pistols firing. An officer stood silhouetted against the sky-line, looking down. He would know what was up. Pat looked around, then launched himself forward once more. The officer turned and saw them. 'It's all right.

You can go back.' Then there was an overwhelming explosion by his side, a blinding flash; the breath was punched from his lungs and he knew that he was being hurled through the air.

A very long while later, Pat Gorman, Ron Jordan and Tom Carpenter sit at a table in the busy Schoonoord café at the crossroads of the Utrechtsweg and the Pietersbergsweg in Oosterbeek, Holland. Uniformly dressed in blue blazers and smartly pressed grey trousers, they are elderly, in their eighties, and each has a discreet winged parachute badge pinned to his lapel. They talk quietly, occasionally lifting a glass of Amstel lager, nodding and saying hello to other men and women as they pass their table. Ron Jordan, tanned and slim, still with a twinkle in his eye for the ladies, occasionally leans forward to catch what one or other of his companions is saying. Pat Gorman is the shortest of the three, but even at his age solidly built, and the quietest of the group. Tom Carpenter is the tallest, thin and still deserving of his old nickname 'Long Shins'. It is Sunday evening, the end of a warm, balmy weekend in September, and the three men are tired, content to reflect on the events of the past three days and the reason why they are there.

They all travelled to Holland the previous Friday for the annual ceremony of Remembrance for those who died in the Battle of Arnhem, on the banks of the Rhine. Here, in September 1944, 10,000 soldiers of the British 1st Airborne Division had landed by parachute and glider, 63 miles behind German lines, in an attempt to capture the two key bridges that crossed the river.

The Rhine brings barge traffic north from the industrial towns of Germany to the great port of Rotterdam, but a few miles before Arnhem the stream of heavy barges diverts on to the wide, fast-flowing River Waal, which passes through the town of Nijmegen, some 9 miles south of Arnhem. The Rhine at Arnhem is narrower than the Waal, but is still about 180 yards across, with a strong current, and smaller barges navigate the marked channel to Amsterdam.

The effort to capture the road and rail bridges at Arnhem was the final piece of a massive airborne operation that promised the seizure not only of the huge road bridge over the Waal at Nijmegen but of a further six bridges over rivers and canals further south, at Eindhoven, Grave and Son. The hoped-for simultaneous capture of these key bridges and the roads that connected them was to provide a route for the rapid advance of the British Second Army into Germany. If the plan succeeded, it would, according to the senior staff, shorten the war by six months.

So it was that, in September 1944, Tom Carpenter, Pat Gorman and Ron Jordan of the 1st Airborne Division landed in fields and open countryside some miles away from Arnhem. The airborne troops found that they had to make their way through the adjoining village of Oosterbeek to reach their target. When they dropped out of the skies, Oosterbeek still looked as it had before the war – a small, prosperous village surrounded by hilly woods dotted with substantial villas for retired colonial administrators and rubber-growers from the Dutch East Indies; it was a popular resort for walkers and ramblers.

There was some desperate fighting around the road bridge in Arnhem, but the battle soon spread west-wards. It reached the outskirts of Oosterbeek and then, like a giant rampaging monster, it hit the centre of the village. The headquarters of the 1st Airborne Division was set up in a hotel barely 100 yards from the Schoonoord café. Gradually the German forces squeezed the troops in Oosterbeek into a smaller and smaller area. Casualties were extremely heavy and many men died at the very crossroads where, fifty-five years later, the three veterans now sit quietly sipping their glasses of lager. The ground floor of the Schoonoord had served as a main dressing station for the British troops – a place of great pain and suffering.

The fighting between the British paratroopers and the occupying German forces caused many Dutch civilian deaths and wrought enormous destruction in both Arnhem and Oosterbeek. Despite this, the local population was deeply moved by the fact that so many young men of the 1st Airborne had fought and died to liberate them. The first memorial service for those soldiers who died in the battle was organized by the local authorities just a few years after the war, coinciding with the creation of an official war grave for the dead on the northern outskirts of Oosterbeek. Many veterans of the landings were invited to Arnhem for this memorial service and this started the tradition of an annual commemoration that continued, past the fiftieth anniversary and then the sixtieth, with the numbers of old members of the 1st Airborne Division slowly dwindling. Despite this, the people of the area have been determined to keep the memory of the battle alive, and each succeeding generation makes sure that the commemoration is as well organized as ever. The ceremonies take place over a long weekend, and the Schoonoord café becomes for those few days the meeting point for the remaining veterans of the Battle of Arnhem.

Most of the veterans arrived early on Friday, as had Ron, Pat and Tom, and they had settled quickly into a routine with which they were now very familiar. They had gone that Friday evening to the bridge over the Rhine in Arnhem. Much of the old stonework still showed the scars of fighting, and Tom Carpenter could still pick out the grooves and marks in the steps where a 6-pounder gun had been man-handled up an embankment on to the road. Here the veterans took part in a brief ceremony on the bridge itself, where the old battle standards of the 1st Airborne were carried on parade. Then they walked to the civic centre to be addressed by the mayor and other members of the local council, before standing to attention while wreaths were laid on the nearby war memorial.

The next morning, Saturday, they travelled out of Oosterbeek to one of the drop zones, DZX, where 500 paratroopers from the current 4th Battalion the Parachute Regiment were due to put on a display. It was a fine day, with clear skies and almost no wind, perfect for a parachute drop. A crowd of almost 20,000 people had assembled there, and the hubbub in the catering tents and marquees had almost drowned the noise of the approaching aircraft, flying low, their four turbo-prop engines whistling and their rear cargo ramps open. As the paratroopers stepped out over the ramps into the air, their parachutes blossoming open to let them slowly descend, a silence passed over the crowd and the white canopies fell to earth in a moment of quiet and individual reflection.

The three veterans had mingled with the throng of locals, dignitaries, the young soldiers who had just dropped out of the sky and other members of the Dutch and the British Armies. They accepted the odd drink and pleasantly reminded the fit, polite young men that soldiering had changed a lot since their day.

On Sunday an event was staged to reproduce exactly what had happened at the first memorial. Pat, Tom and Ron could hardly bear to watch it. A thousand children from Arnhem and Oosterbeek, girls and boys ranging in age from ten to eighteen, formed up in a row and moved forward with their wreaths of fresh flowers towards the rows of spare white gravestones. Gently, the young children, in total silence, laid their blooms on the last resting place of men and boys who had died just a few years older than they were. It brought tears to the eyes of those watching, and gripped the hearts of Ron and his comrades.

This was the last formal event of the weekend, and the veterans have now returned to the Schoonoord, where they exchange information and gossip about comrades no longer fit enough to travel, or who have died in the past year. They talk about former companions who are no longer able to make the trip, and about those who died long ago and lie buried in the cemetery across the railway line.

Like many old friends, the three sitting round the table reminisce and tell each other familiar stories. Occasionally Tom Carpenter likes to remind the others that he was the first of the three to land at Arnhem and actually completed the mission. Pat Gorman, in response, usually points out that, if it was a question of being first, he beat both the others to a landing in occupied Europe by several months. Ron Jordan keeps his counsel, but if pressed will argue that his exploits were the most remarkable because he ought never to have been at Arnhem at all, and certainly not in the 1st Airborne Division. In 1944 they were all young men from working-class backgrounds, but they had come by chance and by very different routes to the killing ground of Arnhem. In between the banter, each returns to his own thoughts, remembering who he was and what he had done a lifetime before. Amidst the public gatherings, the veterans have private memories that were roused when the cut flowers dropped on the graves, and when they each made private visits to the cemetery on Saturday evening to pay their own respects to old friends and comrades buried there.

Ron had gone at around six o'clock that Saturday evening with two bunches of flowers. Limping slightly, he walked through the main entrance of the cemetery, past the memorial stone, and stepped on to the green-grassed square in the middle. He walked on for a few yards before turning to the right, then walked through seven rows of graves to one set in the middle of a rank. He stood and put the flowers down gently before the headstone, inscribed I. J. BREWSTER, CRAFTSMAN ROYAL ELECTRICAL AND MECHANICAL ENGINEERS. Ivor Brewster had been younger than Ron, and had been his assistant and mate; Ivor had looked to Ron for advice and guidance. Ron stood for a few minutes, remembering, as though the sixty-five years had passed in an instant, that moment in the casualty station when he had grasped Ivor's hand and poured a few drops of stale water on to the parched lips of his badly wounded companion, the blood seeping from the bandages around his smashed and torn hip and thigh. Ivor had looked up at Ron and, above the crash of the bursting mortar shells and the screams and groans of the wounded in the cellar, he had begged Ron to kill him. The foetid smell of dried blood, brick dust, cordite and fear remains with Ron, as horrifying now as it was then, despite the passing years.

After a while Ron stirred, then, carrying his remaining bunch of flowers, searched out another grave – strangely, amongst those of men of the 1st Airborne Division, that of a member of the Fleet Air Arm, Air Mechanic Kenneth Hooker. Ken had taken up the invitation to fly in a Stirling, a four-engined bomber that had been converted to a glider tug. He, like many people, had thought that the Arnhem operation would be an exciting day out from which he would return that afternoon. He had not, and Ron, being an old Fleet Air Arm man as well as a member of the 1st Airborne, took it upon himself to remember him.

Like all the men who fought at Arnhem, Pat, Ron and Tom had volunteered to be airborne soldiers, although they were quite different from each other in how and why they did so. After the war, they all married and enjoyed the delights of their children and family life, but the Battle of Arnhem and its aftermath had changed them for ever. They saw and did things that no one should have to see or do, and the fact that their separate lives took them to that small Dutch town in September 1944 gave them an unbreakable bond. Each of them was in a different unit. Each saw a different aspect of the battle. But what they have in common is that they can say, 'We fought at Arnhem.' They share that and the fact that, as they grew up and saw a war start once again in Europe, they had no idea of how badly it would affect them, or of the extreme demands of courage and resilience that would be made of them. This is the bond that binds them.

2

A TASTE OF WAR

1938–1940

Ron Jordan was born in a two-up, two-down terraced house in Aston, Birmingham on 5 September 1920, one of twins. His father had been a sergeant in the Royal Garrison Artillery during the First World War, but he remembers little of him because his father died when Ron was three, leaving his mother, Violet, to bring him up with five brothers and a sister. It was, naturally, a tough life. Violet had been trained as a nurse before she got married and knew the value of education, but although Ron did well at school and passed his matriculation exams, there wasn't enough money in the house to send him to grammar school. His older brothers already had jobs in the local foundry, which was heavy and dirty work, but because of his skill at maths Ron was able to find a place in the machine shop at the nearby

Rover car factory. Even then, money was so short that he could not afford to accept the low pay of an apprentice, so received no formal engineering training in the factory.

Life was cramped in the small house in Marryam Close, so at the age of fifteen Ron and his twin brother joined the Territorial Army. It gave them the opportunity to get away from the working-class terraced streets and experience a more active life in the countryside. Whether it was a way to pay homage to his half-remembered father is difficult to say, but as he got older he became increasingly disenchanted with life in the Rover factory and three years after joining the Territorial Army he decided to sign up for the Royal Marines. Like most eighteen-year-olds, he had little idea of what this meant; his overriding motive was a desire for some excitement and glamour. A recruiting poster stuck up outside the local police station showing a group of marines manning a gun-turret, with a background of the Rock of Gibraltar in bright sunlight, did the trick. It seemed a perfect opportunity finally to escape the humdrum routine of clocking in at the factory in Birmingham.

The recruiting officer sat Ron down and set him a few questions to test his basic skills in maths and English. Ron had no problem with the papers and when the chief petty officer gave him some more difficult tests, he had no trouble with them either.

'Son,' the officer said, 'you will be wasted in the marines.'

It was 1938 and the Royal Navy was about to regain control of its aircraft from the Royal Air Force.

'I have just the job for you,' the officer continued. 'How would you like to work with guns and bombs as an armourer in the Fleet Air Arm?'

With the navy Ron would get the opportunity to travel all over the world. It seemed as good as, if not better than, the marines. Ron was also surprised and pleased to discover that he had some talents that others found promising, so he signed up.

His three years in the Territorial Army had already taught him the basics of military life, so he was immediately given the role of leader in his squad of fellow recruits, directing them in the routines of parade-ground drill, presenting arms and so on. He was treated with respect and enjoyed the six weeks' initial training before starting his six-month course at the Royal Air Force Air Armaments school in Eastleigh, near Southampton. He went through a comprehensive programme that taught the repair and maintenance of various machine guns, and the storage, carriage and fusing of bombs, bullets and torpedoes – any type of weapon, in fact, that could be fitted or used by an aircraft in the navy. It was these skills, learned when he was just eighteen years old, that led to his eventual arrival at Arnhem. Even now he can identify a bullet or shell with one glance.

Ron's course was just about to end when Germany invaded Poland and the British government declared war. It was 3 September 1939. The following day he was woken in his barracks at 4 a.m. and the whole armaments school was ordered to pack in preparation for evacuation. Not only their own kit but the bedding, equipment, desks and blackboards were all loaded on to a waiting train, where they were told they were to be relocated to the Isle of Sheppey in the Thames estuary. The train journeyed throughout the day, stopping in sidings, reversing for hours, until they arrived, not on the Isle of Sheppey but in a new airfield in Wales, at Pembrey.

Ron and his mates had enjoyed their time at Eastleigh. It had been a well-run establishment where there was a cloth and a vase of flowers on each of the mess tables. Pembrey had not achieved such refinements, but in two weeks they had completed their course and were then to discover what a hardship post really meant.

The main base of the Royal Navy's Home Fleet was the open anchorage in the Orkney Islands, Scapa Flow. Earlier in 1939 work had started on an airfield at Hatston, near Kirkwall on the Mainland of Orkney, which would be a base for anti-submarine aircraft and provide some air defence for the fleet. The work had not been finished by the time the war started, so when Ron and two others from the course arrived they found to their disbelief that their living accommodation was a row of bell tents.

Just before they arrived, a German U-boat had penetrated the anchorage of Scapa Flow and fired torpedoes at a veteran First World War battleship, HMS *Royal Oak*. The submarine had escaped and its captain, Günther Prien, was hugely feted in Berlin. This propaganda blow, as well as the loss of the ship with 833 casualties, spurred plans to enlarge the base at Hatston. Consequently, for much of the winter, which was one of the hardest on record, the air station was a sea of mud. For months Ron never wore anything on his feet except Wellington boots. Apart from this discomfort, he, like most of the young men on his armaments course, had no qualms about the war. It was the chance, he felt, of 'seeing some action', and he got it in the Orkneys.

Ron had proved to be a good marksman in the Territorial Army and he was put in charge of a twin Lewis-gun mounting that had been set up for anti-aircraft protection. There were regular overflights by German aircraft. Some were spying on the fleet, but there were also some raids by German bombers, mainly single hit-and-run raids, but sometimes a section of three planes making low-level daylight bombing runs on the runways. These incursions were Ron's first real taste of warfare, the Lewis guns hammering away as he fired. The gun was so loud that on one occasion he didn't even hear the explosion of a bomb that landed barely 30 yards away from him. The first he knew of it was when he turned and saw the crater behind him slowly exuding wisps of smoke from the pulverized earth.

Life was extremely uncomfortable at Hatston over

that winter – muddy, cold and wet – but the worst aspect of Ron's time there was boredom. The raids were infrequent, and checking the guns and depth charges of the Swordfish aircraft that set out on their regular anti-submarine patrols soon fell into a monotonous routine. There were too few opportunities to attack the enemy as far as Ron was concerned. However, this changed on 9 April 1940 when German forces invaded Denmark and Norway. Two squadrons of navy Skua dive-bombers – 800 and 803 Squadrons – were temporarily based at Hatston and on 10 April they combined to carry out a dive-bombing attack on a German cruiser, *Königsberg*, at anchor in Bergen harbour in Norway. The warship was severely damaged, set on fire and sank two hours later. It was a first for the fledgling Naval Air Service and a great boost for morale, particularly at Hatston.

Ron had enthusiastically fused the bombs for the raid, but he knew that both these squadrons were shortly going to be based once more on aircraft carriers at sea and he wanted to go with them. He and a fellow armourer named Hollingsworth badgered their senior officer for a posting on a boat – a phrase that didn't go down well: Ron was continually being reminded 'They're ships, not boats'. Nevertheless, their persistence eventually paid off. One morning shortly after the mission against the *Königsberg*, the petty officer marched into the armourer's office and told them, 'You want to go to sea, well, get your kit double quick. I've got two posts!' Within a day, they were on board HMS *Ark Royal* as part of the complement of 800 Squadron.

Neither Ron nor his mate Hollingsworth had ever been to sea. Ron was amazed at how crowded the ratings' mess decks were and at the lack of personal space. They slung their hammocks above the mess tables, which he found disconcerting. 'At breakfast you could be eating your boiled egg and suddenly a great hairy matelot's foot would be standing next to it. But you got used to it.'

They were treated to all the tricks that were played on new recruits. The first night a lump of rancid bacon was hung up by the air vent to see if it would encourage any feelings of seasickness, but they survived and quickly became part of the company. As armourers on the squadron, they were separate from the routine of the ship and were allowed to stay in their hammocks if they were off duty. The decks were cleared and swabbed beneath them.

Serving on *Ark Royal* had a profound effect on Ron. In the Territorial Army the equipment he had used had been from the First World War, or else a rough-and-ready expedient. Artillery carriages had been mule-drawn limbers that had been modified so they could be hitched up to a 15cwt lorry. Sometimes on exercises removal lorries had been employed to help carry the kit and tow some of the trailers, so Ron had developed a poor opinion of the general level of mechanization of the armed forces. Even at Hatston, the machinery was primitive. On the *Ark*, however, everything was modern and efficient, and for the first time Ron was confident that the war would go well. There were no time-servers on board quick to find a reason not to do anything; almost all the crew, from the junior ratings' mess decks to the captain's bridge, were, he felt, determined to give the task in hand a hundred per cent. He felt confident and buoyed up. It was a good thing that he did, because he was about to learn what the front line was all about.

Ron's role was to be the armourer on the Skua of Captain Dick Partridge, commanding officer of 800 Squadron. The *Ark* was carrying out operations in support of the British Army that had landed in Norway after the German invasion. Patrolling north of the Arctic Circle, the *Ark*'s aircraft were flying raids against German forces, providing air cover for British troops on land and for the naval support ships and supply vessels patrolling along the coast and navigating the fjords. As the year advanced from spring to summer, the days lengthened until it was possible for operations to be carried out around the clock. The Luftwaffe (Germany's air force) also benefited from this, launching air strikes throughout the twenty-four hours. *Ark Royal* was a prime target.

The first few air attacks Ron experienced were gut-wrenchingly frightening, in part because there was nothing for him to do except wait out the attack inside the hangars. The noise of bombs exploding nearby was accompanied by the clatter of shrapnel against the hull and on the flight deck. The 4.5in anti-aircraft guns would be blasting away, and the pom-pom, a gun made up of eight linked Vickers 2-pounders, would start firing as the bombers came closer and closer. Ron would be sheltering in the hangar, trapped between the closed fire curtains, next to high-octane fuel pipes and trolleys carrying 500lb bombs, listening as the explosions got closer and closer.

The anxiety that Ron felt when the *Ark* was under attack never went away, but he learned to put it aside. As soon as the guns stopped firing, he would be called upon to spring quickly into action and prepare aircraft for ranging on the flight deck. There were also plenty of other things to do during lulls in the action. The guns of returning aircraft had to be inspected and their ammunition panniers reloaded. A mixture of various types of cartridges – tracer, ball and armour-piercing – was poured into special machines on the hangar deck that would automatically make up cartridge links of 600 rounds apiece. Sometimes after a very heavy attack Ron had to go out on deck and shovel away the cartridge cases from around the pom-pom mount. The *Ark* always came through unscathed, but Ron knew that the battle was being lost. There were many incidents when aircraft would return trailing black smoke, with bullet holes in the wings and fuselage and with a wounded pilot or observer. Then the flight deck would be quickly cleared and the damaged aircraft given priority for landing.

Often aircraft would just not return, but there was, Ron remembers, a regular rotation of aircrew who had been shot down over Norway and had managed to parachute to safety. If they evaded the German patrols they were often able to escape and would appear on board again a week or so later. The heaviest losses of the Norwegian campaign, however, occurred in the attack on the German cruiser *Scharnhorst*, and that operation is a particularly vivid memory for Ron.

Ark Royal was operating off the Norwegian coast in company with another, older aircraft carrier, HMS *Glorious*. On 10 May 1940 the German Army launched its rapid advance into Belgium, Holland and then France, and in doing so quickly shifted the emphasis of the British war effort. A plan for British troops to seize the Norwegian port of Narvik from German occupation had been developed, but it was now radically altered in the light of the German invasion of the Low Countries. The landings were to go ahead, but the troops were merely to destroy the port facilities before abandoning the town. They landed on 28 May and by 8 June the last of the troops were embarking. *Glorious*, accompanied by two destroyers, HMS *Acasta* and HMS *Ardent*, was heading back to Scapa Flow with a squadron of Hurricane aircraft on her flight deck. A German flotilla led by the cruisers *Scharnhorst* and *Gneisenau*, on its way to intercept the convoy carrying the last of the British troops, came across *Glorious* and started a pursuit. The two British destroyers bravely attacked the German warships but in the process were both sunk.

Glorious had none of her Swordfish aircraft ready to fly and was defenceless. *Scharnhorst* opened fire and within twenty-five minutes *Glorious* was on fire and sinking. One thousand five hundred sailors were killed.

Scharnhorst continued her patrol, but after failing to find the troop ships that were being escorted by *Ark Royal* she sailed on and berthed in Trondheim Fjord. The Admiralty thought that this would provide an opportunity to sink her and asked *Ark Royal* to mount an attack with a large force of Skua dive-bombers. The target was kept secret, but Ron and the other armourers and riggers knew that something out of the ordinary was being planned. Fifteen aircraft were to be armed and ranged on the flight deck ready for take-off – a far higher number than normal.

Captain Partridge was going to take off last and his Skua was therefore at the very end of the flight deck. As the aircraft started their engines, Ron was assisting the observer, Lieutenant Robin Bostock, to strap in and check his rear-firing Vickers gun. The lead aircraft had started their engines, running up to full power before the pilots signed Form 700 to accept the planes from the maintenance crew. The noise was rising and the wash from the propellers was powerful. It was going to be a lengthy flight to the anchorage at Trondheim and back and Bostock wanted extra tins of yellow dye to mark the waypoints on the surface of the ocean. He mouthed his request to Ron, who jumped off the wing and threaded his way through the assembled aircraft to a locker at the side of the flight deck. On his way back he had to keep his head down and fight against the current of air that was being blasted over the flight deck by the Skuas' propellers. He climbed up to the cockpit and, as he handed the tins over, Captain Partridge pushed the throttle of his own aircraft forward. Ron was blown back off the wing. He hit the deck and rolled under the tail plane, finally tumbling over the rear of the flight deck into the safety nets, from where, looking down, he could see the white, boiling wake from the propellers as the *Ark* itself gathered speed. He lay bruised and grazed as the fifteen aircraft took off and formed up, then it was safe for some of the deck ratings to come down and haul him to safety. Attacks by German bombers on the *Ark* had become so frequent and threatening that Ron had taken to carrying a small hip flask of brandy with his life jacket in case he had to abandon ship, but he thought that now was as good a time as any to have a hefty swig.

He had recovered sufficiently to be waiting for the call to the flight deck to assist in the recovery of the returning aircraft, make sure that the guns were safe and get them into the crowded hangar decks. It had been a long wait, and the mood on the *Ark* darkened as the first Skuas were seen approaching.

Many had been hit and showed signs of damage; far fewer arrived back than had taken off. Only eight managed to land. The *Ark* stayed on station for another forty-five minutes, but no more aircraft returned. Seven had been lost. Ron waited in vain for the return of Captain Partridge and Lieutenant Bostock. Partridge, it would later transpire, had been taken prisoner, but Bostock had been killed by gunfire from a German Messerschmitt 109. Despite the loss of fourteen aircrew, dead or captured, *Scharnhorst* had emerged from the attack undamaged.

Some of the personal belongings of the missing non-commissioned aircrew were raffled off to raise money for their families. The destruction of almost half the *Ark*'s Skua force on one inconsequential mission was a heavy blow and the carrier departed for the UK with the crew in a sombre mood. In the few weeks that Ron had been on board the *Ark* he had seen and experienced the real face of war. The fear he had felt during the first air attacks had subsided, and he was now glad to be where he was. The *Ark* was a fine ship with a good crew, and he could not imagine going back to a life based on shore again.

They sailed south, into warmer weather, and before long the old hands on board were informing everyone that they were bound for Gibraltar. They were right – by 27 June the *Ark* was tied up at the mole by the huge three-legged crane and Ron was enjoying the Mediterranean sun. This was what he had joined up for. It was a welcome respite from the stress and effort of the fighting in Norway, at least for a few days. On one manoeuvre, Ron saw a large passenger liner, heading west, all its lights blazing and passengers on the promenade deck, with the sound of a dance band carrying across the water. It sailed, unchallenged, oblivious to the great darkened warships a few cable-lengths away, and Ron, fresh from the turmoil of the Norwegian campaign, looked at it as though it were a vision of a mythical past. It was headed, he assumed, to America, to peace and safety.

The *Ark* was to see some hot action in the Med, but it was the events of a routine patrol that would change the course of the war for Ron. It was September and a flight of Skuas was returning to the *Ark*, one of them showing signs of engine trouble. One aircraft had already landed and Ron helped manhandle it on to the lift to take it down to the hangar. There was some urgency to get the lift back to the flight deck so that the second Skua, which by now had smoke pouring from its engine, could get down. Moving around the main landing gear, Ron slipped on the oily, salty deck and his foot fell under one of the Skua's main wheels. The pain was excruciating – and he saw that a glistening white bone had pierced his canvas deck shoe. He lost consciousness at that point, and awoke to find himself recovering from an anaesthetic in *Ark Royal's* sick bay.

This was the start of several extremely painful

months, during which surgeons, first in Gibraltar, then on a hospital ship, then again in Broad Green Hospital in Liverpool, tried to rebuild the crushed bones. The final operation required a long period under anaesthetic. When Ron awoke he discovered several orderlies pinning him down while he shouted out, 'Load, you buggers, load.' In a half-waking nightmare he was desperately firing one of *Ark Royal*'s 4.5in guns at an attacking German bomber. The stress of the constant air raids in the Norwegian sea had finally surfaced.

Ron spent five months in hospital. At the end of this period of sometimes painful treatment, the surgeon told him his foot was now almost healed and should present no further problems. He went to the Naval Hospital in Gosport, where after a few days he was told to put on his uniform and report to a chief petty officer.

After being told that he had over £30 back pay owing to him, he was ushered into a boardroom where he was astounded to see a vice-admiral, two captains and an officer surgeon. The surgeon asked him how he felt, then told him that he had been assessed at 40 per cent disability and was therefore discharged from the Royal Navy. Ron was utterly shocked. He could not believe his ears. 'I cried real tears. I asked if there was a position on shore that I could take up. No, they said. I was stunned. Despite the horrible times in Norway, I loved the life, I loved it.'

Dismissed, he walked in shock back to the ward, where the sister gave him a travel warrant and told him that he had a month's leave. He returned home, still dazed at his sudden dismissal from the navy. Travelling through the blitzed streets of Portsmouth and Birmingham, it was obvious that Britain was still in the middle of a deadly war. The newspapers were describing the bombing of Malta and the success of the German general Erwin Rommel against British troops in North Africa. But here he was, back on civvy street. It seemed to Ron that his days in the forces were over.

3

Pat Joins the Airborne

1940–1942

The German Blitzkrieg across Europe, from Norway to Belgium, in April and May of 1940 revealed that Germany had created a strong force of airborne troops, dropping behind enemy lines via parachute or glider. They were used to very good effect. German airborne troops – or *Fallschirmjäger* – which were under the command of Hermann Göring, head of the Luftwaffe, had captured important airfields in Norway at the beginning of the invasion and reinforced their mountain troops at Narvik, helping to seal their occupation of that country.

The use of gliders and paratroopers to help smash the defences of Holland and Belgium startled the world. On 10 May the invasion opened with airborne troops seizing bridges over the Rhine estuary, then attacking Rotterdam and The Hague. Those paratroops who dropped on The Hague were cut off and taken prisoner, but in Belgium a stunning and audacious victory demonstrated the potential of airborne troops. Planned by General Kurt Student, the operation called for ninety men to land on the roof of the fortress of Eben-Emael by glider. This they did, and held on for a day until relieved by advancing troops. At the same time, other airborne troops captured two bridges that crossed the Albert Canal. The apparent success of these unconventional forces impressed Winston Churchill and in a memorandum to the War Office in June he called for the creation of a similar British force of 5,000 parachute troops.

There were few resources available for this, with the need to rebuild the army after Dunkirk and make hasty preparations to repel a possible German invasion, but some action was taken and the task of creating the new airborne forces was given to two men, Major John Rock of the Royal Engineers, and Squadron Leader Louis Strange of the RAF. They set up an embryonic organization known as the Central Landing School at Ringway Airport near Manchester. It had a dozen staff and one Whitley bomber. In the beginning, the Whitley was modified for parachute training by removing its rear gun-turret and replacing this with an open platform. The novice parachutist was expected to hoist himself through the gap at the rear of the fuselage, stand on the platform between the two tail planes, pull the ripcord of his parachute pack and be snatched away from the aircraft as the parachute unfurled. Surprisingly, the first few trials went well, without any casualties.

Pat Gorman was still a lad of sixteen when these small steps to create a force of British airborne troops started. He was young, but tougher and wiser than his years. He was the eldest of seven children, living in Workington in Cumbria. The family was so large that his five sisters lived with their grandparents in the terraced workman's cottage next door, while he and his brother lived with their parents. His father was unemployed and there was never enough money, so Pat started working as soon as he could find a job. At the age of thirteen he would rise at 5.30 in the morning to start work in a local fish-and-chip shop, cutting the potatoes for that day's supply of chips. Then he would return home for a breakfast of bread and jam, then go off to school. In the evenings he worked in the local theatre, operating the stage lights for variety and musical productions.

He was an intelligent boy, but like Ron Jordan his family couldn't afford to send him to grammar school, so his formal education finished at the age of fourteen. It was a hard life, and the working-class districts of Workington were tough. Pat was short and had always had to stand up for himself, learning to box at the Catholic boys' club. He was fit and courageous, and at the age of fifteen he was offered the opportunity to box professionally. He was under the legal age limit of sixteen, but he was a good boxer and his manager, an uncle, found it easy to lie about his age. He fought four fights, for which he earned £5 a match. It was good money, but Pat knew it was not much of a future, so when he was offered an apprenticeship as a pattern-maker for a local foundry, he took it. The pay was poor, though, so he supplemented his earnings by teaming up with a local travelling fairground. The boxing booth was a big attraction in those days. Local men who had paid a shilling to enter a marquee and crowd round the boxing ring would be challenged by the resident boxer to go three rounds with him and anyone who managed to knock him down would receive £1. When the fairground set up in Workington, Pat had volunteered and beaten the boxer. Handing over the pound note, the sideshow owner had suggested that Pat might like to join them as they travelled around the towns in the Lake District, volunteering from the crowd and taking it in turns with the professional boxer to lose. They split the take and this boosted the money that he could pay his mother over the summer, but he was not prepared to leave home when the showmen moved on, so he was back to his apprentice's wages.

The outbreak of war was a godsent opportunity for Pat and his family. The local steel works, the biggest employer in the area, started on a government contract to manufacture artillery shells and the work-force they employed almost doubled overnight. Pat gave up his apprenticeship and moved to the steel plant, and his father found a job there as well. The family income was now larger than it had ever been.

At the age of fifteen, Pat was too young to be called up into the armed forces, but several of his more distant family had volunteered. One, Johnny, a cousin from Whitehaven, had joined the Royal Air Force. He was an air gunner in Bomber Command and Pat admired him immensely. As Pat grew older, he could see that the war was not going to be over soon and knew that he too would have either to volunteer or be called up, as his job at the steel works was not a reserved occupation. It was possible to volunteer at the age of seventeen and a half, then enter the services promptly on reaching eighteen.

In January 1942 Pat's cousin Johnny was shot down over Germany in a raid on Bremerhaven, and the loss of this slightly older relative whom he had admired so much prompted Pat to volunteer for the RAF. This decision caused him a lot of trouble with his family, because his mother was angry that she would lose his wage of £10 a week. Pat's relationship with his mother was a strong one. As the eldest son in a family whose father had been demoralized by continuous unemployment, he had been the sole breadwinner from an early age and had played the role of a quasi-head of the household. But he believed that it was better to volunteer and so try to exercise some control over what he did in the war than wait to be drafted into the army. Despite his mother's protests, he went to Warrington for the RAF selection board. To his intense disappointment, his vision in one eye was not up to standard and he failed the medical. It was, of course, the first time that he had ever taken an eye test.

So Pat returned to his family, but their relief was shortlived. Six months later he received his call-up papers for the army and was directed into the Royal Artillery. He served his basic training in Northern Ireland, then went to a Royal Artillery camp at Rhyl in North Wales, where he learned to drive, use Morse code, operate field radios and become part of a gun team. He found it interesting but not particularly challenging. While he was in the camp at Rhyl, he noticed a poster calling for men to join the airborne forces. It may have been the prospect of something more adventurous than the artillery, or the hangover of a desire to join the RAF, but Pat immediately went to his staff sergeant and said that he wanted to volunteer.

He did not volunteer in complete ignorance of what he was doing. The existence of British para-troops had been widely publicized in March when the newspapers had carried stories about a raid they had carried out in France. On 27 February 1942, a small group of men had mounted an audacious operation which had helped to restore some of the morale of the British people. These soldiers parachuted into occupied France to capture parts of the German radar transmitters that were providing early warning of Bomber Command raids. This was the first visible success of the small programme that had been started under the impetus of Churchill's memorandum in 1940.

The first rudimentary system of dropping parachutists had been rapidly improved. A static line, which was fastened to a wire inside the aircraft and which opened the parachute automatically at the start of the descent, had been introduced, and a hole had been cut in the bottom of the Whitley through which the trainees jumped out. These improvements, however, didn't make the first experience of parachuting very much easier. The first group of trainees was selected from No. 2 Commando, fairly tough, trained men, but out of 500 only 21 officers and 321 men completed the training; the rest refused to complete the parachute jump.

Those who had made it were formed into the No. 11 Special Air Service Battalion, and by December 1940 they were considered ready for active service. Churchill was constantly pressing for aggressive action to show that Britain was still a force to be reckoned with, so the search started for an operation that would test the new airborne forces.

The target selected was an aqueduct in southern Italy. This carried water for the province of Apulia, with a population of two million people and with Taranto, an important and strategic naval base in the heel of Italy, as its provincial centre.

The operation was probably more to test the equipment and techniques developed in training on a real mission, and to help boost the spirits of 11 Special

Air Service, than for any strategic advantage. A force of just thirty-eight men was selected for the raid and started training in January 1941. The base of operations was to be the island of Malta, from where six Whitley aircraft would carry the men – called X Troop – to their target. They would place demolition charges in the columns supporting the aqueduct, then withdraw a distance of 50 miles across enemy territory to the coast, where a submarine, HMS *Triumph*, would pick them up.

First, however, the troop had to fly over France and the Mediterranean to the airfield in Malta, a journey of 1,600 miles, which they accomplished, remarkably, without any incident. In Malta they had their first opportunity to examine reconnaissance photos, which revealed that there were in fact not one but two aqueducts. They made a decision to attack the larger, and on 10 February, as darkness fell, the six Whitleys took off.

The crew of the first five aircraft succeeded in reaching the drop zone, accurately delivering their paratroopers to within 250 yards of the aqueduct – quite an impressive feat of navigation. The final aircraft, however, failed to find the drop zone and these paratroopers dropped about 2 miles away from the target. They were the Royal Engineers who were tasked with setting the demolition charges, and the containers that dropped with them held most of the explosives for the operation. The paratroopers who had landed close to the aqueduct then discovered that their own aircraft had not dropped all their containers and some of their explosives were missing. Finally, on closer inspection of the structure, the men realized that the aqueduct was not made of brick but of reinforced concrete. Major T. A. G. Pritchard, in command of the operation, decided to set all the explosives that he had around one supporting structure, in the hope that the blast would be sufficient to destroy it. They detonated the charges and, with a loud crack and a rumble, the aqueduct started to collapse, breaking in half. Water poured on to the valley floor. Despite the initial obstacles, the raid looked to have been successful. All that was now left to do was to make the rendezvous with the submarine, so the paratroopers split up into three parties and headed for the coast. None of them made it. Units of the Italian *carabinieri* (paramilitary police) or the Italian Army intercepted each group.

There was clearly a good deal to think about in Ringway after this operation. Intelligence about the target had not been good. Poor navigation on the part of the aircraft crews could badly affect the outcome of a mission, and the failure of some of the containers to drop also needed to be fixed. It was clear that the chances of a small group of lightly armed men making it back to a rescue point would always be slim. Nevertheless, the training and organization of paratroopers continued. The fact that if used in large enough numbers they could be decisive was underlined when *Fallschirmjäger* spearheaded Germany's invasion of Crete in May 1941. The entire German 7th Air Division managed to hold out against British and New Zealand troops until they had seized the airport, which enabled more German reinforcements to be flown in. It was a serious defeat for British forces in the Mediterranean. The Germans, however, had suffered heavy casualties to their Parachute Division in Crete and Hitler vowed never to use them again. This change of heart was not known by the British; training at Ringway continued apace and the size of the airborne forces grew.

The 1st Parachute Battalion was created out of the Special Air Service Battalion in September 1941, with the 2nd Battalion formed in November of the same year. The intention was to establish a parachute brigade numbering around 3,000 men, with the aim of eventually creating an airborne division of four brigades. Training for the 2nd Battalion started at the newly established headquarters in Hardwick Hall near Chesterfield. Men from this battalion formed the core of a raid on the Bruneval Radar Station, on the French coast near Le Havre, in March 1942. It was carried out by a company of paratroopers drawn from the 2nd Battalion, along with a group of sappers from the Royal Engineers whose job it was to find and remove the key pieces of the radar transmitter. They were led by Major John Frost, commanding officer of the 2nd Battalion, who was destined to play an outstanding role at Arnhem.

Not only did this operation provide valuable

information about Germany's air defences, it was also a stunning success at a time when Britain had had too few of them, and it seemed to confirm the correctness of expanding the airborne troops. Recruitment by now was proceeding apace, and training for a third battalion would soon get under way.

Pat arrived at Hardwick Hall for his initial training. It was extremely demanding, designed to sort out quickly those who were not physically capable of meeting the very high standards. Tough as he was, Pat found it extremely rigorous. He was given instruction in rope climbing and abseiling among other skills, but the course was primarily geared to test endurance and self-reliance, both physical and mental. It ended with the recruits having to complete a 7-mile run in one hour while carrying their full kit, including personal weapons and ammunition.

This load was considerable. Paratroopers needed to be self-sufficient for a period of several days until they were relieved by regular forces, or resupplied by further air drops. The standard infantry weapon, the Lee-Enfield bolt-action rifle, was impractical. It was cumbersome to carry, particularly for someone dropping from an aircraft, and its rate of fire wasn't high enough. The Sten gun, a small automatic machine gun, was developed at the end of 1940 by the Royal Ordnance factory at Enfield and became the standard issue for paratroopers. The magazine held thirty-two 9mm bullets and the gun had a rate of fire of about 500 rounds per minute. It was shorter than a rifle and the butt could be folded away during the jump. It still weighed over 7lb, and an extra seven magazines that fitted in a standard bandolier considerably increased the weight. Pat's load was topped up by a combat knife, grenades, water and rations for several days, plus a field-dressing kit for first aid, and his helmet.

At the end of the run, even the toughest were finding it hard going. Pat passed, however, and would normally have then gone on to do his parachute training, but the trainees from Hardwick Hall were seconded to Fort William in Scotland, to the commando training centre at Achnacarry Castle. Pat remembers that it was an isolated, desolate spot with a few Nissen huts and a canteen. Here, under the tuition of commando instructors, as well as learning a variety of survival techniques in enemy and hostile territory, Pat was taught the black arts of silent killing using a knife, a garrotte or even his bare hands – '101 ways to kill a man' is how he describes it. This course lasted just two weeks and the final qualifying test was an exercise in escape and evasion. He was released from the camp with no money or papers and instructed to return to his unit at Hardwick Hall within forty-eight hours. If the civilian or military police intercepted him, he would fail the course.

Pat travelled at night, climbing aboard goods trains heading south. It didn't take him long to arrive in Barnsley, from where he made his way to his grandparents' house. He stayed there for two days, and Pat thinks that they suspected he was absent without leave. He told them nothing, but had a decent rest and cleaned up before moving on. His grandmother slipped him 10 shillings and advised him that it would be better if he returned to his unit. He promised them that he was all right and left. From then on, by taking buses and hitching lifts, he found it easy to make his way back to Hardwick Hall. He had taken three days, but he passed the course anyway. He never found out why he was sent on it, though he thinks that it may have been because at the time the 21st Independent Company was being set up, a unit that would act as the spearhead of any airborne operation. They would land first and mark out the drop zones for the main force, suppressing any enemy opposition, or, if this turned out to be too fierce, would attempt to secure alternative landing areas. Whatever the reason for his secondment, Pat found that having the course on his record was an advantage. He was treated with slightly more respect and was never considered for the menial fatigue duties that were allotted to others.

Within a few days of his return to Hardwick Hall, he began his parachute training at Ringway, joining a course of around 500 people. The first part of the training was dropping from a high platform with a cable attached to a harness strapped around him. This was meant to simulate the impact on the ground after a real parachute descent. Pat was told how to keep his feet together and how to roll into the landing.

For his first parachute drop he was taken up in a basket suspended beneath a tethered balloon. Trainees had to complete two of these drops and in his view they were the worst. The basket contained four trainees and an RAF instructor, and Pat was the first to go. 'It's a horrible experience, because the balloon is not very high, and I dropped for two hundred feet before the static line opened the parachute.' It seemed to Pat that the parachute would never open, and there was barely time to gather himself before he hit the ground. He felt like kissing it when he landed. There was a small hut and a mobile canteen on the ground where the trainees could have a cup of tea after the jump. Pat could not hold his cup and saucer together. His hands were shaking so badly that tea was spilling out of the cup, which he could barely raise to his lips. In a short while he realized that everyone's reaction was the same.

The second parachute drop the next day was again from the balloon. Yet already 200 or so had left the course – men who had refused to jump the first time or were not prepared to make the second. The thinning out of volunteers continued as the course progressed, first jumping from a Whitley bomber in the day, then carrying out two night jumps. Dropping from the aircraft was less stressful, according to Pat, though not all the trainees might have agreed. The static line came into play almost as soon as the parachutist was clear of the hole in the fuselage, and there was more height above the ground. By then, of course, a certain familiarity had taken over, although there was, Pat believes, always a residual surge of fear and adrenaline in any parachutist as they stepped out of an aeroplane.

After his eight drops, Pat was given his wings and the coveted Red Beret – which was actually maroon – and went on a week's leave, where he basked in the admiration that his status as paratrooper aroused in the local girls. He discovered on his return that he had not yet been allocated to a regular unit, but stayed at Hardwick Hall as part of a holding company. Then, with fifty others, he was sent to Liverpool, where he boarded a ship and, after several days, landed at the port of Alexandria in Egypt.

On his arrival he found that no one knew why he was there. He was still only eighteen years old and should not have been sent for duty overseas until his nineteenth birthday. Pat was clearly well trained, however, and in the absence of any alternative was sent to speak to the commanding officer of the Long Range Desert Group, an irregular unit that operated behind German lines in the desert. Pat clearly had some of the requisites of a covert soldier, especially with his qualifications from the commando course. So he boarded a small vessel and sailed west along the coast to the port of Tobruk, then drove down to the LRDG forward base at Derna, in Libya, where they had commandeered a villa that once belonged to the Italian dictator Mussolini. The major was dumbfounded at Pat's arrival. He was short, just

5 foot 6 inches, and this made him seem even younger than his eighteen years. When the major heard that Pat had been given Morse and radio training in the Royal Artillery, however, he realized that he could use him, as Pat could free up their existing radio man to take part in some of the raids that they were still conducting against German units in the desert.

Pat was overjoyed. He found it a marvellous outfit to be part of. There was absolutely no formal discipline, and from what he could see his fellow troopers in the LRDG wore whatever they felt most comfortable in. When they went out on 'bashes', as they called their operations, in their jeeps and Packard lorries they looked, according to Pat, as though they had stepped out of the film *The Sheik*. He loved the dash and glamour of it all.

After two months, the major told him that they were moving on to Benghazi in Cyrenaica, now Libya, and it would not be possible for him to remain as part of his irregular force. He told Pat that the 4th Parachute Brigade was forming in North Africa and advised him to link up with one of the new battalions, so he made his way by road to Cairo and joined the 11th Battalion, the 4th Parachute Brigade, his first official posting in the 1st Airborne Division. It was the beginning of July 1943. He had joined the battalion just in time to take part in the parachute drop on the Greek island of Kos.

4

THE SAPPER'S TALE

1942

Tom Carpenter, the third veteran sitting at that table in the bar in Oosterbeek, was born in Small Heath, Birmingham, where Ron had ended up when he left the Fleet Air Arm. Like Pat, he was too young to enlist at the start of the war, but had already been a messenger boy with the local ARP, the volunteer Air Raid Protection wardens. Tom's father had been a guardsman in the Coldstream Guards before the First World War and was wounded in the Battle of the Marne in 1914. He recovered and returned to the front, but after overstaying a period of leave he was punished with forty days' detention and then sent to a Guards pioneer battalion, who were the soldiers ordered to go into no-man's-land and repair the barbed-wire defences after they had been shelled. The chances of survival were low, but he made it, serving four years in the trenches. Tom is still bitter about the fact that his father, after all that service, was struggling in the 1930s to raise a family of five children on a wage of £1.10s a week.

Tom remembers that there was a lot of talk of war when he was growing up, although he was not really worried by it. It was even part of popular entertainment. He can still recall the lines of a well-known song that was sung when Italy occupied Abyssinia (now Ethiopia) in 1935: '*Will you come to Abyssinia, will you come, Bring your own ammunition and your gun, Mussolini will be there shooting bullets in the air . . .*' War and its terrors seemed remote at the time.

When it did start in 1939 Tom's father was a senior warden in the ARP, and for a brief period they spent a lot of time in each other's company after work. Then, with the evacuation of British troops from Dunkirk, Tom volunteered for the newly established Local Defence Volunteers, which was shortly to become the Home Guard. He received a rifle and started some basic weapons training, as well as being told how to make Molotov cocktails. Ultimately the Home Guard became a well-organized force, equipped with mortars and Vickers machine guns, and Tom enjoyed learning how to use them.

They were threatening times. On four occasions he was mobilized to move to Home Guard headquarters because of fears that a German invasion was imminent, and in November 1940 Birmingham and the Midlands started to experience the full impact of the air raids carried out by the Luftwaffe. A major air raid on 19 November lasted for thirteen hours and caused considerable damage and heavy casualties to the BSA factory close to where they lived and where Tom's father was now working. Tom had two periods of guard duty at night, sleeping for a couple of hours between them on a billiards table in a local drill hall. He was usually dog-tired after six nights of this, but the night of the big raid the adrenaline kept him going, rushing to assist the fire brigade and to rescue victims from the rubble. The raid came in two parts with a pause for an hour and a half at midnight. Towards the end of the night so many water mains had been destroyed that it was impossible to fight the fires. The next day he was called on to help dig emergency wells for drinking water.

Tom had started working as a delivery boy for a local trader, Mr William Keighley, who specialized in renovating bomb-damaged furniture. Keighley's eldest son, Billy, had joined the RAF and was serving as an air gunner in Bomber Command. One day Billy returned on leave and told Tom that the previous night he had been flying over Berlin. As with Pat Gorman, this association with somebody in the air force had a strong influence on Tom. Billy also went out with the most glamorous girl in the area, a dancer known as Betty Fox. Tom looked up to him.

But then Billy died in a raid over Bremerhaven in 1942. Tom can still remember the day that he heard the news. He was standing in the yard when a car drove up and a padre and an officer in RAF uniform got out. They asked Tom where they could find Mr Keighley. Tom took them over to the workshop and saw his employer's face change to a chalk white at the sight of the two visitors. He knew, before they had a chance to speak, that they were going to confirm what he dreaded to hear about his son.

Tom knew that soon he would receive his call-up papers, but the morning after he learned of Billy's death he went to the army recruiting office and explained that he wanted to join the Coldstream Guards, the regiment that his father had been in. The sergeant refused to listen. There was an urgent need for engineers, so Tom was sent instead to the Royal Engineers.

He served his period of basic training at Formby, before going to Chatham in Kent, a naval training base but also the home of Kitchener Barracks. There he was given the standard engineer's training, which lasted for fourteen weeks. It was comprehensive, ranging from the provision of water supplies, including digging wells and laying pipelines, improvised bridge-laying, road and building construction, explosive demolition, and mine warfare, which included laying and clearing mine fields. This last was particularly challenging, as the Germans had developed sophisticated mines that they used widely in the North African desert. One innovation was the Teller mine, which could not be easily located by normal mine-detection equipment because it was made of glass. Locating and clearing these mines was carried out by probing the ground gently with a bayonet and carefully excavating around it. Another nasty weapon in the German mine armoury was the S-mine, an anti-personnel mine loaded with ball bearings, which sprang into the air before exploding at waist height. The range of these small metal projectiles was enough to cause injuries to a whole platoon.

When Tom was nearing the end of the course two officers visited the barracks and asked for volunteers for the airborne forces. With the promise of an extra 2 shillings a day for those who did, about eight on the course, including Tom, decided to give it a go. At the end of their training as sappers they were directed to the HQ of the 9th Field Company at Tattershall and from there Tom went to Hardwick Hall for basic airborne training.

The 9th Field Company was set up to provide the engineering and sapper support to an airborne battalion. Each platoon of sixty men was attached to a battalion of 800 soldiers. As well as having engineering skills, the sappers would also carry out the tasks of regular infantry. On some occasions they would be selected for special missions where knowledge of machinery and demolition skills were vital. One such operation, known as Operation Freshman, was the raid on the Norsk hydroelectric plant at Telemark in Norway. This plant, constructed in the 1930s, assumed a vital strategic significance in the war because of its production of 'heavy water'.

Germany had started work on building a nuclear reactor and the British government was convinced that German scientists would use the Norsk Hydro plant's output to develop a reactor that would enable them to build an atomic bomb. Heavy water, which occurs naturally, is water whose molecules contain atoms of hydrogen with an extra neutron in the nucleus, making it twice as heavy as ordinary hydrogen. Heavy water can be used to control the speed of a nuclear reaction, but it requires a large amount of energy to extract it from ordinary water. The plant at Telemark could produce enough electricity to do this, and before the war produced heavy water to supply most nuclear laboratories throughout Europe. When the plant came under the control of the German Army, British intelligence learned that its output of heavy water had risen quite dramatically. This appeared to confirm their worst fears, so it seemed vital to destroy the plant and its stockpiles of heavy water in order to prevent the Germans from pressing on with their nuclear plans.

The remote, mountainous location of the plant posed several problems. It was a difficult target to hit from the air, and a bombing raid would cause many casualties among the local Norwegian population without any certainty of having destroyed the plant. The terrain would also cause problems to a team of saboteurs dropping by parachute. The forest and steep hillsides would make it difficult for them to rendezvous and also to locate the containers of demolition equipment. The only solution was to drop a group of well-trained engineers from the 1st Airborne Division, flying in the recently developed troop-carrying gliders. They would land, together with their equipment, at a convenient area of open country near the dam that fed water to the hydro-electric plant.

The German *Fallschirmjäger* had performed a similar feat in 1940 when they had landed by glider on the roof of the Belgian fort at Eben-Emael – the operation that had so impressed Churchill. But this was the first time that British troops had attempted such a thing. The development of British troop-carrying gliders had started in 1940 and the first model produced, a canvas-covered aircraft called the Hotspur, was poor. The American Army produced something similar called the Waco, and Tom flew in one of these during his training. Under tow in the air, the outer skin of the glider appeared to be breathing and it seemed to Tom to be dangerously fragile. The Hotspur could carry only eight passengers, which was far too small a number, so the next design, the Horsa, was far bigger and more robust. Constructed from plywood, it could transport up to thirty soldiers and was also able to carry equipment containers mounted under the centre section of the wing. The Horsa was towed into the air by a powered aircraft, usually a converted bomber, and took off on a nose wheel and two main wheels mounted under the wings. These main wheels were jettisoned in flight, the glider landing on the nose wheel and a skid mounted under the fuselage. Ultimately, these gliders were modified to carry vehicles and artillery, with a hinged cargo door and a ramp in the side of the fuselage. The manufacturer was a company called Airspeed, but much of the construction work was subcontracted to various furniture-makers. The gliders had been produced very quickly, within eleven months of the very first specification issued by the government in October 1940, and the Telemark raid was their first, and quite severe, test in action.

The plan was that two Horsas towed by two Halifax bombers would fly over the North Sea, carrying between them thirty-four Sappers and their equipment. So that they would know exactly where the demolition charges needed to be placed, the men of the 9th Field Company were taken on various visits to hydroelectric plants in Scotland and shown around equipment in a Lever Brothers soap factory that was similar to the condensers producing heavy water. The other important training that they received was designed to make sure that they could survive in the bleak landscape of southern Norway in winter and evade capture. This was tough. They spent nights on mountains in freezing conditions, made night marches with 90lb packs, and learned unarmed combat techniques. In order to maintain secrecy, the men were split into separate teams and told that they were in preparation for a competition, although very few believed it. Their fears were confirmed when, just before the mission, they were ordered to remove their red berets and Pegasus shoulder flashes – usually a sign that a special operation was about to begin.

On 19 November 1942, the two gliders and their tugs lined up on the runway at RAF Skitten near Wick in the far north of Scotland to make the three-and-a-half-hour journey across the sea. It was a desperate venture, requiring great fortitude on the part of those taking part. Even before take-off, things started to go wrong. The communication cable that connected the Halifax flown by Squadron Leader Wilkinson to Sergeant Strathdee, the pilot of the glider he was towing, was unserviceable. There was no replacement, so they managed to work out a rough system using navigation lights. This took some time, and the flight eventually departed thirty minutes late. The weather forecast was that cloud would reach 4,000 feet over the sea, rising to 10,000 on the approach to the Norwegian coast, but the landing site would be clear.

The first Halifax flew into thick clouds and ice formed on the aircraft, the glider and the two ropes. They lost height, then the tow rope parted. Squadron Leader Wilkinson believed that the glider had gone down in the sea, but in fact it crashed a few miles inland. Unable to do anything more, and thinking the worst, he flew the Halifax back to Skitten. The second Halifax and Horsa combination fared no better. The Halifax released the glider suddenly at altitude, then it disappeared. Later, after the war, it was learned that the Halifax had crashed. So too did the

Horsa, whose crew became disorientated in the clouds and lost control. After Wilkinson returned, nothing more was heard until the Germans broadcast two days later that a bomber and two gliders had been found. Their mission had failed.

Two members of the 9th Field Company who had been trained for Operation Freshman had not at the last minute taken part and were still part of the company when Tom joined it. They were tough men, but Tom thought that everybody in the 9th was fighting fit and remarkably well trained. In his opinion any one of them could have been selected for an operation like the raid on the Norsk Hydro plant at Telemark and would have been able, and more importantly prepared, to carry it out.

The outcome of the operation was a mystery to the men of the 9th, and remained so until after the war. When the Allies liberated Norway in 1945, questioning of German prisoners of war finally revealed that some of the sappers had survived from each glider crash, although those that did so had been captured, interrogated and subsequently tortured to death or executed.

The poor outcome of the operation did not affect the expansion of the glider-borne forces and Tom did all his training in gliders at Thruxton airfield. They were flights in a Horsa, fully loaded with twenty-nine men, towed up by an aircraft to 3,000 feet. Then after a circuit of the airfield, the pilots would land the glider, descending first to 500 feet, then making a final approach to the runway, speed brakes out, struggling to control both the speed and the angle of descent. The main wheels were retained for these training flights, and after a heavy landing the gliders could bounce 25 feet into the air before coming to a stop.

The schedule was three flights a day for a week, and by the end of the week Tom had learned how to organize the load in different battle orders, depending on what had to come out first. The usual fit was twenty-one men with eighteen folding bikes, three small motorcycles and 200lb of other equipment. Tom liked flying. He also understood that the great benefit of the glider was that it could bring its load down on one spot, whereas a stick of paratroopers and their equipment containers might be spread over a mile. In his view, the glider was a packing case with wings – although, as the raid on Telemark demon-strated, getting the packing case to its destination was a very dangerous process for which there was no readily available solution. All the first operations of the airborne troops, in Italy, Bruneval or Telemark, had shown that the key to success was getting men and their equipment as close to the target as possible. Failure to do this would prove deadly in the later invasion of Sicily – and it was a lesson still ignored at Arnhem.

5

CIVVY STREET

1941

Birmingham in 1941 had changed radically since Ron Jordan had left it two years before. Whole streets and districts were scarred by blasted ruins from the German air raids of November 1940. Weeds and wild flowers had already started to colonize the piles of rubble and the cleared gaps of wasteland in between the tight-packed rows of red-brick terraced houses. Buddleia sprouted from the cracks in the upper storeys still partly covered by peeling bedroom wallpaper.

There had been other transformations as well. Men of Ron's age had largely left to join the forces. The factories of Morris Motors and BSA were now full of women, who were working lathes, presses, drilling machines, for three shifts a day. This enormous influx of women into the factories, undreamed of in peace-time, kept industry pouring out a stream of armoured vehicles, engines and ammunition for the war.

Entering the Labour Exchange in Aston, Ron discovered that the knowledge and skill as an armourer that he possessed were highly desirable. He was immediately offered a job at the BSA factory, once the largest producer of motorcycles in Europe but now manufacturing armoured vehicles and machine guns. Within a few days he was installed as an inspector and progress-chaser on the production line. He found himself surrounded by women, whose boyfriends and husbands were miles away in North Africa or based in some training camp in Scotland. He was young, fit and wounded from the war, and he could have taken out a different woman every night.

The BSA factory had received a direct hit from a large bomb in the air raid on 19 November. The night shift was still working and the top floors of the factory had collapsed on to the floors below, trapping hundreds of workers under piles of rubble and machinery. Thirty-six men and women had died. The threat of the German bombers had since receded a little, but there were still air-raid warnings and the night shift now didn't hesitate to rush to the shelters. Huddled in the dark, Ron was the permanent butt of innuendo and suggestions from the sixty women in the shelter. It was a hard life for them. He remembers how they stood by their machines, hair piled up in turbaned headscarves out of harm's way, their hands chapped from lubricating oil and their fingernails broken and split from metal swarf. They were exhausted, but after finishing a long twelve-hour shift would then have to get home to their children and cook. Even finding food in the shops took hours of queuing and traipsing from shop to shop with a ration book. Despite their flirting with Ron, he knew that most were anxious about the fate of some man or other who might, because news travelled slowly, already be dead.

All this would have been impossible without the support of the working-class families and neighbours in the mean streets around the factories – the various grannies, aunties and extended families who were pre-pared to offer a helping hand with domestic chores. Ron came from a family like this and he knew how it worked.

Many men would have been eager to be in his shoes. He was well paid, the work was undemanding and the occasional air raid posed little real threat for him compared to his close encounters with the Luftwaffe on board *Ark Royal*. But he was far from happy and many aspects of his current position were contributing to his increasing unease. He was aware that there was considerable waste and corruption in the factory. Most of the contracts for war work were paid for on a cost-plus basis, and there was little effective audit of the amount and quality of the material produced. He didn't think that very much effort had been put into training the new female workforce; moreover, many single women had been recruited from far afield, with no thought to where they would live. One night he found a group of them sleeping in the warehouse and they told him that they had been living there for over two weeks because they could find nowhere to rent in the city. They were tired and dispirited, and much of their work was not up to standard. But there was no attempt to rectify the problems. Vast amounts of output were dumped as waste in the canal behind the factory and figures were inflated by recycling production through different shifts. Whenever Ron said anything about the problems he was ignored and there was a lot of pressure from management not to rock the boat.

All this nagged at Ron and left him unhappy. He knew that men in the forces had a hard time. Britain's lifeline was the sea and he was well aware of the cost in lives and ships of maintaining the convoys that brought food and raw materials to its shores. To see any waste or disregard of this made him angry.

After his accident on *Ark Royal* there had been some victories in the war that provided the British people with some optimism. The immediate threat of a German invasion had receded and the Luftwaffe had not succeeded in bombing Britain into surrender. In North Africa, the Italian Armies were halted in their advance towards Egypt, and the British Eighth Army had taken Benghazi, capturing thousands of Italian prisoners of war.

This was as good as it got. The news deteriorated in 1941, as the Germans appeared able to advance on all fronts. Their invasion of Russia seemed to be sweeping all before it, and in North Africa the British Army was pushed back almost to the gates of Cairo. Greece, Yugoslavia and the island of Crete fell in quick succession to Germany.

Every day Ron went to the factory, inspecting with his micrometer the output of machine-gun barrels, breech blocks and chambers, working twelve-hour shifts, taking out his girlfriends to the pub or the cinema, then once more clocking on for work, while the British Army seemed incapable of reversing their defeats. Although in the context of wartime Britain it would have been thought laughable, Ron was profoundly depressed. He hated being a civilian and he hated working in a factory. He had lost what he valued most – the sense of solidarity, trust and an unclouded sense of purpose that he had discovered in his squadron on the *Ark*.

When *Ark Royal* was sunk in November 1941, the news hit him like a poleaxe, and for two days he couldn't bear the thought of going to work. All these feelings came to a head a few weeks later when his tram was stopped in a queue of traffic outside the Austin Motors works in Alum Rock while a convoy of lorries carrying Bren-gun carriers left the factory. A large, elderly man sitting in front of Ron complained bitterly about the delay. Ron remembers that he railed against the waste of effort supplying any sort of machinery to the troops, saying that they were useless, incapable of fighting, and were not a patch on men like himself who had fought in the First World

War. 'I came that close to hitting him, and I'm sure that if the girl I was with hadn't stopped me I would have been in serious trouble. I gave him a mouthful at any rate, and then got off the tram. The following Monday I made up my mind. I knew the navy wouldn't have me back, so I went to the recruiting office and said I wanted to join the army.'

Ron was asked about his background. His present job was a reserved occupation, crucial to the war effort, so the recruiting officer had no reason to ask him what he had been doing in the war up until then and Ron saw no reason to mention anything about the navy. On the face of it, he was a perfect recruit: he had some Territorial Army training and clearly knew his way round most types of infantry weapons. The medical officer was more sceptical, worrying about the scars of several operations and the slight limp that Ron could not disguise. The colonel in charge, however, returning from what Ron assumed was a 3-pint lunch, had no qualms and brushed the medical officer aside. He signed Ron up on the spot, telling him he would be invaluable as an armourer in the Royal Army Ordnance Corps. His second military career was about to start.

6

OAKS FROM ACORNS

1943–1944

After Ron Jordan had been accepted into the Royal Army Ordnance Corps he did a period of basic training and was then posted to a Combat Training School in Armagh, Northern Ireland, very close to the border with the South. Here he found he was in sole control of the armoury workshops. He had his own Nissen hut, where he worked and slept; he had the run of the firing ranges to test and zero the sights of the weapons he repaired; and he was able to visit the mess whenever his work allowed. It was many soldiers' idea of paradise, but one evening when Ron was on his own having a late tea, two men caught his eye. They were putting up posters asking for volunteers for airborne forces. It stirred in Ron's mind memories of his happy times working on aircraft in the Fleet Air Arm. The next morning he approached the staff sergeant on the base, told him about the posters and that he would like to put in an application. The sergeant said, 'You've got to be out of your bloody mind. You're sorted here, aren't you?'

Ron had to admit that that was true. As an excuse, he claims now that he would sometimes put a small detonator in a practice grenade and throw it into the nearby river, stunning the fish. He would then gather up those that were edible and take them to the cooks. Ron had been spotted doing this by a corporal in the Regimental Police, who had filed a report about his unauthorized use of explosive. As a result, Ron felt under some unknown threat and instinctively believed that his cushy number would not last.

Whatever the true motive, two airborne sergeants arrived a few days later to interview him. Ron wondered why he was so important. They asked him if he knew anything about containers and explained that these were carried under the wings of some of the paratrooper transport aircraft. After three para-troopers had jumped out of the plane, the containers were released and then the rest of the paratroopers completed their jump, so that their equipment fell in the middle of the stick and was easier for the men to locate. The army had recently become responsible for loading and mounting these containers on the air-craft but were experiencing problems getting them to fall accurately. Ron told the men what he knew about mounting bombs on bomb racks and coordinating the release switches, and within three days he learned that he had been accepted into the airborne forces and was issued with a travel warrant for Salisbury Plain.

Ron never worked on the containers. His travel warrant was changed to Barton Stacey and when he arrived there he was immediately given a pass for seven days' leave. On his return, he discovered that he would be going to North Africa attached to the 1st Airborne Division and he sailed to Oran in the former liner *Stirling Castle*.

In November 1942 the 1st Parachute Brigade had also travelled by sea to Algiers as part of the British First Army, which with US forces was to advance eastwards towards Tunis and Bizerte. Originally, there had been a plan for the brigade to drop on Tunis and prevent the Germans from entering Tunisia, but they had reacted quickly to the landings in Algeria and the opportunity had been lost. During the campaign in North Africa various battalions had dropped on key areas, but their success, and the reputation they gathered, was less because of victories in their deployments than because they fought dogged, hard battles against some of Germany's best troops in the cold and rain of winter.

As the Allies advanced, Ron spent the next few months in Oran and then was stationed further along the coast at Bizerte. It was while the workshops were being organized in Oran that he met up with a young recruit, Ivor Brewster, who had joined as a boy soldier and was just nineteen years old. He had been born in Dover and the Ordnance Corps was his first posting. He had the impetuosity of youth and a reckless courage that both infuriated and amused his older comrades. While he was in Africa, Ivor volunteered for service in a unit similar to the Long Range Desert Group, but was stopped by Ron's CO. He was quickly given the nickname 'Buffalo', after the Brewster Buffalo, an American fighter used by the RAF. Because of Ron's experience and more mature years, Ivor looked up to him, and Ron found himself keeping a watchful eye on 'the lad', as he thought of him, making sure that he didn't get into too much trouble. It was a hard job. One night, Ron recalls, before they took off for Arnhem, they were drinking in a pub in Sleaford when Ivor took down the pub's curtains and proceeded to drape them over a prominent statue in the town square. Climbing the 20 feet or so to the statue's head carrying the heavy material was quite a feat.

During Ron's stay in North Africa, the Allies invaded Sicily and this – Operation Husky – saw the first large-scale deployment of paratroops and glider-borne soldiers by Britain and the US in the war so far. It was a disaster. A combination of poor navigating skills and inexperience on the part of the US pilots led to the release of gliders far out to sea, or para-chutists being dropped miles from their objective. Casualties were severe: 400 men of the 1st Airlanding Brigade drowned in the Mediterranean on the first night, with similar losses hitting the rest of the airborne operations. Remarkably, even in the face of utter chaos, some objectives were captured. John Frost, the hero of Bruneval, held on to a key bridge with just a tenth of his original force until he was relieved by the advancing Eighth Army. The invasion of Sicily demonstrated once again how dependent airborne operations were on the quality of the pilots and aircrew who carried them into battle. But it had also shown how small groups of men had succeeded in carrying out missions that had been planned for a whole battalion. The rapid insertion of forces behind enemy lines caused disruption far beyond their numbers to the enemy – a testament to the training and commitment of the airborne troops themselves.

Much of this activity bypassed the newly formed 4th Parachute Brigade, carrying out its training in Kabrit just outside Cairo, where Pat Gorman had been sent by the Long Range Desert Group. The 4th Brigade was commanded by Brigadier John 'Shan' Hackett, a respected veteran of the 8th Hussars, an armoured regiment. Hackett had fought with them in the African desert and had been badly wounded when his tank was hit during the first British encounter with Rommel's Afrika Korps. After recovering from his injuries he had been assigned to the General Staff in Cairo before being put in command of the new parachute brigade.

The 11th Battalion of the 4th Brigade, to which Pat was assigned, was a mixed bag of recruits and had quickly developed a reputation as a difficult group of soldiers to manage. Pat did not find it a problem, save that he felt that he was better trained both mentally and physically than many of his fellow paratroopers. He joined the unit's boxing club and had to do a daily 11-mile runs as part of his training, but otherwise he was content.

In September of 1943 the other battalions of the brigade – the 156th Parachute Battalion and the 10th Battalion – went by sea to take part in the landings on the mainland of Italy. The 11th Battalion remained behind in Egypt to finish its training. The 2nd and 4th Parachute Brigades, less the 11th Battalion, had been sent to strengthen the Eighth Army and on 9 September the commanding officer of the 1st Airborne Division, Major General George Hopkinson, the advocate of glider-borne landings, took the surrender of the Italian garrison at Taranto. Ron Jordan sailed with them and found himself moving up through Italy. He was busy, as the 4th Brigade under Brigadier Hackett was engaged in some stiff fighting. It was his unit's job to refurbish and repair all the weapons as each unit returned from the front line to regroup and replenish itself. General Hopkinson died at the town of Castellaneta, near Bari, shot while he was observing the 10th Battalion advance to capture it. The brigade then moved north and mounted a night assault against the town of Gioia del Colle, capturing it and its nearby airfield on

16 September. In the next two days the RAF moved into the airfield and were able to provide forward air support for the British forces.

After this short but successful campaign, the 4th Brigade handed over responsibility to the 1st Airlanding Brigade and embarked for the United Kingdom. Ron was particularly unlucky. He had embarked on a Free French ship that broke down off the coast of Sicily and wallowed in the swell for three days before being taken under tow by a destroyer. Ron got off in Bizerte, then moved by train to Oran before arriving back in the UK in January.

Pat did see some action, however, despite the 11th Battalion languishing in Egypt. After the Italian government capitulated in September 1943, German forces rushed to fill the gap left by the Italians in the Axis occupation of Greece and the Balkans. A German armoured brigade quickly captured the island of Rhodes and, in an attempt to head off any further advance, Special Boat Service units landed on the island of Kos, taking the port and the airfield close to Antimachia. A Company of the 11th Battalion was selected to drop on to Kos to provide support to the initial landings and Pat Gorman was one of the men chosen. They dropped at night from six RAF Dakotas and the operation went very well, with the crews carrying out their mission accurately. Pat landed safely and moved with the rest of the company to the port where more reinforcements were arriving by boat. These were the 1st Battalion the Durham Light Infantry. An RAF regiment had flown into the airfield with their anti-aircraft guns and the South African Air Force had landed a squadron of Spitfires to provide air cover. It seemed that the small Greek island was securely in British hands.

The Germans had other ideas. They flew in re-inforcements for the Luftwaffe on Rhodes and commenced a bombing campaign on Kos's airfield and port. Soon the number of serviceable Spitfires was reduced to four and the airport was frequently put out of action by anti-personnel bombs dropped by German dive-bombers. The rocky ground made it difficult to dig in and the ground troops started to suffer casualties. Pat could not understand why there was such a lack of Allied air cover. He had no reason to know that the operation had caused a split in the Allies, with General Eisenhower, Supreme Commander of Allied Forces in Europe and North Africa, refusing to sanction any diversion of forces from the Italian theatre for what he saw as a Balkan adventure.

The situation seemed tough, but to Pat's disgust A Company was evacuated on 25 September, ten days after they had parachuted in. 'We got away all right, by boat, would you believe. The poor bloody Durham Light Infantry stayed. And they got captured.'

German paratroopers landed west and south of the airfield at Antimachia on 3 October, and a *Kampfgruppe* (battle group) of around 1,200 troops with artillery and armoured cars landed by boat at the port and on other parts of the island. The battle was over by 4 October, and 1,388 British troops, along with 3,145 Italian troops who had willingly surrendered to Pat and his comrades in A Company, were now in the cage.

Pat landed at Cyprus, then went on to Palestine from where the whole battalion embarked for the UK, landing at Liverpool on 27 December. After a fortnight's leave, he went to join the rest of the battalion in various billets around Melton Mowbray before moving into a central barracks. Throughout this time, the members of the parachute battalions continued their programme of training. Pat was still in the boxing team, so had a 10-mile run every day, but he enjoyed it, and anyway he was given, like other airborne troops, double rations because of the extra physical exercises they had to carry out.

In the first half of 1944, all three men were in England and enjoying their time in the airborne forces. Ron, as usual, had found himself in a comfortable billet with a great deal of freedom. He was based in a requisitioned shop in Sleaford, Lincolnshire, and travelled around the various battalions in the division in a jeep, servicing and testing their weapons. He was able to get into Birmingham every weekend on leave and had a very comfortable existence. It was a great change from the flies and sand of North Africa, or the sparse accommodation in Italy. He was also posted for a while to Saltby, a large US airbase in Leicestershire, to carry out some engineering work, fitting small lights on to air-dropped containers so that they could be found in the dark.

Just as this work came to an end, he was approached by a young American pilot who asked him and his mates if he wanted some cigarettes. They were interested, but wanted to know what the catch was. The pilot explained that the small US gliders, the Wacos, were delivered in crates and assembled on the base, but they had to have a brief test flight afterwards. In order to add a realistic load for each test, a concrete block was placed at the centre of gravity in the fuselage, but the pilot was tired of manoeuvring this about from glider to glider. If Ron and his mates were prepared to sit in the gliders, it would save him a lot of effort and he would give them a carton of cigarettes for each test. It was highly unlikely that the gliders would crash; in fact, it had never happened.

The three English soldiers could see nothing wrong with the plan, so for the next week Ron and his friends were towed into the air in newly constructed Waco gliders, then cast off, the glider pilot performed a loop and landed, and they each received a carton of American cigarettes. The arrangement lasted until they had to return to Sleaford, by which time they didn't know where to put all the cigarettes they had accumulated, but they came in extremely useful in bartering for anything they wanted in the next few months. Not only that, they had all loved the exhilaration of the launch and the loop, and Ron was convinced that he had made the right choice in joining the airborne forces.

Tom Carpenter was also enjoying his rather different life in the 9th Field Company. It was energetic and not always comfortable, carrying out training exercises on the North York Moors, but Tom was young and anyway he was part of a small flexible unit. He enjoyed the challenge and fun of erecting Bailey bridges and demolishing them, and found the live firing exercises exciting. These helped to supplement their rations, as sheep often seemed to stray into the line of fire. He remembers with glee one night when a large number of out-of-date explosives were destroyed. They were all collected into one place for a controlled explosion, but the process got out of hand and the quantity was far greater than it should have been. There was a problem with the cable from the plunger and it took some time to find the break in the circuit, with the result that it was nightfall before the pile was detonated. The explosion created an enormous blast, which echoed across the moors and smashed windows in several villages a few miles away. Nobody was disciplined, however. There was a sense that something big was coming up, and these things were bound to happen.

Pat Gorman continued his rigorous training schedule, but one day he was told to be ready to go to a firing range with some other paratroopers. On Kos he had been equipped with the automatic Sten gun that was standard issue for parachute battalions, but he was now introduced to another weapon. With some others from the battalion he was driven to a large weapons testing range and shown something called a PIAT, which he was told stood for Projector Infantry Anti-Tank. It was a metal tube, just over 3 feet long and about 8 inches in diameter, with a folding hand grip with a trigger in the middle and a curved, padded shoulder rest. It was designed to fire a charge at the side of a tank but, instead of using an explosive propellant like an ordinary shell, it had a large, powerful spring that, when released, fired a pin into a small propellant in the base of the round. The round left the tube at fairly low speed, but the weapon didn't rely on its energy to penetrate armour; instead the warhead was designed to hit the side of a tank and, using a shaped charge, direct a narrow explosive blast through the armour, sending a spray of hot flakes of metal into the interior of the tank's hull. The PIAT had seen service in Italy, but it was new to Pat. It seemed there was some doubt about how effective it would be against the newer German tanks with tougher armour.

Pat lined up with the other paratroopers and they each fired a round from the PIAT at a large sheet of thick steel, while a group of officers and civilians looked on. The results were not impressive and Pat noticed that the faces of the senior officers looked grim. When it came to his turn to fire the weapon he asked the sergeant in charge if he could stand closer to the sheet of metal. With an oath, the sergeant told him under his breath he could stand where he liked. Pat realized that firing from too far away sometimes prevented the warhead from hitting squarely against the target, with the result that the force of the explosive charge was deflected. To load the weapon the spring had to be pulled back into the firing position with both hands, with the far end of the PIAT held against the ground or a wall. It could only be done standing up and took a lot of effort, especially as Pat was short. Placing the round into its slot in the front, he advanced as close as he dared to the sheet of steel. The recoil of the spring gave a nasty jolt against his shoulder, but the round struck true and smoke and flame exited from the far side of the metal.

The party of observers cheered up and a few of them actually clapped. The sergeant told Pat that he had done a good job and he felt pleased with himself. When he found out later that he was expected to be one of the battalion's PIAT gunners and thought of how heavy a weapon it was to carry about on a battlefield, he was not so happy.

7

D-Day

June 1944

Pat Gorman, like many people in the 1st Airborne, was given a forty-eight hour pass on Thursday, 1 June 1944. He would have to be back in camp on Saturday night, the 3rd, but this wasn't really enough time for him to get home to Workington in Cumbria and then return to camp, so instead he arranged with his mate 'Jonty' Herbert to go home with him to London for the two days. Jonty carried the spare rounds and detonators for Pat's PIAT on exercises and they had become quite good friends, despite the fact, as Pat says, that Jonty was 'a real Cockney, always plenty of backchat'. So Pat went to Shoreditch, quite happy to sleep on the couch in Jonty's front room for two nights.

On its return from Italy and North Africa, the 1st Airborne Division had been billeted in various parts of south and central England. Eventually everyone knew that a landing was going to made in France, but the division could do little about it except maintain the exceptional high level of fitness and training that was the hallmark of the airborne troops. Whatever had gone wrong with airborne operations, nobody had ever called into question the ability and determination of the troops once they were on the ground. During this period of waiting, John Frost (now a lieutenant colonel) instituted a regime in his 2nd Battalion to hone the various skills that he thought crucial. He demanded high standards of shooting, and firing practice was relentless. He insisted that all radios and signalling equipment were in first-class condition and that people knew how to use them. Finally, he believed that physical fitness was absolutely essential. Everyone should be able to march 30 miles a day with a half-hundredweight pack on their back.

This routine of training was not always sufficient to keep the men occupied. Frost himself remarked that there were always a number of hard cases in the battalions who did not set much store by obeying regulations, and absenteeism was high if there was no prospect of an operation. The problem was endemic throughout the airborne forces. Tom Carpenter overstayed his leave one week: instead of returning to camp on a Friday, he decided to stay at home for the weekend, hoping that if he made it to the camp by the first parade on the Monday morning nobody would notice his absence. Unfortunately, on Saturday the 9th Field Company moved to Bournemouth to enlarge the airport for the D-Day landings and Tom's absence was obvious. On Sunday morning two policemen came to his back door. Tom saw them from the window and hid under the kitchen table. His father went to the door. 'My father said he's already gone back, he went back this morning.'

'Make sure he's out of Birmingham by two o'clock today' was the reply, which Tom assumed was the time their shift ended, and the police left. Tom left shortly after to return to his old camp in Tattershall and was lucky, as he approached the camp at midnight, to be picked up by one of the last 9th Field Company vehicles on its way to Hurn Airport. On his return, he received a punishment of fourteen days confined to camp and loss of pay.

The same mood affected Pat and Jonty on their leave in London. On Saturday morning Jonty announced that he was not going back – he wanted to stay on over Saturday night to celebrate a cousin's marriage, then return on Sunday. Pat thought it was a good idea and that it would be OK to make some excuse about not being able to find transport when he got back to camp. The wedding reception was a loud affair, and despite the circumstances of wartime, watered-down beer and rationing, everybody had a lot of fun – 'a right old knees up' – and Pat was glad that he had stayed.

On the Sunday morning Jonty's father asked him to

go round the corner to a tobacconist's to see if he had any cigarettes – 'Just tell him it's for Bill Herbert.'

Jonty's father never saw his cigarettes. As he left the corner shop, a packet of ten Park Drive 'off the ration' in his pocket, Pat saw a green Humber saloon car parked in the street. Two large men in trenchcoats and trilby hats approached him and asked to see his pass. They showed him their warrant cards to prove they were in the Royal Military Police. Pat had clearly overstayed his leave, and there was nothing he could do in the face of authority. He was ushered into the car and driven to New Scotland Yard. Pat tried to persuade some of the uniformed police there that he had to get back to his unit and that he had been delayed through no fault of his own, but no one listened to him and he was kept in a cell all day.

Later, one of the plainclothes officers came for him and he was taken to a car. There was another paratrooper in it who had obviously also been slammed up in a cell and who said that he was in the 1st Battalion. Pat asked the plainclothes man what was happening. 'Your colonel's volunteered you,' was the reply, but he would say nothing further.

The two men were driven to an airfield, where they were issued with parachutes, Denison smocks and kitted out for a role as pathfinders – men who land first to mark out the landing zones for the main airborne forces. The sergeant in charge briefed the two of them and another six men on the mission, told them where they were to go when they landed and what time to ignite their magnesium flares. They were also issued with torches to signal over the landing zone. Beyond the bare bones of what he had to do and when, Pat wasn't told anything else. This did not surprise him. 'It was best not to know anything, because as you were the first to land, if you got captured you might reveal to the enemy where the landing zones were and when the rest were coming in. So know nothing.' The pathfinder task was usually carried out by either the 21st or the 22nd Independent Parachute Company, but clearly others were needed for the major operation that was looming. Pat was nonplussed about what was expected of him, but it wasn't anything that he hadn't been trained for, so, apprehensive about the prospect of landing in occupied France, he went to the mess, had a meal and waited for their take-off time.

The flight out, shortly after dusk, was calm, with no anti-aircraft fire over the French coast. Pat went out of the door of the aircraft into the rushing darkness and felt the sharp tug as his parachute opened. It was impossible to see the ground until the very last minute and he landed with a bone-shaking thump, but nothing was broken. He quickly got out of his harness and released the parachute, all the while expecting to hear the rapid fire of a German machine gun, but nothing came. The drop had gone surprisingly smoothly and the small group quickly assembled at their rendezvous point. Pat knew where he had to take up his position, but apart from knowing that he was in occupied France he had no idea where he was. 'I knew where I was to go, and what time to light the flares and switch on the torch. I didn't need to know much else.'

On that night, 5 June 1944, as Pat took off on his quite unexpected and mysterious journey, the Allies began their long-anticipated operation to land in Nazi-occupied Europe. It was a vast undertaking, with 130,000 soldiers carried across the English Channel to the beaches of northern France. Almost 5,000 ships and landing craft formed up in choppy seas south of the Isle of Wight before setting course for the five separate landing areas, escorted by over 500 vessels, ranging in size from enormous battleships to small minesweepers.

Everyone living in the south of England had noticed the huge troop movements that had taken place in the days leading up to the launching of Operation Overlord, as it was called, although its exact date was uncertain. However, the constant drone of aircraft engines over the towns and villages on this particular night seemed to suggest that now was the time. The aircraft flying low over their heads were not the large four-engined bombers that had been flying with increasing frequency to attack targets in France; instead they were transport aircraft, twin-engined C-47s – 1,200 in all – carrying the largest number of airborne troops ever used on a single mission.

Some lessons had been learned from the airborne landings in Sicily. The transport planes would be flying over the biggest fleet of warships ever assembled, and to avoid the awful losses caused by friendly fire that had happened on Operation Husky, all Allied aircraft had large alternate bands of black and white stripes painted around their wings and fuselage as an obvious means of identification. Unavoidably, to ensure maximum surprise the landings were still going to take place in the dark. The US 101st and 82nd Airborne Divisions were to drop inland of the US landings at Utah Beach to capture important road crossings, while the British 6th Airborne Division would land to the east of the French town of Caen to protect the left flank of the British landings at Sword Beach. An important part of their mission was to knock out a massive bunker at Merville, which the planners believed housed large-calibre artillery that threatened the invasion fleet. The 1st Airborne Division had no place in operation Overlord. They were going to be held in the UK as a strategic reserve and to maintain the fiction that the real landings were going to take place in the Calais area.

Cradling his Sten gun, crouched in the shelter of a hedge in a field in Normandy, Pat kept alert for any enemy troops that might be approaching. At 2.30 in the morning he moved out to the middle of the field and lit his magnesium flare, then retreated to cover.

He waited and waited. He could hear the noise of aircraft in the distance and the faint sounds of a bombardment rumbling away. Otherwise, there was nothing but the wind in the hedgerows. He waited for over two hours, but no gliders came. Eventually the sergeant arrived and told him to extinguish what was left of the flare and form up with the rest in the corner of the field. They were no longer needed. Pat was disgusted. 'Locked up, flown into France for D-Day and then told it wasn't necessary. Christ, what a performance.'

The sergeant was the only one who had a map and he set out, heading for the landings on the beachhead. It was becoming light and they could hear the sound of fighting to their west, a mixture of machine-gun fire and bombs. Pat thought that they would inevitably get caught up in the German front line. Advancing along a lane, they came across an enemy patrol. The Germans were taken by surprise, and Pat and his small group immediately opened fire, then took cover. So too did the German soldiers, who must have retreated, because Pat saw no more of them. They didn't find out if any of the enemy had been wounded or killed, but melted into the hedgerows and kept on their course.

Pat doesn't know why the gliders that he expected to land on the field he was marking did not arrive. There was, however, considerable confusion that night. The Rivers Orne and Dives were hard to distinguish from the air at night, so several advance parties dropped in the wrong place. The main forces of the 6th Airborne Division were also scattered by high winds. The very first British troops to land in France were the paratroopers of D Company and two platoons of B Company from the 2nd Oxford and Bucks Light Infantry, and a platoon from the Royal Engineers, all under the command of Major John Howard. A glider-borne force, their job was to seize the Bénouville Bridge over the Caen Canal, and the nearby Ranville Bridge over the River Orne. By holding both these bridges, the airborne troops would enable the British and Canadian troops of the British Second Army landing on the beaches to move eastwards quickly. One glider out of the six in this operation landed 7 miles from its objective, but the other five landed extremely close, barely 50 yards from the Bénouville Bridge. Both river crossings were captured within ten minutes with the loss of just two men, one of whom drowned in the canal. Elsewhere, things did not go so well.

The eastern approaches of these two bridges that had been so easily captured ought to have been defended by 4,000 men of the 3rd and 5th Parachute Brigades. Some units of this force were detailed to destroy several other bridges to hinder any possible German counter-attack against the eastern flank of the landing areas. In the event, the aircraft carrying the two brigades met strong winds which scattered the force and many dropped miles from their intended targets. At the eastern extremity of the drop zones, a lot of men landed in low-lying areas along the River Dives that had been flooded by the Germans. Men had to abandon all their equipment to avoid being drowned, and some who were not quick enough didn't survive. These units managed to form up, but with as many as 60 per cent of the men unaccounted for. Part of their task was to destroy bridges over the Dives at Robehomme and Varaville, and they still succeeded in doing so, in part because any resistance from the German forces was slow in coming.

The other key objective was the destruction of the long-range gun battery at Merville, an operation that was to be carried out by the 9th Battalion. The battery was defended by 130 soldiers with strategically located machine-gun posts and it was surrounded by a mined area between belts of barbed wire. In addition, an anti-tank ditch was built around one side of it. A raid by a squadron of Bomber Command Lancasters a few hours earlier ought to have destroyed the minefields and wire fences, but the bombs had been dropped far off the target. Despite their lack of mine detectors and demolition charges, the reconnaissance group cleared a way through the wire and then the minefield with their bare hands. They had cleverly located the positions of weapons points around the walls by listening to the conversations of the German soldiers manning them. With a line of attack now open, marked by lines scraped in the ground, the rest of the battalion were preparing to start their assault when a German sentry spotted their shapes in the dark and raised the alarm. The machine guns opened up and the paratroopers charged, hurling grenades and firing on the run. Reaching the concrete gun emplacements, they managed to breach the doors with grenades and poured through to begin hand-to-hand fighting with the defenders. Sixty-five of the men from the 9th Battalion were killed or wounded in the assault, while only six of the German garrison escaped unhurt. The attackers were dismayed to find, however, that the guns were of much smaller calibre than they had been led to believe.

By the end of the day the various elements of the 6th Airborne Division had carried out all their main tasks and were holding out against attacks from the enemy. The men of the 7th Battalion at the Bénouville Bridge were reached by infantry from the Second Army, but on the far-left flank of the British landing area the 6th Airborne Division continued to fight for the next few weeks.

Pat and his small group of ad hoc pathfinders met up with some advancing British airborne troops, who directed them to a rendezvous point where members of the 22nd Independent Company were forming up. Pat was slowly passed back down to the beach and ended up near Ouistreham. There he waited for four days before he was allocated a berth on a returning ship. Back in the UK he was given a travel warrant to Melton Mowbray. Despite having taken part, albeit in a small way, in the largest airborne landings of the war, approaching the camp Pat's natural distrust of authority came to the fore. All he could think of was that he had been absent for over a week and that the battalion was bound to throw the book at him. At the camp gate he was told in no uncertain terms to report to the regimental sergeant major, who told him that Lieutenant Colonel George Lea, the battalion commanding officer, wanted to see him. Pat stood to attention while Colonel Lea told him that he was a disgrace to the battalion and could have severely let down his comrades. They had been called to stand by on the Sunday morning, but 'You, Gorman, were absent, having failed to return at the end of your leave.'

Pat stood there expecting at the very least the loss of several weeks' pay, but the colonel stopped his diatribe and said, 'I knew where you were, Gorman, and I told them that they could do what they wanted with you.'

'Yes Sir!' said Pat, and then Lea dismissed him. Pat saluted and turned to leave the room, but as he did so he heard the colonel say, 'Well done, Gorman. See the staff sergeant. You're owed a week's leave.'

Pat could not believe his ears. He left the office as though he were on air. He got home to Workington, this time – but made sure that he returned to camp on the dot.

8

ALL OR NOTHING

July–September 1944

It was just over a hundred days between Pat landing in Normandy and his second parachute drop. Despite the 1st Airborne Division's role as a reserve force, the delay between D-Day and their descent into action at Arnhem was longer than anybody had anticipated.

The Allied landings in Normandy were followed by extremely bloody fighting. The German armies poured in reinforcements to contain the bridgehead, but the Allied troops succeeded in breaking out of Normandy and German resistance collapsed. They had been overwhelmed by the weight of the Allies' artillery and tank forces, and of course by their mastery of the air.

The impact of Allied firepower and the 2nd Tactical Air Force on two SS Panzer divisions, the 9th

'Hohenstaufen' and 10th 'Frundsberg', for example, was devastating but not out of the ordinary. The 9th SS Panzer Division had left the Russian front to take up its position in France with 18,000 men, and a complement of 170 tanks, twenty-one self-propelled guns, which were large artillery pieces mounted on tracked and armoured chassis, and 287 armoured troop carriers. On 26 June both divisions were placed under the command of Lieutenant General Wilhelm Bittrich to form II SS Corps, and they were then ordered to attack the British 11th Armoured Division. Failure to hold their line would allow the British to break through to the brutally contested Normandy town of Caen. The 9th and 10th had some initial success, halting the British advance, but later, under the weight of both artillery and naval gunfire, the Panzer divisions lost thirty-eight tanks. The battle lasted for two days; as well as the tanks, they lost many men and much of their equipment, supplies and personal belongings.

By 25 August they were in full-scale retreat, attempting to cross the Seine. Between them, the two German divisions were reduced to just 3,500 men and a handful of tanks. Thousands of other disorganized and beaten soldiers from German units were also struggling to cross the river and escape to Germany. A junior officer in the 10th Panzer Division recorded in his diary, 'all approaches to the river are hopelessly jammed. We estimate that 5,000 to 7,000 vehicles are three deep on the roads. Officers of the Waffen SS direct traffic with drawn pistols, a group of eight men on the bridge has the job of tipping off any vehicle that has broken down.' There was little leadership. Officers who attempted to rally the retreating troops, and to create some form of defensive line, were sometimes shot by their own men.

Paris had been liberated to scenes of wild euphoria, with wine flowing and flowers strewn in the path of the French and US troops who entered the city. A briefing written for General Eisenhower described the German Army as 'no longer a cohesive force but a number of fugitive battle groups disorganised and even demoralised, short of equipment and arms.' This was true. In the period between D-Day and 31 August, the Germans had suffered 23,019 deaths, 67,240 wounded and a massive 198,616 men were missing or taken prisoner. Many of the German units had been cut down to a tenth of their size. The Assistant Chief of the Imperial General Staff, Major General John Kennedy, wrote in his diary that the Allied forces should be in Berlin by the end of September.

As the rout continued, Hitler replaced the Commander in Chief West, Field Marshal Günther von Kluge, with Field Marshal Walter Model. Model had risen to his very high rank extremely quickly under Hitler's patronage. He had seen action in the invasions of Poland and France, and subsequently fought successful defensive retreats in Russia and on the Eastern Front. It was now his task to defend the western border of the Reich. He issued instructions to create a defensive line along the Belgian–Dutch border. General Kurt Student, the founding genius of the German airborne troops and the victor of Crete, was sent from Berlin with some headquarters staff to assemble a 1st Parachute Army and create a defensive line along the length of the Albert Canal in Belgium. SS troops, conspicuous by their shoulder flashes and special uniform, were pulled together and directed to assembly points where they formed rough and ready units or *Kampfgruppe*. At the same time, men from the German Navy and the Luftwaffe were organized and drafted into General Student's new Parachute Army, which, despite its title, was barely much larger than a division. Nevertheless, however seemingly inadequate, these hastily implemented measures were soon to pay off because the British forces were beginning to run out of steam.

The collapse of the German Army after the breakout from Normandy had allowed the British XXX Army Corps under the command of Lieutenant General Brian Horrocks to advance at great speed, making almost 50 miles a day in the direction of Antwerp and Brussels on a front that was 50 miles wide. The Guards Armoured Division, the spearhead of XXX Corps, captured Brussels on 3 September. The next day the 11th Armoured Division entered Antwerp.

The speed of this advance actually caused problems for the Allies. They had failed to capture a major port. Field Marshal Montgomery had left the French

Channel ports in German hands, and they were now small isolated pockets that were being liberated by the Canadian Army. Nearly everything that the advancing Allied forces needed, ammunition, fuel, spare parts and replacement equipment, as well as food, was being brought by road from the artificial harbours built on the landing sites in Normandy, which was now 300 miles or so in the rear. The Allied bombing campaign had destroyed much of the rail network, and the advancing armies could not ignore the demands for food from the newly liberated civilian population, so there was a developing crisis in the supply chain. The liberation of Antwerp should have solved the problem, but its lengthy estuary would take several months to clear of mines. The problem of supplies had become so acute that on 4 September General Horrocks's XXX Corps received orders to halt its advance. This allowed the German 11th Armoured Corps to escape and retreat eastwards; more importantly, it gave a short but vital breathing space for Model and Student to organize their ad hoc forces without the pressure of an advancing front. It was all they needed. By the time XXX Corps were allowed to advance once more, on the 6th, they ran into stiff resistance from the newly cobbled-together German units. It took the Guards Armoured Division four days to fight their way the short distance to the Meuse-Escaut Canal on the Dutch border, where they were once more brought to a halt. The Germans had managed to bolt the door.

* * *

Montgomery had previously expressed disagreements with Eisenhower's strategy and these differences were now coming to a head. At the time that Montgomery's Second Army had taken Brussels, he had tried to put to Eisenhower an idea of a single major thrust that would strike at the Ruhr, Germany's huge industrial region to the east of Holland. The capture of this vital area might shorten the war and bring it to an end in three months. An added advantage would be that this thrust through Belgium and Holland would outflank the German Siegfried Line, a defensive structure of gun emplacements and walls that ran the length of Germany's border with France. There was also another factor in Montgomery's thinking. While US forces were still pouring across the Atlantic, Britain had no more men to commit to the battle. The share of the burden of the Allied war effort was shifting, and the longer the war continued, the more British influence over the political landscape of post-war Europe would diminish.

Montgomery needed Eisenhower's approval for his plans because in order for this thrust to succeed he would have to be given priority for the supplies that were still snaking their way across France from the Normandy beaches, and in addition he would need to be put in overall command of the US First Army to defend his southern flank. It would also mean that General George S. Patton's Third Army, advancing on Germany to the south, would have to halt. This was a major difficulty for Eisenhower. Patton would object vociferously at this seeming favouritism towards Montgomery and it would cause political problems for Eisenhower in the United States. Eisenhower was in any case dubious about the value of 'lightning thrusts' and remained committed to the idea of a 'broad front' – the steady advance of all his armies into Germany. Montgomery, however, was determined to get what he wanted.

The two men met on 10 September at Brussels airfield on board Eisenhower's plane. It was a tense affair, with Montgomery allowing his impatience and disregard for Eisenhower's military qualities to get the better of him. Eisenhower managed to control whatever feelings of anger he may have felt at this show of insubordination, however, and they went on to discuss a plan that Montgomery's staff had been working on for the last few days. The kernel of it was the issue of what to do with the 1st Airborne Division. This had remained in Britain, ready to be used to assist the advance of the British Second Army, which had landed in Normandy. Throughout the summer, while Pat, Ron and Tom had kicked their heels in the UK, seventeen different plans for their deployment had been quickly worked up, only to be cancelled at the last minute as the rapid advance of the Allies rendered them unnecessary. Now, at last, with a bold plan to advance across Holland to Arnhem, the 1st Airborne could be thrown into the fray to solve many of Montgomery's problems.

The men of the division had been prepared for action ever since June and had lost count of the number of operations that had been cancelled. Tom Carpenter in the 9th Field Company came out of breakfast on D-Day itself to be briefed by his platoon commander, Captain Eric O'Callaghan, who as a lieutenant had won his MC in Sicily. They were told that the 6th Airborne Division had landed in Normandy as part of the Allied invasion. It wasn't a place with which they were at all familiar, but they were ordered to be ready to move by 10.00 that morning and were taken by lorry to occupy the camp at Bulford in Wiltshire that had been vacated by the 6th Parachute Brigade the day before. They were placed on a two-day standby, and from then on Tom is sure that up to seventeen operations were planned then scrapped at the last minute.

It was remarkably frustrating. Although their deployment and the tasks they were to be prepared to carry out were often the same for each mission, the gliders had to be unloaded after each cancellation because the extra weight would eventually distort the airframe. Very often the news that the operation was a no-go was delivered when they were sitting in the glider waiting for the tug to begin. There would be a bang on the side of the fuselage and an 'OK, chaps, it's off.' The unit's war diary beginning on 1 September records that on that day the gliders were loaded for Operation Linnet, which was cancelled on the 2nd, but that the company remained on standby for a further operation, which was cancelled later that day.

On the 7th the camp was again sealed. The company was briefed for Operation Comet and went to Harwell, while Tom with 2 Platoon went to Broadwell transit camp. On 8 September they were told that the operation had been postponed for forty-eight hours; the next day there was another postponement of twenty-four hours and then of forty-eight, and then on the 10th it was cancelled and the gliders were unloaded. Tom remembers the end of Operation Comet particularly well. The plan was that they were going to land on the bridge over the Waal at Nijmegen in Holland as closely as possible, in a *coup de main* or swift, surprising show of force. The rest of the division would land on the bridges at Arnhem and Grave. The general opinion was that a single division would be far too small to accomplish this and there was considerable trepidation. When Captain O'Callaghan banged on the side of Tom's glider, shouting, 'Come on, chaps, it's off!' he added, for all to hear, a heartfelt 'Thank Christ!'

Major General Roy Urquhart, in command of the 1st Airborne, thought that many of the plans were badly thought-out, mainly motivated by a desire to commit the division to action, whatever the possible outcome. In his view, 'there was a growing sense of the naiveté of the planning staff about airborne operations'. However, on 4 September Eisenhower had placed the US First Allied Airborne Army, commanded by Lieutenant General Lewis H. Brereton, under Montgomery's command. This army contained two US divisions, the 101st and the 82nd, veterans of landings on Crete and in Normandy, and a Polish airborne brigade. Suddenly the resources for a bigger version of Operation Comet were available, providing further support for Montgomery's vision of a lightning thrust to the north into Germany.

Montgomery's staff had taken this new force and incorporated them into the existing plans for Comet, so that it now became a substantial operation, the largest airborne mission yet seen. It was named Operation Market and would be supported by a ground operation of the British Second Army to be called Garden. This was the plan that Montgomery presented to Eisenhower at that acrimonious meeting on 10 September.

Perhaps to Montgomery's surprise, Eisenhower appeared to welcome the proposal. It solved for him the problem of what to do with the large Allied airborne forces that had not yet been committed to the battle. It was bold and imaginative, and would show that the huge resources that had been devoted to the development of airborne forces were going to make a significant contribution to the defeat of Germany. Montgomery immediately despatched Lieutenant General Frederick Browning, now in charge of the US forces as well as of the British Airborne Division, back to the UK to brief the various commanders.

Montgomery hoped that the operation would start on 17 September. The largest and most complicated airborne operation in the history of warfare was to be finalized in just seven days.

Events moved very quickly. Later that same day, at 14.30 on 10 September, General Browning landed in England and by 18.00 he was outlining the plan to thirty-four commanders and staff officers who had been called in to Brereton's office at the First Allied Airborne Army HQ in Sunninghill Park, Ascot.

There was an enormous amount of work to do for an operation that one participant described as one of unprecedented complexity and boldness. Montgomery's Second Army would advance northwards from their current positions on the Belgian–Dutch border towards the shore of the Ijsselmeer, the large body of seawater enclosed by the Dutch polders. There were three corps in the Second Army. XII Corps would cover the left flank to the east, while VIII Corps would cover the right flank to the west. The main advance in the middle would be by XXX Corps, which would advance to Eindhoven, then Nijmegen and on to Arnhem, with a potential finish line for the Guards Armoured Division around the Dutch town of Apeldoorn, cutting off any possibility of the German Army in Holland retreating to the east.

The path for this rapid advance by XXX Corps was to be prepared by three key landings by airborne troops. The corridor between Eindhoven and Veghel was to be secured by parachute and glider landings by the US 101st Division. They would capture bridges over the Wilhelmina and Willems Canals. Further north, the US 82nd Airborne Division would land and seize the bridge over the River Maas at Grave and that over the River Waal at Nijmegen, while the British 1st Airborne would land and seize the bridges over the lower Rhine at Arnhem. Montgomery likened the airborne landings to carpets over which the advancing XXX Corps could walk, and this terminology took hold. The role of the airborne troops, then, was to assist the advance of the main units, yet their ability to hold on to their objectives would depend on the speed of advance of the main ground forces.

The distance from the start line of XXX Corps' advance to Arnhem was 65 miles, and Montgomery told Browning that it would be necessary for his airborne troops to hold on to the bridges at Arnhem for two days. Browning's reply was that they could hold it for four, but that 'it might be a bridge too far' – a phrase that has cascaded down the years to sum up the operation at Arnhem.

Browning didn't repeat this remark to Major General Urquhart at the briefing later that day; instead, according to Urquhart, Browning drew the third circle on the map in front of them, fixed Urquhart with a stare and said bluntly, 'Arnhem Bridge – and hold it!' So instructed, Urquhart left the meeting and started his own planning. Some of it was easy. The number of troops and amount of equipment that could be lifted by aircraft and gliders were well known, and the configurations of various combat teams were also worked out. However, Urquhart discovered that he was not necessarily going to get the number of aircraft that he would like, so he would have to get his troops and equipment into their landing areas in three separate waves. His aircraft were being provided by the 9th US Troop Carrier Command, as well as by the RAF. 1st Airborne had at its command ten squadrons of gliders and tugs from 38 Group RAF and six squadrons from 46 Group, while the 9th US Troop Carrier Command was laying on the C-47 Dakota transports for the paratroops. It was calculated that each parachute brigade needed 130 of these aircraft, so lifting the 1st and 4th Brigades would require the available aircraft to make two drops, with the Polish Parachute Brigade requiring a third one.

The RAF were prepared to attempt two waves on the first day, which would have entailed the initial wave taking off at dawn from airfields in the UK, with the follow-on troops lifting off in the afternoon. At this time of the year there was still sufficient daylight to accomplish this. The Polish Brigade would land on the morning of the second day. The US commander, however, was not prepared to do this, arguing that he had insufficient maintenance staff to mount two sorties back to back, so the arrival of the 1st Airborne Division would be spread over three days. It was hardly the 'thunderclap surprise' that Montgomery had first suggested.

The other problem was one that exercised Urquhart a great deal. The RAF had been persuaded that the landings should take place in daylight in order to avoid poor nighttime navigation dispersing troops over a wide area, but they were adamant about doing all they could to avoid the added dangers daylight might bring. RAF planners suspected that the German Army had placed anti-aircraft guns near the bridge at Arnhem and they wanted to avoid both what they believed were heavy anti-aircraft emplacements north of the town and the German fighter airfield at Deelen. This led them to select parachute-drop and glider-landing zones to the north-west of Arnhem. The advantages of these locations, according to Urquhart, were that they were flat and open and would allow troops to form up quickly. The disadvantage – and it was a huge one – was that between the landing zones and the bridges lay 8 miles of intensively cultivated farmland, woods and built-up areas. Also, because the arrival of Urquhart's forces would be spread over three days, troops would have to be kept in place to secure the landing zones. His forces would be split for some time, and Urquhart summed it up succinctly: on the first day, the effective strength of his 1st Airborne Division against the main objective would actually be just one parachute brigade. Urquhart pestered Browning for more aircraft, but was told that the operation had to be planned from the bottom up. There was little to be gained if, in maximizing the effort for Arnhem, the resources needed to capture the bridges at Grave or at Nijmegen were compromised. The relief of the troops at Arnhem depended on the success of these other operations – a truth that was to be brought brutally home to Urquhart later.

It was useless to argue. Urquhart had no other option but to make plans to fit in with the resources he had available. On the first day, the pathfinder force of the Independent Company and the 1st Parachute Brigade would land from 155 Dakotas from the 9th US Troop Carrier Command, and the bulk of the 1st Airlanding Brigade would descend in 358 gliders, towed by their equivalent aircraft from the RAF. The 1st Parachute Brigade would strike out for the bridges, while the landing areas would be defended by the 1st Airlanding Brigade. The next day, the 4th Parachute Brigade and the remainder of the 1st Airlanding Brigade would arrive, freeing the 1st Airlanding Brigade to move out and defend the left flank of the captured bridges, while the 4th Parachute Brigade would take up a defensive position to the north. With the anti-aircraft guns near the bridges put out of action, the Polish Parachute Brigade would be free to land immediately south of the town of Arnhem and cross the bridge to occupy the eastern outskirts of the town on the right flank. Within twenty-four hours of that, the Guards Armoured Division would arrive and advance through Arnhem to Apeldoorn.

Lieutenant Colonel John Frost, still in command of the 2nd Battalion of the 1st Parachute Brigade, was informed of the plan in the orders group meeting conducted by the brigade's commanding officer, Brigadier Gerald Lathbury, on 15 September. As Frost wrote after the event, 'We were highly delighted to be given a really worthwhile task at last. This was the genuine airborne thrust that we had been awaiting and we felt that if things went according to plan we should be truly instrumental in bringing the war to an end in 1944.'

Frost, however, very much from the view of someone whose job it was to take the bridge, immediately saw the glaring snags in the plan. From his wide experience, he knew it was essential to get troops on to both sides of the bridge straight away. Taking bridges, as he said, is very difficult. If your forces are on one side only, the defenders can concentrate their fire on all the approaches and on to the bridge itself from the comparative security of the other side. He also realized that there would be a long march from the drop zones to the bridge. The brigade's Reconnaissance Squadron, in armed jeeps, would make a speedy dash for the road bridge and, having secured it, the battalions would take three different routes to reinforce them. Frost was told that it was his task to seize the main railway bridge as well as the road bridge, and to create close bridgehead garrisons and hold them. Frost wanted to secure the rail bridge first and send a detachment of troops along the southern bank of the Rhine so that they could move to join up with the Reconnaissance Squadron, who would have approached from the northern side. Between the railway bridge and the steel-arched road bridge was a third crossing – a narrow road bridge supported by floating pontoons that opened and closed to allow passage for river boats. It was probably too flimsy to support heavy loads like tanks or artillery, and it wasn't thought to be an important objective.

The Royal Engineers were going to be important players in the mission. It would be their job to advance on to the bridges and ensure that any demolition charges placed there by the Germans were neutralized. The commanding officer of Tom Carpenter's 9th Field Company, Major Jack Winchester, had attended a briefing on Operation Market on 12 September. He was told that it was his job to send a small detachment with the main Reconnaissance Squadron to remove any demolition charges that were attached to the main road bridge. He was also ordered to provide a second force to seize and hold the railway bridge over the Rhine. He decided to nominate Tom Carpenter's unit, 2 Platoon, for that task.

Doubts about the extended lift, and the distance that lightly armed soldiers would have to travel to reach their objectives, were allayed to some extent by intelligence that the Arnhem area was only lightly protected by units of the Hitler Youth and a battalion of troops who were not fit enough to be front-line soldiers. The Dutch Resistance, however, had passed information to the British that in fact some remnants of SS Panzer divisions, still with some of their armour, were stationed in the area around Arnhem. One intelligence officer, Major Brian Urquhart, who was no relation to the general, took this information seriously. On 12 September he asked for photo-reconnaissance flights to take place, and the pictures he received three days later revealed the presence of tanks near some of the 1st Airborne's landing and drop zones. His efforts to disseminate the information to the divisional HQ and alert the staff to this potential danger did not meet with any success. He was advised, after a strained meeting with General Browning, to seek leave on medical grounds.

It was hard to interrupt an operation the size and complexity of Operation Market Garden. After a certain point, such things have a momentum of their own. Anyway, there was little that the senior planning staff could do. There were no more resources to allow radical changes to the plan. At this late stage, the operation had either to go ahead as planned, or be delayed, perhaps for ever, with all the possible repercussions that that might have for the course of the war, and on relations between Montgomery and Eisenhower. From the moment of their meeting at Brussels airport on 10 September, the die had been cast.

* * *

In fact, British Signals Intelligence at the code-breaking centre in Bletchley Park had followed the movements of the 9th and 10th SS Panzer Divisions all the way from their defeat at the hands of the British in the Battle of the Falaise Gap in Normandy to their reception areas near Arnhem. It was the presence of these armoured units, revealed in the reconnaissance photos, that so alarmed Major Brian Urquhart. The 9th and 10th Panzer Divisions, the two sister divisions of II SS Corps, had been re-organized into two *Kampfgruppe* that had been so reduced in the fighting that they now numbered just over 5,500 infantry. The 10th was slightly better off in terms of equipment than the 9th, because in the retreat they had come across a supply train carrying new 88mm guns, which were very effective anti-aircraft artillery and also good anti-tank weapons. They had taken all that they could before continuing on their retreat. The 9th had around 20 Mark V Panther tanks, a few self-propelled guns and armoured cars, and forty armoured personnel carriers. The 10th, however, apart from its new 88mm artillery pieces, had very few vehicles of any sort. Lieutenant General Bittrich had received orders to prepare the two divisions for rest and resupply in Germany, and so ordered them to positions east and north-east of Arnhem in preparation for their move. The 9th was scheduled to move back to Germany first, but Bittrich was uncertain where the next British thrust would come, so wanted to maintain a reserve force in readiness for as long as possible. Before the 9th left for Germany, he instructed them to hand over their weapons to the 10th, and made sure that the administrative and support staff were the first to make the journey back. The fighting elements of the 9th that stayed were unhappy about releasing all their weapons to the 10th, and managed to hold on to a few tanks and armoured personnel carriers, which they claimed were unserviceable. They remained in place just thirty minutes by vehicle from Arnhem and were scheduled finally to leave their positions on 17 September.

By then the planning for Operation Market Garden was finished, the orders were issued and the gliders were loaded.

9

THE FIRST DAY

Sunday, 17 September

On 16 September, the 9th Field Company was in a transit camp at Blakehill Farm in Wiltshire and everyone was briefed on Operation Market. Most of them were doubtful that it would ever take place. 'It'll be another false alarm, we won't be moving out,' thought Tom Carpenter. Nevertheless, they memorized their 'chalk' numbers – the numbers written on the side of the glider that they were meant to board the next morning – then went through their instructions and the rendezvous details for their landing zone, looking at the large-scale maps of the area in the briefing tent. The sappers then checked their weapons and equipment, making sure that everything was in order and properly packed away. This was now so routine that they could have done it in their sleep.

Perhaps, however, there was a gut feeling that this

time it was really going to happen, because that night several men in the company – Tom thinks it might have been about twenty of them – broke into the NAAFI tent and started rifling through the stores, breaking open crates of beer and settling down for a party. The gathering grew raucous and the drinking session was eventually broken up by the arrival of the Military Police. Everyone scrambled back to their tents, crashing through guy ropes and creating mayhem, pursued by the beams of the MP's torches. Reveille was at five o'clock the next morning and they awoke, some with sore heads, to a decent breakfast, then at 08.00 hours they climbed on board their lorries and headed out to the airbase at Keevil in Wiltshire, where their gliders and the tugs were waiting.

Each platoon had five gliders and the number of sappers in each glider depended on the amount of stores and other equipment that was also loaded. One of the gliders assigned to 2 Platoon carried a jeep, a 10cwt trailer, a motorcycle, four folding bicycles and 200lb of stores, plus a captain and five sappers. Tom's glider had eighteen bikes, two lightweight motorcycles, one heavy motorcycle and 200lb of equipment, plus twenty-one sappers. The equipment, which was stored in containers under the wing centre section, held shovels, demolition explosives and other weapons like Hawkins grenades, which were rectangular charges shaped like large hip flasks. These were detonated by a small chemical igniter that was set off when a tank or other vehicle drove over it. As part of his training, Tom had been taught how to place a grenade underneath a tank track or wedge it on top of one. The crew of a tank, he had been told, had a blind spot that stretched for about 75 feet around the vehicle – an area where an infantry man could operate with impunity. 'Get in close and it was easy to place a grenade. This was why tanks worked in company with other tanks, or with infantry. The crew can't see, and they hate it.'

Tom, like most other airborne troops, was loaded with his own kit and personal weapons. As he stepped up into the glider, he was carrying three bandoliers of .303 rounds in clips of five – a total of 150 rounds; four Bren-gun magazines in the pouches of his smock; eight Sten-gun magazines; two hand grenades and two smoke grenades; two Hawkins mines; and he was also responsible for a tube of three PIAT anti-tank rounds. He also carried his personal weapon, which was a rifle and bayonet, and he had his small pack in which went his rations, mess tin, water bottle, shaving kit, any spare clothes that he wanted, an entrenching tool, gas mask and a gas cape, which doubled as a rainproof poncho.

An extra piece of equipment was the Denison jump smock, which was made of heavy, windproof denim that covered his battledress, and which had a flap at the back that went between his legs and attached to the front with press studs.

Once they had boarded the gliders with all that

equipment there was little room to move about. They sat waiting, as they had many times before, only to hear the bang on the side of the fuselage and 'It's off, boys!' They waited, but this time Captain O'Callaghan came and tapped on the side, shouting, 'Chaps, we're on our way. See you over there. Good luck!' At last! It was on! Tom felt a thrill like electricity go through the men in his glider – a mixture of adrenaline and sudden anticipation of what lay ahead. For Tom it was his first action, and he could only imagine the landing behind enemy lines.

The four engines of their Stirling tug picked up speed and the glider rocked in the backwash. Tom felt the vibration as the towing cable snaked out, then came a short jerk and the glider accelerated, faster and faster, the wheels rumbling until they were airborne, at last.

These men had every reason to be fearful and anxious, about to journey over the North Sea in a fragile wooden glider and attempt a landing in enemy territory, thrust into a battle with almost no mental or physical adjustment. It was one of the great disadvantages of airborne troops, that they could not observe their enemy before the action started; there was no physical reconnaissance or observation of the terrain in which they were about to start fighting. They dropped from the sky into a ready-formed battlefield and had to impose themselves on it immediately, or perish. The men in Tom's platoon, however, were not afraid. They were excited, eager. Some of them started singing as they rose into the air. 'We were in good form. We were fit, really fit, in tip-top condition, and if you're feeling fit you're feeling great.'

They climbed in the air to 3,000 feet. The weather was fine and through the small portholes some of them could see England spread out below them in the morning sun. The flight was smooth, the glider pilots keeping station just above or below the tug's slip-stream to avoid any turbulence. First they turned west, flying out over Gloucestershire and the Severn estuary to form up with the other gliders and their tugs taking off from airfields scattered throughout the south-west. Apart from Keevil, from where Tom took off, six other airfields were dedicated to launching the gliders, while the parachute aircraft took off from three airfields in Lincolnshire. US troops who were landing at Eindhoven separated from the stream of air-craft and formed up over Manston in Kent before heading towards Belgium and then crossing the front line. The US 82nd Airborne Division, bound for the bridge at Nijmegen, flew in the stream heading for Arnhem before breaking away for their target over Holland.

More than 3,500 aircraft took off for Operation Market Garden that day. It was an impressive and amazing sight. The giant airborne armada formed three lines of aircraft 1½ miles apart and nearly 100 miles long. All along its route, people on the ground left their houses to look up at the huge stream of planes and gliders flying above their heads, the roar of the engines filling towns and villages for over an hour, even after the main force had passed. Unlike the nightly flights of bombers heading for Germany, and the enormous activity for the D-Day landings, these aircraft and their gliders were flying low and in daylight, for all to see – the greatest airborne operation ever. It was obvious to those on the ground that another major offensive had started and that victory could not be far away. After five long years of war, no one could look up and not be filled with pride and hope.

Tom's glider turned east over Weston-super-Mare and with the other syndicates, as the glider-and-tug combinations were called, headed to join the main stream that was to turn again over Hatfield and head down the eastern side of London. Tom had seen the town spread out below him, and at about eleven o'clock he remembers one of his mates suddenly shouting, 'He's going down, he's going down!'

Tom looked and just saw a glider, chalk mark 390, carrying Sergeant Arthur Oakey and twenty sappers of 1 Platoon, break in half. The rear fuselage fell away and soldiers spilled out, helpless as they fell to the ground 3,000 feet below. The nose and wing section, still attached to the tow rope, started to fall, then the tow rope broke and that too plunged to the earth. The wreckage fell close to the village of Paulton, near Weston-super-Mare. There were no survivors. The

Stirling aircraft towing the glider landed back at Keevil and the crew commandeered a jeep to drive to the spot where they believed the glider had hit. The rear gunner, Sergeant Wally Simpson, saw the wreckage and thought to himself, 'It looks like a matchbox that's been stepped on.'

On Tom's glider, the mood changed swiftly. There was no more singing. People were mulling over the fate of the sappers on board, and the brief glimpse that Tom had had of the glider falling apart was to haunt him in later life. 'I had nightmares of being in that glider and sitting for probably five minutes while it's spinning, and you've got to sit there, and know you were just going to your death.'

The now quiet sappers sat in their glider until they were crossing the coast. It was a wonderful day for flying; the sea was placid and it was a comfortable flight. They saw more gliders in trouble, breaking away and ditching into the sea, but there was a long chain of air-sea rescue boats that stretched along their route over the North Sea. Some of the tugs experienced engine trouble, and in some cases the tow rope separated unexpectedly, but the glider pilots were able to put down close to a rescue vessel and almost all the soldiers and crews were rescued, except for one who was killed when his glider hit the sea.

The journey from the English coast to the Dutch landfall was 94 miles – about forty-five minutes' flying. Halfway into the journey the three huge columns of C-47s, Stirling tugs and gliders were joined by 874 fighters from the US Army Air Force and the RAF, whose task it was to guard the airborne troops from German fighter planes. Tom could look out of the nearest porthole in his glider and see a vast expanse of aircraft stretching into the distance, the gliders gently rising and falling behind their tugs, the sun overhead striking blinding reflections off Perspex windscreens. It was a strangely beautiful sight to see at such a time.

As they neared the Dutch coast, some flak ships anchored near Schouwen Island started firing and the explosions caused more alarm, but they were soon past the coast and the gunfire faded away, then all that Tom could see was the red-tiled roofs of houses surrounded by water. The whole area over which they were passing had been flooded by the Germans, who had opened the dykes on the Ijsselmeer. The water seemed to go on for mile after mile.

Finally, snaking beneath them and glinting in the sun, were the three great rivers, the Maas, the Waal and the Rhine.

There was a command from the front to be ready to cast off, then the noise of the tugs' engines fell away and there was a silence, apart from the air rushing past the fuselage. As they got lower, Tom remembers that there was the sound of a sudden burst of machine-gun fire, random, fired by whom at what he never knew. Then the glider pilot descended rapidly, in 500-foot swoops, circling as he looked for a landing spot, getting lower and lower with the options rapidly disappearing, clutching now at straws. There were about ten other gliders trying to get into the same space, and in the final drop the pilot was now committed. He had no power – a glider pilot can do no more than keep the glider straight and level, hoping for a smooth landing run with no hidden obstacles or sudden gusts of wind. Tom's glider hit and bounced once, a section of the fuselage splintered away and then they were sliding along the ground, bumping and jolting for almost 100 yards before it came to a halt. Someone flung the door open and the platoon started to clamber out. This was the most dangerous part of the landing, as enemy troops could be in position ready to open fire as the airborne troops stumbled out of the doors, disorganized and laden with equipment. There was fighting in the woods next to the landing zone, but it was spasmodic fire between the South Staffordshire Regiment troops who had landed in the same zone and a few German soldiers who had been on a routine patrol.

Tom had landed in Landing Zone Z, alongside the 1st Parachute Brigade, who dropped in their Drop Zone X, to the west of them. Immediately further west was another landing zone, LZX, where part of the 4th Parachute Brigade had come in. They had landed on ploughed fields, although Tom cannot remember any crops; he believes they were lying fallow. To the south of the landing zone was the village of Heelsum, and on the north-east border was the village of Wolfheze. The landing zone itself was a picture of complete confusion, littered with gliders, with men gathering around them trying to get out jeeps, trailers and the 6-pounder guns of the Royal Artillery Anti-tank Battery that had come in with the 1st Airlanding Brigade, whose job it was to protect and defend the landing sites for the second lift the next day.

The company's rendezvous point was at the southeast of the landing zone, and as they assembled there they learned of the losses that had taken place. Not only had the glider carrying members of 1 Platoon broken apart over Weston-super-Mare, but another glider carrying a detachment from 3 Platoon, which was to have gone forward with the Reconnaissance Squadron to take the road bridge in Arnhem, had had to slip their tow and land in the UK. The final casualties from the glider of their CO, Major Jack Winchester, which had broken up on landing, were: the wireless operator, Sapper Holdstock, who was thrown out as the fuselage hit the ground and died soon after; Sergeant Paffett and Sapper Robertson, whose ankles were broken when a landing wheel came up through the floor; and the pilot, who was hurled through the rear of the cockpit and hit the jeep that had been lashed down in the fuselage.

At around 14.15 the company was assembling at the rendezvous point. Major Winchester took stock of the situation, trying to work out how to accomplish all his allotted tasks with two platoons missing. He ordered a section of 2 Platoon to join up with

1 Platoon to capture the Wolfhezen Hotel, which he wanted to use as the company HQ. Captain Maurice Heggie and eleven sappers were sent off with two jeeps to meet up with the Reconnaissance Squadron, who were to make the quick advance to the Arnhem road bridge, while Tom's 2 Platoon, under Captain O'Callaghan, was sent to capture and secure the rail bridge.

On their way to the rendezvous point, Tom had come across some of the inmates of a nearby mental asylum, who had escaped when the asylum had been bombed that morning. They stood there in their white hospital smocks, staring at the activity around them, some gesticulating and laughing. The members of the platoon were taken aback at this, but they saw no reason to interfere with them, so they continued on their way.

The platoon set off into Heelsum from the rendezvous point on their folding bikes, with a jeep and the demolition equipment with them. It was now three o'clock in the afternoon. As they cycled along a path in the woods they were fired on, the bullets thudding into the trunks of the trees, and Tom and the rest of the platoon threw themselves to the ground. The firing sounded as though it was coming from a Bren gun, which had a slightly slower rate of fire than the German MG42 machine gun. All the troops landing at Arnhem carried a yellow cloth as identification, so Tom tied his to his rifle and waved it in the air above him. There were cries of 'OK, mate' and they rose to find that they had crossed the path of the 1st Parachute Battalion, who were making their way to take the most northern route into Arnhem.

They passed through each other and continued on their respective ways, Tom's platoon finally reaching Heelsum. The Dutch civilians in the area had been expecting the Allied armies to arrive for some days. They knew about the rapid advance of the British Army across France and Belgium and had witnessed the German troops retreating, obviously in a state of disorder. The sudden arrival of thousands of men by parachute and glider in the nearby fields had taken them completely by surprise, however, but now they were excited to have an army of liberation in their midst. They came out of their houses to greet the airborne troops, offering drinks, apples and whatever food they had to hand. So when Tom walked into the village, he was met with offers of cups of tea and home-made apple juice. He was also met by fire from two snipers.

The bullets came whistling past and one of the snipers, who had fired from behind a chicken coop, attempted to roll away from his position, but he was immediately hit by fire from several rifles and he sprawled lifeless. At the opening shots, however, the villagers fled back into their houses, leaving the streets deserted.

It was just as well. They had no time to waste before getting to the railway bridge. Although they did not know it, John Frost was relying on capturing the bridge intact so that he could send a detachment along the south bank of the Rhine to take the southern end of the road bridge.

The longer that 2 Platoon took to reach their objective, the more time the Germans guarding the bridge had to make final preparations to their demolition charges. They had several miles still to go, and with the skies above black with gliders and parachutes, the German guards were not going to be taken by surprise. At Heelsum, Tom's platoon had orders to liaise with the 2nd Battalion under John Frost, who was taking the lower route to Arnhem along the northern bank of the Rhine. When they met up, Frost told Captain O'Callaghan to slot the platoon in between his A and B Companies, with A Company in the lead. The 2nd Battalion, numbering only 481 men, was smaller than the other battalions in the 1st Parachute Brigade, but it was accompanied by the 1st Parachute Squadron of the Royal Engineers and some of the 1st Airlanding Anti-Tank Battery, with four 6-pounder guns towed by jeeps.

The woods were closed in around their path and there was the occasional hold-up as they encountered enemy fire, which was very sporadic but enough to make them pause, dribbling away the precious time that they needed to reach their objectives. This was Tom's first taste of action, and he was struck by how organized everyone was. The opposition was briskly dealt with and the column re-formed, but the dense trees and woodland meant that progress was cautious and slow. They passed through the houses of Doorwerth, then Heveadorp. A Company of the 2nd Battalion was well ahead, Tom remembers, setting a cracking pace, extremely well trained, firing effectively at any opposition, and occasionally he saw the dead bodies of the German soldiers they had shot lying in the grass or by the side of the road. Tom continued down the road, coming to the high ground at Westerbouwing, very close to the river, which afforded a view, for the first time, of their objectives – the railway bridge, and the road bridge further down river. The rail bridge was a three-arch span, each span extending about 50 yards, so that the bridge itself was about 150 yards long, with the railway tracks approaching on a long embankment over the low ground to the north. It was still intact.

At this sight, they felt elated, although they still had almost a mile to march before they could reach the embankment. By now they were pushing their cycles as they continued eastwards along the road, following the sound of the Sten guns from A Company in the lead, and hearing also the noise of fighting coming from the north, where the other parachute battalions were heading towards Arnhem along the northern and middle routes.

The column was on the Benedendorpsweg, in Oosterbeek, and Captain O'Callaghan took the opportunity of a short halt to talk to Major Douglas Murray, who was in charge of the small detachment of Parachute Squadron Royal Engineers, to outline his plans for the capture of the railway bridge. They started again, but just as they passed the old church at Oosterbeek, a German armoured car nosed out of a side street and started firing at them. Once again, they flung themselves to the ground while the 20mm rounds flew over their heads. A call went down to B Company to bring forward one of the 6-pounder anti-tank guns, while a few grenades were hurled and small-arms fire peppered the turret of the armoured car. The gunfire and the blasts of the grenades, followed by the crack of the 6-pounder and the report of the shell hitting the armoured car, created sufficient din to alert anybody on the bridge, if they needed any alerting at all. Smoke poured from the armoured car and none of the crew got out. Tom picked himself up and went on. Despite the fighting, he still felt as though he were on an exercise, and this feeling continued even when an 88mm artillery piece mounted on a tracked chassis fired two shots, the high-pitched crack of the gun scattering them again before it withdrew. The platoon was taking everything in its stride; the atmosphere was 'We're going forward, press on.' The bridge was still there; they were gradually getting closer.

As they did so, Tom's platoon separated from the 2nd Battalion and made their preparations to take the railway bridge over the Rhine. The plan was to proceed with as much stealth as possible, with one section to keep an eye out for guards while others searched for wires and fuses leading to any demolition charges so that they could be cut and the charges rendered safe. Benedendorpsweg passed through a concrete archway under the railway line, and just before this a lane turned off, running down by the side of the embankment leading to the river. Captain O'Callaghan left his jeep and trailer just past the entrance to the lane, under the arch out of sight, and ordered the rest of the platoon to stack their bicycles by the embankment. They took grenades, ammunition and a couple of Bren guns and rifles, then struck off along the side of the embankment. After a few hundred yards they climbed up the slope of the embankment under the cover of bushes until they reached the rail tracks. There was an abandoned two-car electric train on the rails, looking as though it had been shot up in a raid on the anti-aircraft guns by the side of the bridge. These also appeared shot up and abandoned. The sappers crossed over the rails and started to move along the other side of the embankment. They were in excellent cover, and Tom continued moving forward until he and his fellow sappers were about 20 yards from the start of the first span.

It appeared that the German defenders were all on the south side of the bridge. Captain O'Callaghan observed the situation closely. The anti-aircraft guns around the bridge had been hit by ground-attack aircraft. One of the positions was little more than a twin 20mm machine-gun mounting fixed on the back of a half-track vehicle. It had obviously caught fire. The other more fixed positions on the north side were also deserted. There was a pillbox on the north side, and another one on the south side, which was occupied, although the nearest one to them seemed to be empty. Also on the south side next to the railway, on the eastern side of the line, were two houses that had been turned into a defensive position with sandbags around their entrances and the windows taken out. German soldiers were working on the southern end of the bridge, and it was obvious that they were laying some sort of charges with their associated wiring. They were roughly 150 yards away from Tom's position. The bushes and shrubs on the embankment had shielded his platoon from view and the Germans, about twenty of them, were oblivious to their presence.

It was a tense moment. Each of the sappers had marked his target, ready to shoot the Germans if they noticed them. Their first, extremely urgent, task was to check for demolition charges and attempt to neutralize them. It was vital that the bridge be captured intact. O'Callaghan looked through his binoculars to see if he could spot any fuses and wiring set along the bridge. Suddenly, the stillness was broken by a platoon of paratroopers who stormed up the embankment from Tom's right and surged forward on to the railway line.

As soon as this happened, firing broke out from the other end of the bridge and Tom's platoon went forward, Captain O'Callaghan in front and Tom following him. They moved rapidly forward for 50 yards, making their way along the side of the bridge, taking cover from the girders. They saw some wiring and snatched at it, quickly cutting it while the others in their platoon gave them covering fire. The leading paratroopers, who had advanced on to the railway line in a frontal assault, started to go down under the weight of enemy fire. The sappers stayed on the first span, while machine-gun fire from the pillbox and the two houses on the south bank opened up with even more ferocity. Then the bridge under Tom's feet shook, there was a massive explosion and the middle span over the water lifted high into the air amidst a cloud of smoke and dust. Pieces of debris hurtled high above the river. For a moment, Tom thought that it would continue to rise and topple on to them. The huge metal arch stayed poised in the air for a moment, then crashed, buckling, into the Rhine, with gouts of water mingling with the smoke and debris from the demolition charges that had been set off. The bridge was wrecked.

They had no time to contemplate this disaster. The machine-gun fire from the south bank was intense, but mortars from the paratroopers behind them were now being directed at the two houses and smoke grenades were providing some cover. Then a shout went up, 'Off the bridge!' and Tom, O'Callaghan and the rest rushed for the embankment. Tom remembers going so fast that he could have been flying, tumbling down some steps that he had not noticed before, in fear of the span that they were on blowing up. But, of course, they had in fact succeeded in cutting the demolition wires, so the third span remained in place.

The paratroopers who had rushed the bridge were a platoon of C Company from the 2nd Battalion, who had been ordered independently to capture the railway bridge. Several of them, including the CO, Lieutenant Peter Barry, were wounded and one was killed by the German fire. They withdrew to join up with C Company, then with the main battalion.

Tom's platoon remained where they were. O'Callaghan sent some sappers to look for further demolition charges along what was still accessible of the bridge and the railway line. The bridge would need to be rebuilt and the advancing British troops would need to know that it had been cleared of explosives. They found nothing. The platoon set up a defensive position around the embankment and O'Callaghan radioed back to company headquarters: 'Objective lost, seek further instructions.' The message was sent repeatedly, but there was no reply. O'Callaghan got slightly impatient with the wireless operator, but he wasn't to know that communications were failing across the whole division. It was nine o'clock at night on the first day, it was dark, the radios were not working, and the railway bridge had not been captured. It was time for another plan.

Both Ron Jordan and Pat Gorman had missed all the action on the first day. While Tom was on the alert at the foot of a railway embankment behind enemy lines, Ron and Pat were back in the UK, just finishing their supper. They were due to go in the second lift and would not follow Tom over the North Sea until the following morning.

10

FORWARD OR BACK?

Sunday, 17–Monday, 18 September

Tom's platoon stayed at their post on the north side of the railway bridge. Captain O'Callaghan knew that the platoon was serving no useful purpose there, but he was experiencing what was to affect everyone in the division over the next thirty-six hours. He was in complete ignorance of the current status of the operation and had no idea what was happening to the other units.

After he had left the 9th Company rendezvous with 2 Platoon, the company commanding officer, Major Winchester, set about trying to move his company headquarters to the place that he had selected, the Wolfhezen Hotel. This was in its own grounds some way outside the village, which was on the north-eastern edge of the company's landing zone.

The 9th's intelligence officer, Lieutenant Edgar

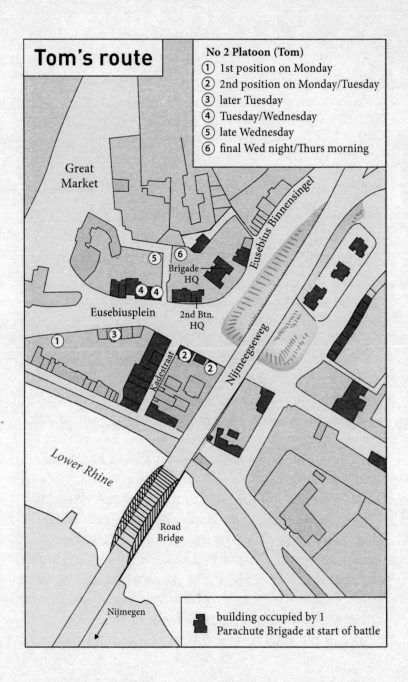

Tom's route

No 2 Platoon (Tom)
① 1st position on Monday
② 2nd position on Monday/Tuesday
③ later Tuesday
④ Tuesday/Wednesday
⑤ late Wednesday
⑥ final Wed night/Thurs morning

Great Market

Eusebius Binnensingel

Nijmeegseweg

Brigade HQ

2nd Btn. HQ

Eusebiusplein

Kadestraat

Lower Rhine

Road Bridge

Nijmegen

■ building occupied by 1 Parachute Brigade at start of battle

Tom Carpenter was a sapper in the 9th Field Company, Royal Engineers, and was one of the few men in the 1st Airborne Division to reach the bridge at Arnhem.

Pat Gorman joined the 11th Battalion, 4th Parachute Brigade, in North Africa, and parachuted into Arnhem on the second day. His orders were to go directly to assist the defenders at the bridge.

Ron Jordan, an armourer in the REME, landed by glider on the second day to establish an advance divisional workshop. Within hours of his arrival he was on the front line at Oosterbeek.

The Horsa glider *(above)* could carry small vehicles and artillery as well as men. Here a jeep is manhandled on board. Some units loaded and unloaded their aircraft as many as thirteen times in the weeks before Operation Market Garden.

Paratroopers were carried into battle on C-47 transport aircraft *(above)*. The utilitarian cabin quickly filled with men and their kit *(below)*. With so many operations cancelled at the last minute, the order to go on the 17th came as a surprise to many.

The operation filled the skies with aircraft *(above)*. Thousands of men dropped out of the skies not only at Arnhem, but also at other key bridges in Holland. Here, US gliders have landed, and a wave of paratroopers follows them in at Grave, near the River Maas crossing. Gliders were often damaged when landing, but casualties were far lower than expected.

British troops near Oosterbeek *(below)* have unloaded their jeep and trailer, ready to go to their rendezvous point before advancing to Arnhem.

The landing zones were several miles from the bridges at Arnhem, and the columns of British paratroopers became stretched out as they marched to their objectives through the wooded countryside around Oosterbeek *(left)*. The landings were spread over two days. Some of those arriving on the first day had to stand guard at the landing zones *(above)*, like this unit at Wolfhezen. Further south the leading units of the Guards Armoured Division, advancing on the road towards Arnhem, started to suffer casualties *(below)*.

At first, German forces on the ground were taken by surprise. Some of the soldiers were young reservists *(above)*,

and General Kissin, the local commander, was ambushed and shot as he tried to flee from the Wolfhezen Hotel *(below left)*.

However, the remnants of two SS divisions in the area quickly started to mobilize *(below)*.

At the end of the first day Tom Carpenter had reached the road bridge over the Rhine, but there were only a few hundred men holding a perimeter around the northern end. Burnt-out vehicles from the convoy that was attacked on Monday morning are visible *(above)*. The German forces brought up some 88mm artillery pieces like the one shown *(inset)* and started shelling the British positions from across the Rhine. Light tanks were also brought into play by the SS troops, including this captured French Renault *(below left)*, which was knocked out on the Utrechtsweg.

Pat Gorman *(below)* flew in with the 11th Battalion on the second day. He was dropped on the wrong drop zone, but he and the rest of the battalion were told to head for the bridge immediately, and reinforce the men who were valiantly holding on to their objective.

A battery of lightweight 75mm artillery and their gun crews *(above)* had been dropped in gliders and set up in Oosterbeek. These guns, firing from several miles away on to enemy gun emplacements and tanks provided valuable support to the men at the bridge. But it was a risky business, and called for extreme accuracy in spotting the fall of the shells.

Everyone knew how vital it was for the men at Arnhem to be relieved by the Guards Armoured Division advancing up from the south. But their tanks had been delayed reaching Eindhoven, their first day's objective *(right)*, and their progress to Nijmegen *(above)* was also painfully slow. The two key bridges over the Waal had still not been captured by the US 82nd Airborne Division. .

Self-propelled guns and troops of the 9th SS Division *(above)* had created a blocking line between the landing zones in Oosterbeek and the road bridge, and a pitched battle took place on the only two routes into Arnhem.

German officers stand amidst the discarded helmets of British soldiers *(above)*.

The bodies of dead British paratroops lie in the road by the museum, where their advance was halted *(above)*, and, a few hundred yards west, smashed vehicles lie outside the St Elisabeth Hospital *(right)*. Between these two points, Pat Gorman was sent flying by a mortar blast.

The paratroops around the bridge at Arnhem *(left)* were shelled out of their positions building by building, and German troops moved in to clear the road.

Wise, had been one of the first to land and had taken the initiative to go on ahead in a jeep to scout out the route to the hotel. As he and the driver, Sergeant Miller, got to the Wolfhezenweg they ran into a machine-gun post manned by SS troops. The Germans were naturally on full alert and opened fire as soon as the jeep appeared in their sights. Bullets hit Wise in both legs and in his left arm, and his nose was torn open by a fragment of metal. Miller, who escaped any injury, managed to swerve off the road into cover. Wise was extremely fortunate not to have any bones broken, and was still able to walk. They returned to the company rendezvous with the news that the road to the Wolfhezen Hotel was blocked. A group of 300 9th SS Panzer troops, under the command of Major Sepp Krafft, had been conducting exercises in the Wolfheze area when the landings started and he had quickly ordered his troops to set up a perimeter around the village.

Unaware of the extent of the German forces and their preparations, Major Winchester ordered Captain Roger Binyon and the rest of 1 Platoon to clear the route along with Lieutenant Roy Timmins and his section from 2 Platoon. They set off, to be followed an hour later by the whole of the company HQ and the rest of 3 Platoon. This last party had gone only some 500 yards when they were brought to a halt by machine-gun fire coming out of the woods to their south-east. The column took cover, returning fire as best they could through the closely packed trees. Major Winchester ordered a messenger to go forward to discover what had happened to Captain Binyon's advance party. The messenger, Lieutenant James Steel, never returned, although his bullet-riddled motorcycle was later discovered further up the road. Major Winchester then decided to dig in where they were – a crossing in the woods. They had advanced barely 600 yards from the rendezvous point at the landing zone.

Captain Binyon and 1 Platoon had reached as far as the road that passed in front of the Wolfhezen Hotel and could see that it was a large, three-storey building with a veranda running around it. Although it was set in woodland, the grounds surrounding it were open, with little cover. It was, however, spacious and airy, sufficiently attractive to be selected by SS Major Sepp Krafft as his temporary HQ during training exercises for his troops.

Binyon decided to mount an attack, ordering Timmins and a group of sappers to make a right-flanking move. They managed to cross the Wolfhezenweg between the hotel and the junction with Bilderberglaan despite heavy machine-gun fire being directed at them from the hotel. As they moved closer, however, Timmins was shot in the chest and fell to the ground. He shouted out to the section, 'Get back, get back if you can,' then collapsed and died. Sapper Grieg was also hit, receiving a severe wound in his stomach. The section went to ground, taking cover where they could, but it was clear to them that

Grieg was still alive. Lance Corporal William Takle moved forward to try to help him and pull him back into cover, but as he inched forward and tried to drag Greig by the arms, he too was hit by a bullet from a sniper. The section started laying down some strong covering fire and a group of them managed to pull both men, still alive but badly wounded, to safety. Captain Binyon then ordered all his men to pull back to the crossing where the company had dug in for the night. Greig and Takle were taken to the dressing station that had been set up by the 181st Field Ambulance closer to Wolfheze, but both of them died the next day.

The 9th Company HQ and what remained of the sappers spent the night in their positions in the woods. There were occasional skirmishes with German troops, who were passing through the woods to set up positions closer to Arnhem. Only one of these encounters turned into a determined firefight, and the sappers defeated the attack, killing three of the enemy, who they discovered later were in the Hitler Youth.

The headquarters of 9th Company had encountered stronger German forces than they had anticipated and had failed to make it to their first objective. He didn't know this, but if Captain O'Callaghan had decided to go back to report to Major Winchester, he would have been unable to find him. Within a few short hours, the plans of Tom Carpenter's company had been disrupted by unexpected German opposition and the failure of their radio sets. These fundamental problems were to affect the whole operation.

Back on the southern approach to the road bridge, Lieutenant Colonel John Frost, the 2nd Battalion's commanding officer, was approaching the outskirts of Arnhem when he heard and saw the railway bridge collapse in a cloud of smoke. When the smoke and dust cleared, he could see that the southernmost span was lying in the river. It was obvious that C Company would not be able to cross the Rhine by that route. If the pontoon bridge was still intact that might be a way to the southern bank. If it was not, then taking the main road bridge was going to be a very difficult task. As it was, it was extremely urgent to make progress towards it because, with the railway bridge demolished, the road bridge was surely next. Colonel Frost was now also affected by the loss of radio communication. He knew that the Reconnaissance Squadron in its jeeps should have gone straight to the northern side of the bridge and attempted to seize it, but he couldn't find out through the radio net if they had succeeded. It was absolutely imperative to press on, so he moved forward, but to his dismay he found that A Company, the battalion's advance guard, appeared to have ground to a halt.

The reason for this was that Frost's 2nd Battalion was moving along the north bank of the Rhine on a road called the Klingelbeeksweg. This was a narrow road, and ahead on the left flank was an area of high ground marked on their maps as Den Brink. It was wooded and provided good cover for German soldiers who were in machine-gun posts able to fire on anything coming along the road. A Company were advancing straight into the gunfire and were now stopped. Colonel Frost ordered B Company to deal with the problem while the rest of the battalion tried to move on.

A platoon from B Company went along the railway cutting to see if they could outflank the Germans on Den Brink. They advanced rapidly along the railway, but were spotted and fired on from a machine-gun post; Lieutenant Peter Crane, in charge of the platoon, and several others were killed. A Company, under Major Digby Tatham-Warter, started trying to cut through houses and gardens along the road to gain cover from the machine gunners. This stratagem worked, allowing them to start moving again, this time also under cover of approaching darkness, though the rest of B Company was still engaged in trying to suppress the fire from Den Brink. A large column was now following the leading companies of the 2nd Battalion and they were held up whenever progress at the front faltered. The headquarters staff and defence platoon of the 1st Parachute Brigade, under brigade Major Tony Hibbert, were following on, and as well as the Royal Engineers and the anti-tank gunners there was a platoon of the Royal Army Service Corps with jeeps and trailers of ammunition.

Passing Den Brink, the leading men were still 2 miles from the road bridge at Arnhem. It was about 19.30 and night was falling. Frost knew this would give them some extra cover, but there was still no time to waste. Pushing ahead along the bank of the Rhine, past the small terraced houses that lined the road, they passed the pontoon bridge which was, unfortunately, dismantled. Leaving a few men to look at the possibility of finding other boats, Frost went on and they finally reached the road bridge at about 20.00. It was a single-steel-arched suspension bridge and on the northern side the road it carried crossed over the riverbank and the riverside road, then continued on a long embankment that slowly reached ground level and entered the eastern part of Arnhem.

A platoon led by Lieutenant Jack Grayburn reached this embankment first and the rest of A Company quickly followed. As they approached the road underneath the bridge, a convoy of German vehicles, a mixture of armoured personnel carriers and covered lorries, sped across the bridge, heading south. Members of the small group of paratroopers took up positions on either side of the road leading on to the bridge. They tried to remain hidden, lying flat on the sides of the embankment, doing nothing to stop any traffic coming across it for the moment. The key was to secure both ends of the bridge intact. At the same time, platoons from A Company occupied buildings on either side of the embankment, while the HQ company and the other units took over buildings close by so that a small enclave was set up around the northern end of the bridge that could control the approaches to it from the town of Arnhem. There was no sign of the Reconnaissance Squadron, nor of the 3rd Battalion. Frost had received some news from a messenger earlier that the 3rd would remain on the outskirts of the town during the night. This left the 2nd Battalion badly exposed to counter-attack, but there was little Frost could do. At least he had got to the bridge.

Frost quickly called his senior officers together. It was all very well to have men around the northern end of the bridge, but it was imperative to secure both ends and hold the bridge intact. The first attempt to achieve this was by A Company, whose CO sent a rifle section across the bridge, using the girders of the side spans as cover. As they moved over they captured a few enemy soldiers, who seemed to be on guard. This stealthy approach was ruined when the leader, Lance Sergeant Bill Fulton, saw a rifle pointing at him and fired his Sten gun, hitting the German but also receiving a bullet in the top of his thigh. The riflemen retreated and Fulton crawled to safety behind a girder, where he was rescued by some medical orderlies.

Major Tatham-Warter then tried another, stronger attack. A full platoon, with faces blackened and boots wrapped in cloth to muffle their sound, waited until it was fully dark and then set off, as silently as possible, along the side of the bridge. They had managed to get only a short way when the night was split by the gun flashes of a machine gun firing at them from point-blank range. The fire had come from a pillbox situated on the bridge near the north end. The platoon stumbled backwards under the fire, with eight of them, including their leader, Lieutenant Grayburn, injured by machine-gun bullets.

The next attempt was more robust. One of the 6-pounder anti-tank guns was towed by a jeep to the bottom of a set of steps that took pedestrians from street level up the embankment to the pavement of the approach road to the bridge. Then the gun crew physically hauled the gun up the steps, a flight at a time, until it was on the pavement of the bridge and pointing at the pillbox just 30 yards away.

At the same time, a group of Royal Engineers was preparing to attack the pillbox with a flamethrower from a building next to the bridge. They reached their position by 'mouse-holing' – that is, blasting their way through the walls of buildings using PIAT anti-tank rounds. Simultaneously, the enemy attempted to counter-attack the 2nd Battalion positions on the embankment, firing star shells and mortars, then attempting a rush attack, but they were beaten back by strong rifle and machine-gun fire. Then, at the command, the 6-pounder gun crew fired armour-piercing rounds at the pillbox and the flamethrower let loose a blast of searing flame. Utter mayhem followed. The explosions of the shells mingled with the fire of machine guns, and there were shouts and screams from inside the pillbox. The flamethrower crew, however, missed the pillbox and engulfed a wooden shed behind it. This must have contained explosives and fuel, because it erupted with an enormous blast, setting the paint of the bridge on fire. Some German soldiers staggered out of the flames and surrendered. As a platoon prepared to advance across the bridge now that the pillbox had been taken out, four German lorries drove towards them from the south. These were riddled with machine-gun bullets and came to a swerving halt near the pillbox. German soldiers tumbled out of them and were taken prisoner, but the canvas tarpaulins covering the back of the lorries caught fire and they started to go up in flames. The fires on the bridge, from the lorries, the paintwork on the girders and the remnants of the fuel store, burned fiercely, lighting the area as though it were daylight and making the bridge impassable. Any hope of capturing its southern end was now gone, for this night at least.

Frost had one consolation. The Germans could not reinforce that side without having to go through his own positions on the north end of the bridge and the small area around it that he had now occupied. He would have liked to get B Company across the river, in a commandeered barge or other rivercraft, and also to get C Company – who had left Den Brink but were now near the German HQ in the centre of Arnhem, and having a hard fight – to move down to the bridge to reinforce the perimeter that had been established in various buildings around the ramp. But finding a boat was proving difficult, and the radios were simply not working. He had no option but to wait out the night in the hope that the 3rd Battalion and the armed jeeps of the Reconnaissance Squadron would arrive as soon as possible.

While all this was going on, Tom Carpenter and the rest of his platoon were still at the foot of the railway-bridge embankment 2 miles further down the riverbank. They had dug in using the drainage ditches that ran alongside the railway embankment as slit trenches. After innumerable efforts at contacting his company HQ, or the 2nd Battalion, Captain O'Callaghan ordered the wireless operator, Sapper Tom Hyland, to stop trying. O'Callaghan had probably already made up his mind what to do. He had been in tight situations before, and the Military Cross that he had won in Italy showed that his instinct was to press on to the main objective. He knew it was pointless maintaining a guard over the railway bridge, which was now useless to British or Germans, but he knew also that some of the men in the platoon, like Tom, were fresh to fighting. A bridge blowing up in front of you could unsettle anyone. Here they were, a small force, in the dark, isolated in enemy-held territory. They needed to take some action before doubts started creeping in, and he knew what it ought to be.

'We're doing no bloody good here,' he said, then,

keeping the mood light, he joked, 'We'll go for a stroll to Arnhem. It's just the day for it. Keep up close, keep going. We're not going to get bogged down in a fire-fight, we just go for the bridge.'

They moved back to the road and collected their folding bikes. They had to pass under the arch carrying the railway tracks across the Benedendorpsweg, and the German troops in their positions across the river had now fixed their firing lines on to the tunnel entrance. The light was fading, but tracer rounds ricocheted off the stonework of the bridge, followed by the sound of a machine-gun burst echoing across the river. Callaghan mustered the men, and in separate sections they put their heads down and ran. No one was hit and they made steady progress along the side of the river. There was considerable activity to the north, with signal flares lighting up the sky and the sound of gunshots mingling with the stutter of automatic fire but, apart from the occasional burst of machine-gun fire from the road above them, they were not seriously delayed. The road they were on had started a gentle slope uphill to join the Utrechtsweg, the road that leads into the centre of Arnhem.

Fortunately for them, a Dutch Resistance member intercepted them at the junction and explained that there was heavy fighting in the town. He offered to show them the path to rejoin the lower road along the bank of the Rhine, which took them past the pontoon bridge. O'Callaghan took up the offer and they went on. As they approached the site of the old pontoon bridge, with its small harbour cut into the riverbank, there was a sudden shout from the rear of the column and, almost simultaneously, machine-gun fire echoed around them. The men threw themselves to the ground, while O'Callaghan and his section took cover in the doorway of an old building, tracer spattering around them. O'Callaghan shouted out, 'Can you spot where they are firing from?' Tom was lying in a gutter, pressed as close to the cobbles as he could, and all he could see was that tracer bullets were coming from several different positions. A few men managed to return fire at the gun flashes and the machine guns stopped. Remarkably, no one was injured and the platoon was able to crawl forward out of the exposed area.

They had to abandon their bikes, because retrieving them would be too dangerous. O'Callaghan, however, insisted that his jeep was not left behind, so the driver made a dash for it and drove it clear. They went on to reach the pontoon bridge, where they came cross the bodies of four German soldiers and two others who were wounded. They inspected the remains of the bridge. As the 2nd Battalion had found out an hour before them, it was no longer complete; the central pontoon had been removed, according to their Dutch guide, just two days previously and was anchored on the southern bank. Lieutenant Colonel Frost's men had found a barge moored on the north bank and had left a section in charge of it, but neither they nor the barge were any longer to be seen.

The platoon gave what assistance they could to the wounded enemy soldiers and searched for any boats that might be used to cross the river. But anything that had been left on the north bank had had its hull broken and was unusable. Continuing on their way, they found themselves under fire again. The Germans had set up machine guns on fixed firing lines in the side streets leading off the embankment road. Tom remembers that at every junction two machine guns would fire out at knee height. O'Callaghan got the platoon formed up in line abreast, with the jeep at the end closest to the machine guns. At each junction they paused, tense, then, as the jeep shot forward, the men charged, running the gauntlet of bullets, each man waiting for the impact of a 7.92mm round to smash through his legs. They negotiated four junctions covered by German machine guns and each time they miraculously passed through the stream of tracer unscathed. Eventually they came to a big, open square by the old city gate, at the junction of the Rijnkade, as the embankment road was now called, and Eusebiusplein. They could see the bridge in front of them, its arch looming high into the sky, but they were coming under fire from three different machine-gun posts – the square had been set up as a killing ground. O'Callaghan realized that they could not continue on their way to the bridge. They were trapped.

While Tom was crouched down against a shop front on the Rijnkade, with the rest of the platoon spaced along the street on both sides, there was a huge explosion on the bridge and flames leaped into the darkness. The ammunition shed on the bridge had exploded. Tom had no idea what had happened and thought that demolition charges on the road bridge had gone up as well. 'The operation was well and truly f****d. But we had other things to worry about because tracer was coming from all over, and bullets were zipping off the road, off walls ... You didn't know where to go.' The fire to which they were exposed seemed to be coming from several positions around them, as well as from across the river. The huge fire now burning on the bridge illuminated the area in a reddish orange glow, making it hard to identify enemy locations from their gun flashes.

Captain O'Callaghan and his sergeant, 'Sonny' Gibbons, shouted to the men to prepare to make a dash, when they could, to a villa on a side road leading out of Eusebiusplein. To Tom this seemed almost suicidal, but no worse than staying where he was. Then, from the 2nd Battalion positions around the ramp leading up to the bridge, came the sound of tracks and an engine, and a Bren-gun carrier clattered into the Rijnkade. Its crew started to fire at the enemy machine gunners, and with this sudden respite O'Callaghan and Gibbons urged the men towards the big house they had marked out on the corner. Tom and the others needed no further orders. He thinks he must have cleared the iron railings in front of the house in a single leap, propelled as he was by fear and adrenaline, his hobnailed boots striking sparks off the cobbles.

They kicked down the front door and poured into the house. It was a large, well-furnished middle-class house, and the men tumbled into it, their rifles and packs ripping into wallpaper, their parachute smocks covered in mud, smelling of cordite and sweat, their boots digging into carpets and parquet floors. They proceeded, methodically, to smash everything. The windows were punched out with rifle butts, china ornaments, pictures and glass cabinets were broken and reduced to pieces, curtains were ripped down and cushions and carpets were laid over window sills. This orgy of destruction was deliberate and for a purpose. Everything that might shatter with a bullet or piece of shrapnel was broken first, so that it could not add to the lethal debris hurling around a room taking fire. The soft furnishings were laid over sills to prevent stone splinters, and armchairs and sofas were pushed against walls to add protection and firing rests. It took just a few minutes to destroy the contents of the house.

When there was some quiet, they could hear the sound of voices coming up from the cellar. They could not tell the difference between German and Dutch, so Tom and another sapper went down, rifles ready. He was glad that he had not thought to throw a grenade down the cellar steps. A family was hiding there, a man and a woman with two or three children. There was nothing to say, and Tom knew no Dutch. He left them and returned to the ground floor.

O'Callaghan was unhappy with the location of the house: it was still too open to the square and bullets were hitting its front. He wanted to look for a better strongpoint, closer to the bridge and the 2nd Battalion, so he took Tom and Sapper Danny Weddal to start reconnoitring along the back gardens of the houses towards the bridge. They had to climb walls 7 feet high, and after negotiating eight of these they found themselves in the back garden of a house close to the bridge ramp. Going through the house, they could see across the road an area that looked like a factory and courtyard. They raced across and found it was a clog and coffin manufacturer with a timberyard. Tom was sent back to alert Sergeant Sonny Gibbons and bring the rest of the men forward with him. He counted the walls that had to be climbed and when he reached the house got the men assembled and led them back. In the tension and excitement, however, Tom became confused about the number of walls he had climbed over. 'I scrambled over this wall and in front of me was a Jerry. He was crouched down and luckily he had his back to me. I looked round and I thought, Christ, where are the rest of the lads? I must have gone too far.' The enemy soldier heard a noise and turned. Tom was squeezing the trigger, about to fire, when he saw that the German was an older reservist. Tom was reminded instantly of his father, and he paused. The German's life was on a knife-edge. He raised his hands in surrender. 'I was pleased about that. I didn't want to kill him.' Tom gestured, and took his prisoner with his hands up around the corner into the coffin factory.

It was now around 08.30 on the morning of 18 September. Tom and his platoon had been on the move for over twenty-four hours, but O'Callaghan wanted to get a section checking for fuses and demolition charges on the supporting stone piers of the bridge, or at least those they could reach on the northern side. The intense flames from the burning lorries and the ammunition store would have set off any charges, so it was assumed that they had not been planted on the main span of the bridge. They found nothing. Then the platoon set about establishing some strongpoints around the ramp and the buildings in collaboration with the rest of the 2nd Battalion and the mixture of units in the small perimeter. The situation was not perfect, but at least the road bridge was still intact, if not wholly in their hands. Many of the units that had left the drop zones yesterday had not managed to reach the bridge, and nobody knew why, but another drop was due this morning and it would not be long before the Guards Armoured Division of XXX Corps would reach them from the south.

Tom sat down with some of the lads to make tea on their little stoves, which burned solid blocks of paraffin. A brew would be extremely welcome – the first they had had since being given a mug on the airstrip at Keevil. They were thirsty and hungry, and exhausted from the long night. Then there was a shout. 'Enemy armour on the bridge, and hold your fire.'

11

THE FIRST CRACKS

Sunday, 17–Monday, 18 September

M ajor General Roy Urquhart had dealt with the fact that his 1st Airborne Division was to be dropped in Arnhem over two days by splitting responsibilities between the two brigades that would land on the first day. The three battalions in the 1st Parachute Brigade, under the command of Brigadier Gerald Lathbury, were tasked with taking the river crossings and setting up defensive positions around them. So far, only the northern end of the road bridge had been reached by part of John Frost's 2nd Battalion and some other units, including Tom's sappers. The 1st Airlanding Brigade, under Brigadier Philip Hicks, was charged with securing the landing zones for the next day's drop of the 4th Parachute Brigade, commanded by Brigadier John Hackett, in which Ron and Pat would take part. The 1st

Airlanding Brigade battalions (the 1st Border Regiment, the 7th King's Own Scottish Borderers and the 2nd South Staffordshire Regiment – half of Urquhart's available force on the first day) were therefore all deployed to the west of Arnhem, guarding the landing zones rather than supporting the assault on the bridges over the Rhine. The three battalions of the Airlanding Brigade had a few minor skirmishes with some German patrols, but spent a relatively quiet night guarding the open fields and heath of the landing zones.

Brigadier Lathbury had decided to split the 1st Parachute Brigade, with each battalion taking a different route into Arnhem. At the same time, Urquhart ordered the 1st Airborne Reconnaissance Squadron under Major Freddy Gough, which was under his divisional command, to make a speedy advance to the road bridge via a northern route along the railway line that led into the centre of Arnhem.

The Reconnaissance Squadron had twenty-four jeeps armed with twin-mounted Vickers machine guns and these jeeps were split into three troops. It would be normal practice for each troop to provide a reconnaissance unit for each battalion, driving ahead of them on the line of advance to scout out enemy positions. Instead, they were to remain together as a unit for a rapid thrust towards Arnhem. The Reconnaissance Squadron's jeeps had landed by glider, while most of the men had come in by parachute. One of their gliders had aborted the mission over Britain and two had crashed in the landing zone, so there were some gaps in the troops' strength, which caused delays at their rendezvous point. Impatient to start off, Lieutenant Peter Bucknall, in charge of a section of C Troop, decided to set off on his own, telling his radio operator, Trooper Arthur Barlow, to follow him when the other jeeps had assembled. At around four o'clock in the afternoon the rest of C Troop set off. They drove into Wolfheze from the west, crossed the railway line at the crossing, then followed a track that ran parallel to the railway line in a cutting. As they did so, they heard the sound of gun-fire in front of them and they were also fired on from the top of the railway embankment. Lieutenant Bucknall and his section had driven into an ambush and the lead jeep was disabled. Trooper Barlow and the others in the jeep jumped out, rushing for cover on either side of the vehicle. The machine-gun fire con-tinued and each of the men was hit. Trooper Dicky Minns, shot in the hip together with other wounds to his body, was bleeding badly. The driver, Trooper Reg Hasler, was hit in both legs. Lance Sergeant Thomas Macgregor was hit in the face and chest as he raised himself to take stock of the situation. Barlow kept firing, but was hit in the thigh. Eventually, after half an hour, pinned down under fire and with some of them badly wounded, they surrendered.

The main force of C Troop had also dismounted when they came under fire and moved forward on foot. They fired some smoke grenades and tried to move up under cover to help the rest of Bucknall's section, but the machine-gun fire was too heavy. Captain Douglas Swinscow of the Royal Army Medical Corps tried to go forward to help some of the wounded men, but he came under fire and one of the men to whom he was trying to give assistance was killed. They dug in and held on to their position, but the planned route to Arnhem was clearly blocked.

The German unit under Major Sepp Krafft, a depot and reserve unit of the SS Panzer Grenadiers that had been training in the woods around Wolfheze, had responded very rapidly when they first saw the airborne forces descend on the area. Krafft had quickly signalled to his commanders, then organized his men into a temporary force that blocked the railway and the main highway into Arnhem. He knew that it was a race against time before he was surrounded, but he had succeeded. His troops had confronted C Troop's jeeps and halted their advance. The rapid deployment of his men, and the intelligence he passed back to the 9th SS Panzer Division, meant that the German forces in the area – much stronger than General Urquhart knew – were already trying to move to block the British offensive.

Back at the temporary brigade headquarters, close to the landing zones, Brigadier Lathbury was told that there had been a problem with the Reconnaissance Squadron's vehicles and that they were below strength. Believing that they were held up, he ordered the 1st Parachute Battalion, under the command of Lieutenant Colonel David Dobie, to move out. Their objective was not the road bridge; instead, their task was to occupy an area of high ground north of Arnhem to defend the British forces holding the bridge against any attack from the north. Moving out from their assembly point, they advanced to Wolfheze station, where they were told that German forces blocked the railway line. Colonel Dobie thought that the railway line was not the best path to use for his transport of towed anti-tank guns and Bren-gun carriers, so the battalion continued north to the main Amsterdamsweg. They had moved forward just a few hundred yards when R Company, in the lead position, confronted German troops in the woods that lined the road on either side.

A machine-gun post opened up and a member of 1 Platoon was shot and killed. The platoon took cover, with the body of the dead paratrooper lying in the road where he had fallen. In the ensuing fight the Germans were silenced or retreated and R Company pushed on further, but there were constant skirmishes with groups of German soldiers. They were next alerted by the noise of tanks. The company started digging in, getting out their trenching tools and excavating shallow holes so that they could get below ground level but still have a good firing position. The tanks got closer, the clanking of their tracks and the screech of the drive sprockets mingling with the noise of the engines. It was difficult to see through the trees what type of tank they were, but they suddenly opened fire and the woods became a death trap, with shells bursting in the trees, splinters and bullets slicing the air above R Company's heads.

To the rear of the company was the mortar platoon. They attempted to target the tanks with mortar fire, but their radio had stopped working and the fall of shot had to be relayed by a chain of messengers. Eventually, the accuracy of the mortar fire improved and the tanks withdrew, but not before the company had suffered more casualties. The slow progress through the woods and the spasmodic fighting had taken their toll. It was not just a question of casualties, but individual sections had got lost in the woods, and by the time the fight with the tanks had finished, the company was down to about thirty men.

Major Dobie wanted to avoid any more contact with the enemy and hoped that by changing his route he could bypass their position. Moving to the right, he ordered the battalion to follow a track in the woods, but saw five German tanks and around fifteen troop-carrying half-tracks move along the main road about 400 yards away. The battalion had lost contact with R Company, who, because of the number of wounded for whom they had to care, were struggling to maintain any speed along the line of march. The battalion was trying to move through the woods parallel to the main road, but was still 5 miles from its objective, and it was getting dark. The road was clearly blocked by several tanks and armoured cars, and, although Dobie didn't know it, three companies of the 9th SS Panzer Division had managed to move forward to support Sepp Krafft's ad hoc battle group. The prospect of advancing through the woods at night was not promising: it would add to the difficulties of keeping the battalion together, particularly as the radios were working only intermittently.

Then, while Dobie was pondering his options, he got a clear radio message from John Frost with the 2nd Battalion at the road bridge. It said that his force had arrived at the bridge, but that there was no sign of the 3rd Battalion, who should have taken the middle road along the Utrechtsweg through the village of Oosterbeek, and that he needed reinforcements. Dobie quickly called an orders group with his company commanders and battalion staff. The way forward to their primary objective was blocked. Frost had captured the bridge – a key target of the brigade effort – but needed more forces. Dobie decided to change his plans and head for the Arnhem bridge in support of Colonel Frost.

They swung south-eastwards now, heading through more woods, pushing all their equipment, including the tracked Bren-gun carriers and the jeeps, by hand so that the engines would not alert any German positions in front of them. They had suffered 100 casualties and many others were missing, while R Company was still struggling to form up. All through the night they came into contact with German units. At three in the morning they opened fire on an enemy machine-gun post and knocked it out. An hour later, after struggling through the woods, they reached a junction of the Utrechtsweg to the west of Oosterbeek, where S Company, now in the lead, came under fire from more German positions and several armoured cars that were parked off the road. The enemy fire was heavy, with 20mm cannon and mortar shells landing amongst the battalion. S Company moved around to the flank to attack the SS soldiers, destroying their positions on the north of the road. The armoured cars retreated, but still kept up their fire. S Company had received thirty casualties.

At this point Dobie received another message that the 2nd Battalion was in urgent need of reinforcements. His own battalion had taken a battering since they landed. R Company was split, with some paratroopers remaining with the wounded, while a rump was still struggling to join up with the main column. Their fighting in the woods and the latest conflict had also weakened S Company. Dobie decided to disengage from any further fighting with the armoured cars and to press on as hard as he could to the bridge. It was 05.30. His men had had no rest for twenty-four hours and no opportunity for a meal or a hot drink. Their nighttime push through the woods had been exhausting, but this was what they had trained for. They still had a few more miles to go.

The 3rd Battalion of the 1st Parachute Brigade, whose task was to head directly for the centre of

Arnhem, had found the going equally hard. After assembling at their drop zone they had struck out along the central route to Arnhem, the Utrechtsweg, a wide, paved road that passed through the woods and was lined with detached villas set back behind high fences and hedges. The Utrechtsweg went through Oosterbeek, continued on to the high ground above the north bank of the Rhine, then ran past Arnhem station into the town centre. The battalion made good progress, moving fast, the advance company, B Company, organized with its platoons in sections on either side of the road, keeping some separation between them. They were accompanied at the rear by three 6-pounder anti-tank guns pulled by jeeps, various sections of the Royal Engineers, the Royal Army Medical Corps and a group of forward observation officers who would liaise with the batteries of 75mm artillery from the Royal Artillery Light Regiment that had remained at the landing zones. There were also two Bren-gun carriers. The column stretched for a mile. As they went forward, there was the occasional attack from snipers in the woods. They had travelled a few miles and were approaching a crossroads when there was a burst of firing from the front of the column. A Citroën car drove into the Utrechtsweg from a turning on the left side road and the men of the two leading sections, who were just approaching the junction, let fly with their Sten guns and rifles. The car was hit by a stream of bullets, the tyres burst, the windscreen was blown apart and bullets punched through the doors. The occupants of the car were killed instantly. One of the bodies that tumbled out of the passenger door, blood streaming from wounds in the chest and head, was that of Major General Friedrich Kussin, the senior officer in charge of the defence of Arnhem, who had just left a meeting with Major Sepp Krafft in the Wolfhezen Hotel to the north and was on his way back to his HQ in Arnhem.

The leading platoon commander, Lieutenant Jimmy Cleminson, paid little attention to the dead general, preferring to keep up with his men as they continued on their way, pressing ahead to the road bridge, which was still 4 miles away. As they continued, they were surprised again by another vehicle. This was far more dangerous than a Citroën staff car – it was a self-propelled gun, an armoured tracked vehicle carrying a large-calibre gun, similar in size to a tank, but without a rotating turret. With this gun was a detachment of troops and two armoured cars. The self-propelled gun drove straight down the road into the lead section of B Company, its engine roaring, thick diesel exhaust pouring out from behind it. The machine gun mounted on the hull fired at a PIAT gunner who was trying to get his weapon into a firing position. The column scattered and the anti-tank section at the rear manhandled a 6-pounder anti-tank gun, trying to turn it to fire forward. They were too late. The two crew were riddled with machine-gun bullets, one of them, Gunner George Robson, dying immediately from bullets cutting through his chest; the other man collapsed, seriously wounded.

The paratroopers weren't prepared for dealing with armoured vehicles. Their Gammon bombs (grenades made of plastic explosive and particularly effective against tanks) were still in the packs on their backs and all they could do was pour fire on the self-propelled gun and troops with their Sten guns and other automatic weapons. This seemed to have some effect and the gun pulled back, but still threatened the way forward.

During this fighting, the brigade commander, Lathbury, arrived in his jeep at the Wolfheze cross-roads to urge the CO of the 3rd Battalion to move forward with more urgency. Lathbury told Lieutenant Colonel John Fitch that he should try to bypass the fighting and send a company to the road bridge via the northern route. He ordered C Company, under the command of Major Peter Lewis, to move off. They moved through B Company's troops, recovering from the burst of fighting, and went north up the Bredelaan, heading in the direction of the railway line. Lathbury was impatient, and clearly anxious. Lieutenant Len Wright, a platoon commander in C Company, was briefing his men about the change of plans and the new line of advance when Lathbury interrupted him, saying, 'They don't need briefing: just tell them that's the bloody way. Get moving!'

The reason for Lathbury's appearance was the

failure of the various radios over the whole of the divisional area. This generated an anxiety about the outcome of events which both Lathbury and Urquhart felt could be assuaged only by their physical presence with their battalion commanders, so they had left their respective headquarters and driven forward to meet up with the various battalions. At about this time, Urquhart arrived at Fitch's HQ and simultaneously the rear of the column came under fire from the woods to their rear. Mortar shells, which caused several casualties, followed this machine-gun fire and one shell hit the general's jeep, badly wounding his radio operator. The battalion was stuck, unable to go forward and now also coming under attack from the rear.

Lathbury told Lieutenant Tony Baxter in A Company to collect his platoon and clear the wood. They advanced into the woods, not particularly sure about what the enemy positions were or from where the mortars were coming. They cleared a few hundred yards, but then stopped, not wanting to become separated from the battalion. As the lieutenant conferred with his men, the mortar fire started once more and two sergeants were killed, while Baxter, who had already had a thumb shot off, was hit by shrapnel and knocked unconscious. The rest of A Company entered the woods in support and, as well as the two sergeants, they suffered twelve other casualties. A dozen enemy soldiers were captured, but the fighting had delayed them and it was now 21.30.

A Company rejoined the 3rd Battalion, which was now much reduced because of the departure of C Company. It still had a general and brigadier attached to it. The battalion advanced along the road until they came to a large, elegant building on their right called the Hartenstein Hotel. The leading units moved into it, to discover that the previous occupants had got out very quickly. There was food on the table and papers were scattered about. It had been the temporary HQ of Field Marshal Model, in charge of German Army Group B, which was responsible for the whole of the northern part of the German front line. He had seen the parachutes and gliders dropping, and had quickly abandoned the position with his staff, fearing that he would be captured.

Some of Lieutenant Cleminson's platoon stopped to eat the remains of the German staff officer's lunch, but moved out when fighting started in the woods to the south of the hotel. B Company had encountered some German troops, but by this time it was dark, so the firing quickly subsided. Brigadier Lathbury was now able to make contact with his brigade HQ, which had become attached to John Frost's 2nd Battalion and was now at the bridge. The brigade major, Tony Hibbert, suggested to Lathbury that the southern route was still relatively open, so the 3rd Battalion should make a half-mile detour and come along the river route to the bridge. Lathbury ignored the advice. He ordered the battalion instead to overnight near the Hartenstein Hotel. The battalion HQ took over one of the villas on the Utrechtsweg, while the battalion formed a perimeter around it. Major General Urquhart and Brigadier Lathbury stayed with the battalion, and were now effectively cut off from the rest of the Division; worse, no one knew where they were. The 3rd Battalion had stopped on the western edge of Oosterbeek and was still several miles from the road bridge and John Frost's position.

One element of the 3rd Battalion did, however, succeed in reinforcing the position at the bridge. This was C Company, which had been ordered by Lathbury to find a route to the north and press ahead. They advanced to the railway line, then headed east along it. By a stroke of luck, they came on to the railway cutting at a point behind the troops of the Krafft battle group that had blocked the Reconnaissance Squadron's advance into Arnhem.

As they moved along a road parallel to the cutting, they met a British jeep heading towards them filled with German soldiers. It was probably a captured Reconnaissance Squadron vehicle. A short fight ensued, in which one of the company was wounded. The jeep retreated, then two trucks came down the road, which the company ambushed. They were loaded with ammunition and both were set alight. In the fighting, the German occupants were killed but Sergeant Andrew Graham was badly wounded in the stomach. They continued past Oosterbeek station, then on to Arnhem station, from where they struck out for the bridge. They were greeted by two Dutch policemen.

As they walked down the main road, they now met the enemy in numbers. A German car was ambushed, blown up with a Gammon bomb and left burning, but they avoided a large group of German soldiers in the darkness. As they approached the bridge they got mixed up with a group of enemy soldiers preparing to make an assault on the 2nd Battalion's perimeter. Firing started, killing one of the platoon commanders and another sergeant. Unfortunately, in the dark and chaos of the close-quarters fighting, 7 Platoon was surrounded and taken prisoner. The rest of the company were fired on by a machine gun, which caused more casualties. At that point they broke ranks and headed independently to a school building on the eastern side of the road embankment which had been fortified by the Royal Engineers.

The addition to the small number of forces around the bridge was not the complete company that had set out from the woods west of Oosterbeek: only forty-five of the hundred or so of C Company joined up with the 2nd Battalion. Major Gough of the Reconnaissance Squadron had also managed to reach the bridge, bringing the total number of men that John Frost now had at his command to about 740, including Tom Carpenter's platoon from the 9th Field Company.

One other action changed the fortunes of the men

gathered around the northern edge of the road bridge after that first day. Major Dennis Munford, a battery commander of the Light Regiment, Royal Artillery, had come up with the brigade HQ and was perturbed by the fact that none of his radios would work. His battery of 75mm guns, which had been air-landed in gliders, were still at the landing zones, but the plan was to move them forward to Oosterbeek the next morning so that they could provide supporting fire for the forces holding the bridge. Without radios, they would be useless. Munford, with his driver, Lance Bombardier Bill Crook, and one of his forward observation officers, Captain Tony Harrison, drove back in two jeeps to the divisional HQ to collect fresh batteries and re-set their radios. They arrived, driving down the Utrechtsweg without being stopped, told the HQ about the situation at the bridge, then fixed their radios and drove back to the bridge. It was a remarkable effort when most other units had been so thoroughly frustrated in their efforts, but on the return journey Captain Harrison was hit in the stomach and seriously wounded. They managed to get back to the bridge, where they discovered that another artillery signaller had one of the radio sets working and they now had direct contact with their gun crews. It was to prove extremely valuable in the days to come.

Meanwhile, Ron Jordan and Pat Gorman had still not boarded their aircraft for the second lift. If they made it to their landing zones, they would be in for a shock.

12

THE ADVANCE OF XXX CORPS

Sunday, 17 September

The men fighting their way through the woods of Oosterbeek, or, like Tom Carpenter, scrambling into the shelter of buildings around the bridge at Arnhem, were part of an extremely large and complicated operation. Thousands of US airborne troops were landing at the same time in two areas to their south, and a few miles beyond them the massed forces of Montgomery's Second Army were primed to launch a huge thrust into Germany. The size of the effort involved is difficult to comprehend. The main advance along the road towards the airborne forces was to be made by XXX Corps under the command of Lieutenant General Brian Horrocks. The corps was made up of its HQ units, a brigade of Free Dutch troops and three British army divisions – the 43rd Infantry Division, the 50th Infantry Division and the

Guards Armoured Division. Once the battle started, more than 20,000 vehicles would be waiting to move down the road to Arnhem. In the rear of the column, as many as 9,000 engineers were prepared to move up and replace any bridges destroyed by the Germans with prefabricated Bailey bridges.

The Guards Armoured Division was made up of battle groups of the Grenadier Guards, the Coldstream Guards and the Irish and Welsh Guards. At the very tip of this spear were the Sherman tanks of the Irish Guards. Formed up on the north bank of the Meuse-Escaut Canal, having captured the vitally important bridge over the canal seven days earlier, they waited for the signal to start their advance once again. It was 65 miles to the bridge at Arnhem, but several key bridges on the way had to be captured by the 101st and 82nd US Airborne Divisions. Lieutenant General Horrocks was some way away from the tanks of the Irish Guards, having found a viewpoint on a factory roof on the other side of the canal, from where he was looking over the line of advance.

At around one o'clock, the first gliders and their tugs carrying the US airborne troops flew over him, heading towards their drop zones near Nijmegen and Eindhoven. They were followed by hundreds more C-47 transport planes carrying their loads of paratroopers. The arrival overhead of this great fleet was the signal for the start of the ground offensive, and 350 howitzers opened up a barrage of shells on the woods bordering the road down which the Irish Guards were to advance. The onslaught of high explosive continued for half an hour, then this curtain of fire started moving forward and, as it did so, the driver of the first tank, commanded by Lieutenant Keith Heathcote, engaged its gears and moved forward, keeping pace with the barrage. The first few hundred yards were uneventful, but the German defenders had dug in well. They were tough troops; despite the shocking shellfire, they were disciplined enough to leave their cover and open fire with anti-tank guns and Panzerfausts (hand-held anti-tank rockets) as soon as the wave of bursting shells swept past them.

The road was a killing zone. Within a few minutes nine Sherman tanks had been knocked out and were on fire, slewed across the road, their crews and the accompanying infantry scrambling for cover, some of them into slit trenches still occupied by German soldiers. The German positions were attacked again, this time by rocket-firing RAF Typhoons circling in the skies above waiting to be called down, and by more directed shellfire from the artillery in the rear. It took some time and 230 aircraft sorties before the infantry accompanying the tanks went into action, winkling out the German defenders, and the road was open. It was a frustrating delay. Horrocks hoped that the German resistance had been overcome and that it would prove to have been just a thin crust, with nothing more substantial behind it.

The Shermans of the Irish Guards now clanked their way forward once again, but there was continual resistance from small mobile units of German soldiers, who would open fire from concealed positions in ditches and hedgerows before melting away. By nightfall the leaders of the Guards Armoured Division had reached only their first objective, the small Dutch farming town of Valkenswaard. They were still 6 miles short of Eindhoven, where they should have met up at around 17.15 with the US troops from the 101st Airborne. The gap was in fact greater than this, because the 101st had also been held up as it moved south from its drop zones towards Eindhoven, and there was now a distance of 10 miles between the two forces. Eindhoven still had to be taken, but despite this, and the fact that speed was of the essence in this operation, the Irish Guards were told by their divisional HQ to stop at Valkenswaard for the night, re-arm and re-fuel, then prepare to resume their move forward the next morning in daylight. This they did.

The US 101st Airborne's task, after securing its landing and drop zones, was to advance both north and south to secure the highway and its bridges between Eindhoven and Veghel, a town on the South Willems Canal. One regiment, the 501st Parachute Infantry, was to drop close to Veghel and secure the bridge there, while the 502nd and 506th were to drop close to the town of Son. The 502nd Regiment was given the task of seizing the road bridge over the River Dommel and also of guarding the drop zone for the arrival of the 327th Glider Regiment the next day, while the 506th Regiment was to capture the bridge over the Wilhelmina Canal and then move 8 miles down the road to Eindhoven.

After landing successfully, the CO of the 506th, Colonel Robert Sink, split his regiment in order to make a pincer attack on the bridge over the canal. The 1st Battalion of the 506th advanced from the west, approaching through a forest. They made fast progress until they were close to the bridge, where they then ran into three 88mm anti-tank guns stationed on the north side of the canal. One of the guns fired into the trees above the troops, bringing down branches and creating a hail of shrapnel and wood splinters. The battalion kept on advancing, but then started to receive mortar fire. Five men were killed and several wounded in the first fifteen minutes. The leading A Company tried to kill the crew of one of the 88mm pieces with a heavy machine gun, but a shell from the artillery hit the machine-gun crew and killed both the American soldiers. In a final desperate effort, the remnants of A Company fixed bayonets and charged the gun crews, even as the barrel of the 88mm gun belched orange flame, firing directly at them. They overran the gun, bayoneting and shooting the crew, then rushed on to take the second gun.

The third German gun was hit by a bazooka round

fired by a soldier from the regiment's 2nd Battalion, which had advanced straight down the road through the town towards the bridge. But the young German soldiers working the three 88mm artillery pieces had bought their demolition team some precious time. The paratroopers were now barely 200 yards from the bridge when the charges placed under it exploded, hurling pieces of debris high into the air. The men of the 506th Regiment found their route to Eindhoven cut off. The complicated plan that was Operation Market Garden was already starting to show how vulnerable it was to any disruption. Even small enemy units could block vital roads, and every minute's delay had a price.

Over the next few hours the US troops mobilized many of the Dutch civilians in Son, and with timber scavenged from local sources they put together a rough bridge to cross the 50 yards of water. By the time they had accomplished this, and the 2,000 troops of the regiment had made their way across, darkness was falling. They decided, like the Guards Division to the south, to hold off their move into the outskirts of Eindhoven until the following morning.

Further north, the 82nd Airborne Division, commanded by Brigadier General Jim Gavin, not only had the task of capturing the road and rail bridges over the River Waal at Nijmegen, but also had to secure the bridge at Grave that crossed the Maas to the south-west. In addition, he had to capture two other crossings over the Mass-Waal Canal that connected these two rivers. It was a tall order, and it was further complicated by a peculiar instruction issued to him by his British senior officer, Lieutenant General Browning. This injunction was contained in a written set of instructions given to Gavin on 13 September and stressed again verbally by Browning at a conference the next day. Browning told Gavin that it was imperative that an area of high ground to the east of Nijmegen called the Groesbeek Heights and the forested land that extended south of it to the edges of the Reichswald forest were secured before attempting to capture the bridge itself. This gave Gavin and his 82nd Division a perimeter of 25 miles. Some of his paratroopers would drop 8 miles away from the Nijmegen bridge, and would have to travel through thickly wooded country to reach it. On the day of the drop, Gavin decided that just one battalion was needed to secure the bridge, so the 508th Parachute Infantry planned to detach its 1st Battalion to head into Nijmegen directly from the drop zone.

The 82nd Division dropped successfully. The opposition that they did meet was quickly overcome and the bridge over the River Maas at Grave was seized. The 504th Regiment took 400 German soldiers prisoner and a road bridge over the Maas-Waal Canal was in US hands, although two others had been demolished before they could be taken. The high land and forest was also secured, without any fighting, by the 505th and 508th Regiments, but for some reason it took the 1st Battalion of the 508th seven hours before they began their move towards the road bridge at Nijmegen.

The battalion separated into two groups, F Company going towards the road bridge while A and B Companies took a different route through the town. It was growing dark and the streets were quiet and deserted. F Company reached a traffic roundabout just to the east of the railway station without any incident. As they were advancing down one of the roads, however, a German machine gun split open the silence, its muzzle flash just a few feet from the leading column of American paratroopers. Well placed, the machine-gun crew were firing tracers down the street. Bullets ricocheted off the cobbles and the US troops scattered, seeking shelter behind trees and against the walls of buildings. One of them threw a grenade and some rifle fire was aimed at the source of the muzzle flashes, then everything went quiet.

Elsewhere, the other two companies were being guided by a Dutch civilian through the narrow streets of the old town towards the approach road for the bridge over the Waal. As they approached the grounds of an old ruined castle that overlooked the river and the huge, single span that crossed it, they stumbled upon the 9th SS Reconnaissance Battalion. (This unit, led by SS Captain Viktor Graebner, was the one observed heading south over the bridge at Arnhem as the men of John Frost's 2nd Battalion were taking up their positions prior to their attempt to seize it.) The first indication of their presence was again a burst of machine-gun fire that cut two men down and made the rest of the company scatter. A grenade silenced the machine-gun crew, but as the two American companies tried to advance there was more gunfire, then mortars and grenades added to the chaos, killing more paratroopers. The US attack could not penetrate the German defences, despite some brutal and frightening close-quarter fighting with bayonets.

Finally, the US soldiers dug in to wait for daylight and some extra support from their anticipated second drop the next day. The road and railway bridges at Nijmegen were still securely in enemy hands, and further south XXX Corps had still not reached Eindhoven.

At the close of the first day, only a small force had managed to reach the road bridge at Arnhem. The other two battalions of the British 1st Airborne Division, despite receiving calls for urgent reinforcements from the men at the bridge, had found their planned routes blocked by German forces and had halted for the night some miles from the bridge. In the overall scheme of things, the fate of the airborne troops at Arnhem depended on the rapid advance of the British XXX Corps along the road through Eindhoven to Nijmegen, and the swift seizure of the bridge at Nijmegen by General Gavin's US

Paratroopers. Here, too, as at Arnhem, things had not gone as expected. XXX Corps was 5 miles from Eindhoven and the bridge at Nijmegen had not been captured. Time was of the essence in Operation Market Garden, and it was rapidly running out.

13

THE BRIDGE ON MONDAY

Monday, 18 September

Dawn that Monday at the road bridge in Arnhem revealed a scene of chaos and destruction. The previous morning Tom Carpenter had woken to the prospect of a bright summer's day and enjoyed breakfast of a bacon roll and mug of hot tea before climbing on to the lorries that took him and his comrades to the airbase and their gliders. Today he was hungry and thirsty, with the rank smell of burned oil and cordite filling his nostrils. On the bridge over the Rhine were the skeletons of two wrecked German lorries, blackened, smoke still curling off them, the metal of their engines and chassis emitting sharp cracks as they cooled. The paint of the supporting spans of the bridge was scorched and peeling. Tom heard the occasional gunshot from across the river, and bullets winged past or thwacked into the buildings that the soldiers had occupied in the night.

Tom's platoon had taken up positions as a reserve with A Company of the 2nd Battalion, and he had just settled down for his first cup of tea since they had taken off twenty-four hours before. There had been some bursts of automatic fire, and the explosion of grenades in the early hours, but no general 'Stand to!' A small building on the eastern side of the ramp carrying the road to the bridge had been attacked by a section of German infantry. It was quite isolated and the paratroops occupying it, who were part of the 1st Parachute Squadron of the Royal Engineers, had moved to a larger building. Then a lorry drove into the area from the road into Arnhem making a loud, rattling noise. It was a dustbin lorry, but the response was instantaneous. The unsuspecting driver was killed as its 9mm bullets from various Sten guns shot through his cab. The lorry came to a swerving halt against a kerb. Three more came from the same direction – this time German army lorries and they were also fired on and stopped.

All these incidents seemed random incursions; there had been no major German assault on the British troops now ensconced around the end of the bridge. The perimeter held by the airborne troops was a few hundred yards across, with strongpoints set up in various houses around it. Apart from a few anti-tank guns, they were dependent on their personal weapons, some light machine guns and a few PIAT anti-tank projectors. The first task while they waited for reinforcements was to hold on to the perimeter, and this would be greatly helped if they could utilize some of the heavier artillery stationed in Oosterbeek.

Major Munford of the Light Regiment, Royal Artillery, who with his driver had driven from the bridge to the divisional HQ and back again with batteries for his radio, asked Colonel Frost if he could contact the remainder of the Light Regiment back at the landing zones. In fact, the 3rd Battery had set up its 75mm howitzers on the south side of Oosterbeek beside an old church, establishing themselves on a flat area of land that stretched down to the Rhine. Major Munford was given permission to carry out the ranging shots, although there was some nervousness amongst the brigade and battalion staff. They had previously been the victims of friendly fire by British artillery in North Africa and didn't want it to happen again. For safety's sake, Munford was asked just to target the approach road on the south of the river. He climbed up to the roof of the building in which the brigade HQ had been established, where a signaller had fixed an aerial and which provided a good view of the surrounding area. From here it was possible to see the whole of the British perimeter. It did not stretch very far. From the point at which the road bridge crossed over the north bank of the Rhine, it reached about 300 yards along the road heading into Arnhem and 200 yards to the east and west of it. Brigade HQ had been set up in a large detached house that stood back from the road and faced towards the embankment carrying the road up to the ramp leading to the bridge. Ten other houses had been occupied in the vicinity of the HQ, clustered around the Eusebiusplein, as had various industrial buildings underneath and on both sides of the bridge ramp. Tom and his platoon were in this area in the clog and coffin works. The weakest part of the perimeter was on the eastern side of the embankment, where the buildings, which were occupied, were somewhat isolated from each other. It was a small area, and of course the surrounding buildings provided ample cover for any forces getting into position for an attack. Munford knew that the supporting fire from the battery in Oosterbeek might prove very valuable. He radioed to the battery commander, Captain Tony Harrison, who was about 6 miles away, and asked for some ranging shots on the southern bank. It took six rounds for the gunners to get the shells to land precisely on the approach to the bridge and for the battery commanders and Munford to be happy that the howitzers were accurately registered.

The first sign of aggressive intent by the Germans was the appearance of a single German tank, which approached the bridge from the eastern side along a road that ran under the bridge ramp. It was an elderly Mark III light tank, armed with a 50mm gun, and it was supported by a section of infantry. The driver approached slowly, the commander probably unsure of the exact strength of the British forces. The

German infantry came under small-arms fire from various paratrooper locations and they ducked for cover. A 6-pounder anti-tank gun had been set up in the street at the end of Eusebiusplein. The crew quickly manoeuvred it into position to take on the tank, but in the rush it was not properly dug in, with the limber arms just resting on the cobbles. When the gun crew fired at the tank, the recoil threw the gun backwards for almost 50 yards. The shot missed and the tank reversed out of danger. The uncontrolled firing had injured the gun crew, but other members of the battery rushed to replace them, managing to secure the gun properly and reload. Sure enough, the tank nosed out of cover, and this time the crack of the 6-pounder was followed almost immediately by the explosion of the shell against the hull of the German tank, which retreated rapidly, its tracks rattling over the cobbles. This time it did not reappear.

This probing attack and small-arms fire from across the river were ample reminder to the men at the bridge that they were surrounded, and that the perimeter was barely a few hundred yards across. Everyone, however, felt optimistic. There was a general expectation that reinforcements would arrive in another air drop by the 4th Parachute Brigade that morning, and those units guarding the landing sites would be able to push forward to bring more men, ammunition and firepower. Also, again optimistically, they were sure that the advance of the

British XXX Corps up the road from Nijmegen was in full swing. Ignorant of what was happening in the divisional area, and on the road to the south of them, the men believed that British tanks would join up with them in the next twenty-four hours, and it would not be difficult to hold out for that long even if the forces around the bridge were fewer than originally planned.

So when Tom and the others in 2 Platoon sat down to brew up a mug of tea, morale was at a very high level. The lads were tired, not having slept, and were still buzzing from the adrenaline of the dash to Arnhem and the early-morning actions, but they were fully alert. They needed to be.

The group of motorized infantry in half-track armoured personnel carriers and lorries observed crossing the road bridge towards Nijmegen the previous night had encountered and fought some US troops close to the bridge over the Waal. It had been relieved and was now making its way back to the 9th SS HQ in the north of Arnhem.

The approaching column of vehicles was spotted from the high observation post on the divisional HQ building and at first sight – so optimistic was everybody about the success of the operation – it was taken to be an advance party of the British XXX Corps heading up the road to join John Frost's forces. The lookout on the HQ roof then reported that the vehicles were German. The cry of 'Armour on the bridge' was quickly followed by an order to 'Stand to.' The 75mm guns near the church at Oosterbeek were called into action and several shells landed on the southern ramp, but the column was going fast and Major Munford told the batteries to stop firing. Frost thought that the wreckage of the burned-out German lorries would help to block the bridge, but the leading armoured cars smashed into them. With the noise of shrieking metal, the lorries were forced aside. A chain of Hawkins grenades had been strung across the road, but the leading armoured cars wove their way past them. One of the grenades exploded, but it did not stop the vehicle that had triggered it. The four leading armoured cars continued unimpeded, speeding past the paratroopers' positions on either side of the northern ramp and continuing down the embankment towards the centre of Arnhem.

When the remainder of the column was level with the houses, however, the shouted command 'Fire' revealed to the German infantry that they had entered a deadly trap. Everything opened up at once, and Tom recalls that echoes from the space underneath the ramp and from the surrounding buildings amplified the sound of 100 Sten and Bren guns blasting away. It was like being in the middle of an almighty thunderclap. Sten guns, Bren guns, rifles, PIAT charges, the report of 6-pounder anti-tank guns and the blast of the exploding shells all combined to create an overwhelming cacophony of noise.

The gunfire was concentrated on a small stretch of

roadway on the ramp, and the effect was devastating. The 6-pounder anti-tank guns – one firing head on from the side of the road at the steps by the ramp, two others firing from the woodyard by the coffin manufacturers – wreaked havoc on the armoured cars and troop carriers, which slowed and blocked the road, causing the other vehicles to pile into them. One side of the parapet on the ramp had been knocked away so that the 6-pounder could fire up to the road. The gunner was firing blind, relying on signals from another gunner in the attic of a building to tell him when a vehicle was in range. The armoured cars and half-tracks piled up on the road, blasted open and burning. A wheel flew high into the air, followed by pieces of doors and wooden panelling. Desperate to escape death, the soldiers threw themselves out through the doors and over the sides, into the storm of small-arms fire that poured from every window. Grenades were lobbed into the open tops of the troop carriers, whose unprotected inhabitants Tom described as dead meat. It was utter carnage. As the leading armoured vehicles started burning, some of the German soldiers managed to escape when the last two vehicles of the convoy succeeded in reversing back over the bridge to their own lines on the southern bank. The fighting lasted for some time, as desperate German troops tried to fire back from under their lorries or any rudimentary piece of cover they could find. German machine guns from the opposite bank also tried to give covering fire to their comrades, but the situation on the bridge was utterly hopeless. The British ambush destroyed twelve vehicles on the bridge, and the bodies of around seventy German soldiers lay sprawled on the road, or hung like sacks out of cabs and the back of trucks. Some burned with their vehicles.

There was a strange moment of silence after the firing stopped. Armoured vehicles were again in flames, sending thick, black, oily smoke into the air. Tom now has the impression that there was always something on fire on the bridge, from the moment that the pillbox was attacked with a flamethrower on the first night. Added to this was the thick smell of cordite that caught the throat, and the haze of gunsmoke that hung over the area around the ramp.

It was impossible not to feel a sense of elation at the outcome of this battle, but everyone, from John Frost to Tom Carpenter, was forcibly reminded of the precariousness of their position. Mortar fire from across the river now started to hit them, while there were attempts to infiltrate the British perimeter from the north and the east. Snipers also began firing from windows and holes in the roofs of the adjacent buildings, while heavier artillery was firing from a brickworks further along the river. Movement inside the perimeter was almost impossible. One curious incident was that, at the same time as the German mortar crews zeroed in on the paratroopers' positions, the horn of one of the wrecked vehicles on the bridge appeared to sound intermittently. After this had happened twice, some of the soldiers believed that there was a German, still alive, in the wreckage of a vehicle and that he was using its horn to direct the fall of shot on to the target. As the mortar bombs got closer, so the sound of the horn became more intermittent. A sniper crawled forward and spotted a body trapped in a truck. He fired, and the body slumped forward, the horn blaring continuously until the battery died.

Shortly afterwards there were charges by German soldiers into gaps between the houses, or directly at some of the outer positions. These resulted in intense hand-to-hand fighting, but they ended in defeat for the German troops. However, British casualties were increasing, and some more precarious and vulnerable positions in outlying buildings were slowly abandoned. Supplies of ammunition started to get low. The artillery fire from the 75mm howitzers of the 3rd Battery at Oosterbeek church was once more called upon to hit the Germans on the southern bank and succeeded in stopping the fire from their mortars. Shortly after these shells landed, and presumably caused some casualties amongst the German mortar sections, a German 88mm gun took over the fight from the south bank of the Rhine, firing at almost point-blank range at some machine-gun posts in the buildings facing the river on the Rijnkade, which started burning. Another piece of heavy artillery, a 105mm field gun, was brought up by the Germans and placed in the road that led to the bridge from the town centre. This began firing at the divisional and battalion headquarters that had been set up in large buildings overlooking the northern ramp and embankment. Shells ripped into the building, and Major Munford, who was in touch with the guns in Oosterbeek, saw the German gun firing from a mere 400 yards away. He decided to throw caution to the winds and ordered the gunners of the 3rd Battery to shift their target from the south bank. The risk of shells landing on the paratroopers' own position was high, but the gun had to be destroyed. The first round from the battery at the Oosterbeek church landed long, but from there it took just a few more shots to zero in on the German 105mm weapon. Two rounds blew it up and killed the gun crew.

There was no let-up in the German efforts, however. Three light tanks moved in from the east along the embankment road, again accompanied by a section of German soldiers. The tanks started firing at the occupied houses and at a school on the eastern side of the perimeter. They blasted holes through the walls with solid shot, then fired high explosive. Many of the soldiers in the buildings, who were from 8 Platoon of the 3rd Battalion and the HQ defence platoon, were wounded and captured when the buildings were abandoned. Others escaped, but the buildings were lost. Two of the tanks were hit by a 6-pounder anti-tank gun and the PIAT section from 2 Platoon, Tom's comrade Sapper Ed Lyndon being credited with knocking out one of them.

Eventually that attack was repulsed when the German infantry came under very intense fire from an attack on their flank. A platoon from the 2nd Battalion had managed to manoeuvre around them and killed several with grenades and Sten-gun fire. Many Germans surrendered in this close fighting, and the number of prisoners was increasing. Captain O'Callaghan, Tom's commanding officer, recorded in his diary that twenty prisoners had been taken in the morning after the ambush of the armoured cars, and another thirty were captured by the time the German assaults on the perimeter had been fought back. The cellar of the battalion HQ was used to house German prisoners, and it was becoming quite overcrowded. Unbeknown to anyone at the time, two lorries that had been captured in the north of the perimeter earlier in the day were carrying special troops from a V2 rocket battery located in the north of Holland. These soldiers might have been the ones that O'Callaghan reports as clutching leaflets dropped by the RAF which promised them safe conduct if they surrendered. 'They waved these wherever they went,' he said, 'still being uncertain of what would happen to them.'

The incessant mortar fire and shelling had also increased the number of casualties. The 75mm guns at the church in Oosterbeek could deal with some of these threats, but sniping was also killing men inside the perimeter. Some of 2 Platoon were sent out on a sniper hunt. The usual method, according to Tom, would be for a group to take up a position on the perimeter and watch for the flash or gunsmoke that would reveal a German sniper. A favourite place for a sniper to conceal himself was under a roof. He would climb into the rafters and knock out one or two slates to make a firing slit. Once he was spotted, a rapid volley of rifle fire would be directed at the concealed gunman, aiming to kill him, or at least make him move back.

Three sappers on sniper duty were moving past the jeep park, an area of open ground between the back gardens of the houses on Rijnkade and Eusebiusplein, when a German mortar bomb landed on a jeep carrying explosives. The blast threw all three sappers in the air and all of them were badly wounded. Tom helped drag them to their base in the clog and coffin factory, and when the mortar firing lessened they were taken to the casualty clearing station in the cellars of the brigade HQ. At least one of them, Sapper Harry Thompson, survived. Tom met him many years later and heard a bizarre story that resulted from his rescue. He had been afflicted ever since the war with nightmares about being put in a coffin and didn't know why. Tom told him that he had been hit with shrapnel in the head and neck, and seemed conscious, although paralysed. With mortar shells still exploding, Tom had dragged him into the factory and placed him in a coffin until he could be moved to the Regimental Aid Post. The fear, which Sapper Thompson had been unable to express, of being treated as though dead remained with him for years.

The violent events of the morning had shown the Germans that the soldiers around the northern end of the bridge were determined and sufficiently well armed. The anti-tank guns and the 75mm artillery firing from some miles away had accounted for three light tanks, some mortar crews and a 105mm gun and its crew, and was capable of inflicting casualties on the southern side of the river. The loss of Captain Graebner's column on the bridge that morning was the biggest blow. Graebner had been a dashing if sometimes foolhardy Panzer officer and his death, along with the seventy or more troops of his unit, must have created some caution in the minds of other German troops who went into the attack on the British. There were no more direct assaults, but the bombardment with mortars continued throughout that afternoon.

The 1st Parachute Brigade's intelligence officer had interrogated some of the officers captured in the ambush of the armoured cars and they had revealed some worrying information about their unit and what they were doing in the area. That they were from the 9th SS Panzer Division was the first indication to Frost that there were bigger and better German forces in the vicinity than he had been told. The news was serious. Also, by now he should have seen some sign of the 1st and 3rd Battalions of the 1st Parachute Brigade, and the 4th Airborne Division should have landed to boost the forces holding Arnhem and the bridge. What had happened to them?

By the time the German assaults began to peter out in the late afternoon, Pat and Ron were still in the air approaching their landing and drop zones. The 4th Airborne had been delayed by several hours. More critically for the men at the bridge, however, the rest of the 1st Airborne Division had come up against some tough German resistance. Their overnight halts had allowed the enemy to seize the initiative.

14

REINFORCEMENTS

Monday, 18 September

Early on the morning of the 18th, Tom and the rest of the men at the bridge had been taking stock of their situation, checking their sight lines and shoring up their firing posts. Further west, the two battalions of the 1st Parachute Brigade that had failed to reach the bridge on the 17th now started considerable efforts to do so. The two companies of the 3rd Battalion, A and B, under Lieutenant Colonel Fitch, with General Urquhart and Brigadier Lathbury still attached to the battalion HQ, made their move forward at about 04.30, before it was fully light. Colonel Fitch had decided that the battalion would work its way south of his original planned route and try that successfully taken by John Frost's 2nd Battalion on Sunday. They cut across Oosterbeek from the Utrechtsweg, heading south-east down

Julianaweg until they reached the bridge carrying the railway over the Klingelbeeksweg, then continued to march east. B Company was in the lead and making good progress; in fact, they had advanced over 2½ miles without coming under any enemy fire. As they reached the outskirts of Arnhem, however, the light improved and A Company, and the HQ Company, with the mortars and medium machine guns, which were bringing up the rear, started to come under fire from snipers who had taken up positions overnight in trees and wasteland between the railway line and the road.

The two companies halted and the gap between the front and the rear of the column widened. By this time B Company had reached a point where the Klingelbeeksweg joined the Utrechtsweg, just over 1½ miles from John Frost's perimeter around the northern ramp. Instead of taking the right fork and staying close to the river on the Rijnkade, the route that Tom and his 2 Platoon had taken the previous night, they stayed on the Utrechtsweg, which led into the centre of Arnhem. They started to come under what was described as persistent and accurate shelling from 88mm guns, which stopped them from going any further. The leading platoons tried to find a way through by striking out to the left, into rows of houses and narrow streets that led to the railway line behind the large red-brick façade of the St Elisabeth Hospital, which had already started to receive wounded soldiers from both sides. These side roads, however, were also blocked by German troops, who had moved overnight to create another blocking line running north from the river to prevent reinforcements reaching the bridge. This was precisely what Fitch, with all that remained of his battalion – B Company, the HQ Company and the Royal Engineers – was trying to do. Sadly, by now he was cut off from A Company and the mortar sections, the jeeps with their Vickers machine guns and three of the four 6-pounder anti-tank guns that his battalion had landed with.

Fitch and B Company were left with just one 6-pounder anti-tank gun and the two most senior officers of the division, General Urquhart and Brigadier Lathbury, who had stayed with him overnight. They were completely ignorant of events in their divisional area and were not able to communicate with divisional HQ or any of their units. Communication had broken down to such an extent that nobody had any overall view of the disposition of the three battalions that had been charged with securing the bridgehead; perhaps equally important, no one was in a position to make an assessment of the German forces and their movements.

By ten o'clock that morning, because of this disorganized split in his battalion and the strength of the German blocking forces, Colonel Fitch decided that the remnants of the battalion should consolidate their position in six residential houses along the Utrechtsweg and set up a strongpoint. Here German units, strengthened by a self-propelled gun, pinned them down. Their advance had once more reached stalemate and the forward company of the 3rd Battalion was under siege. Mortaring started shortly after midday and continued for several hours, the barrage of mortar bombs varying in intensity. The enemy seemed to have no concerns about shortage of ammunition. At about three o'clock a Bren-gun carrier with a few more hours' ammunition managed to get through to the battalion HQ along with another twenty men from A Company and the HQ Defence Platoon. Colonel Fitch had come to the conclusion that his present situation was useless and wanted to break out of the houses and try to reach the bridge by cutting north and getting into Arnhem along the line of the railway.

At four o'clock they moved out, to find that the enemy had set up machine guns or snipers that could direct fire down every road. The battalion moved slowly, cutting through houses and alleyways, and running across open streets and junctions. The leading platoons reached a street close to the railway but couldn't manage to get any further. Machine guns and mortar fire prevented the rest of the battalion from joining them. The whole force was surrounded and split into two parts, each one amounting to about seventy men. They managed to provide some mutual defence, and the enemy didn't succeed in coming into close contact despite the fact that they made several attacks down various streets. The concentrated fire of the paratroopers always repulsed them; although short of ammunition, they made every shot count. As night fell once more, German tanks moved into the area, but other than firing tracer down the roads at the houses occupied by the paratroopers, they did nothing.

Fitch decided that if there were no more attacks by the enemy that night he would try to break out in the morning, this time moving down to the road by the side of the river and hoping to get through to the bridge that way. The start of the move out was planned to be at 02.30 on Tuesday, 19 September.

The 1st Battalion of the 1st Parachute Brigade, under the command of Lieutenant Colonel David Dobie, had an equally tough time trying to get to the road bridge. The 1st Battalion was also not at full strength because their R Company had been caught in heavy fighting in the woods and had yet to regroup and join up with the HQ Company and S Company, whose 7 Platoon was in the lead as it went through Oosterbeek.

Dobie believed that the 2nd Battalion had taken the Utrechtsweg as a route to the bridge and thought that he too would be able to use it. The road went through a short tunnel under the railway line just before the high ground of Den Brink, where German troops from the 9th SS Panzer Division, under the command of Lieutenant Colonel Ludwig Spindler, had set up positions on the railway embankment. The first two troops to cross under the railway line were taken prisoner as soon as they moved through the tunnel to the other side, while the rest of the platoon, seeing their danger, quickly retreated. The German troops on the embankment then opened fire and three men of the platoon were killed, while the CO, Lieutenant Robert Feltham, was hit in the arm. The company dived for cover and its Bren gunners started to return fire, but Spindler's men had a mortar platoon and their mortar bombs started landing amongst the paratroopers, inflicting more casualties. The fire from the Germans was concentrated and the forward platoon couldn't find enough cover to re-organize and make a charge forward. It would have been suicidal. As it was, seven had been killed and many others wounded. Dobie then came forward and, seeing the extent of the opposition, decided that the battalion should make another manoeuvre and go for the southernmost route to the bridge, the same one that Frost's battalion had taken the previous day and which in fact Fitch's 3rd Battalion had stumbled upon earlier.

At this point, the 1st Battalion ran into the HQ Company of the 3rd Battalion and Dobie took them along with him, their mortar and machine-gun sections giving a much-needed boost to his forces. They worked their way down to the other road tunnel, which took the Klingelbeeksweg under the railway. Unfortunately, in the time that had elapsed since the 1st Battalion passed through it without any effort, Colonel Spindler's men had managed to get their blocking line established in houses along both sides of the road. There were also some tanks on the high ground at Den Brink, which had been turned into the main focus of the strategic area. The German troops did not physically block the road as it left the tunnel and headed towards the junction with the Utrechtsweg, but they totally dominated it from their firing positions 500 yards ahead. When the first soldiers of the battalion passed through the tunnel, the German machine guns opened fire.

Members of T Company took shelter in surrounding houses, storming in, many of the buildings still occupied by Dutch civilians who watched in horror as paratroopers smashed windows, climbed up into attics and knocked holes in the slates in an attempt to get some fire back on the German machine gunners. The Germans returned fire vigorously and the houses were blasted with bullets from German snipers and the fast-firing MG42 machine-gun posts.

Dobie's reading of the situation was that the SS troops controlled the area. As well as the high ground at Den Brink, and the houses on the road ahead, his assessment was that a tank and armoured cars were stationed at the road tunnel on the Utrechtsweg, seemingly manoeuvring between this position and Den Brink. A disused factory on the southern side of Den Brink housed mortars and possibly some 88mm guns. Moving forward was going to entail some very serious urban fighting. Dobie had decided against a frontal assault on the German troops blocking his way in Oosterbeek earlier that morning, but at this point he had very little option. He called a briefing meeting of senior officers in the back garden of one of the houses along the Klingelbeeksweg and ordered T Company to mount an attack on the occupied houses ahead of them. The mortars and 6-pounder guns of the 3rd Battalion's HQ Company were to provide some supporting fire.

The attack was led by Lieutenant Eric Vere-Davis, and about fifty men from the company charged up the road, into sniper and machine-gun fire, but with mortars and shells exploding on the German positions. The Germans fell back and T Company took the first occupied houses on the road. Two platoon commanders were wounded and there were many other casualties in this attack. The battalion consolidated their position, but still needed to take on the Germans in the disused factory if they were to get any further in bringing reinforcements to the men at the road bridge.

They pushed forward along the road but were fired on by 20mm anti-aircraft guns from the south bank of the river. The fire was too strong to move forward any further. Colonel Dobie then met the commanding officer of the 3rd Battalion's A Company, Major Mervyn Dennison, who had with him part of the company that had become separated from his battalion. He and Dobie worked out a plan to attack the factory, which required A Company to attack along the edge of Den Brink, while T Company moved up the road supported by mortars and Vickers machine guns. At two o'clock in the afternoon they set off into heavy fire from the Germans. Bullets whistled through trees and thudded into brick walls, while mortar bombs exploded amongst them. They pressed bravely on and one of the 6-pounder anti-tank guns scored a direct hit on a concrete pillbox in the factory grounds, wiping out the gun crew that was in it, and an armoured car was also hit and knocked out. They killed a lot of the SS troops in the factory and the remainder retreated in the face of these casualties.

By three o'clock the combined men of T and A Companies had forced their way forward, bypassed the disused factory and were advancing up the hill of the Utrechtsweg towards the St Elisabeth Hospital. The enemy now really poured everything they had on to the British troops; shells from 88mm guns, mortar fire and machine guns were all directed at the road up which they were struggling to advance. They were also being fired on from the anti-aircraft guns by the river and the 1st Battalion HQ Company directed mortars and machine-gun fire on to these in return. They scored direct hits and Dobie recorded in his diary that the Vickers machine guns shot down the gun crews that were trying to flee: 'Good work.'

But the struggle was an unequal one. The speed of advance was slowing, and a man died for every yard gained. They could not get past the road junction on the western side of the St Elisabeth Hospital. Tanks and self-propelled guns were now firing at them and a Bren-gun carrier that tried to move up was knocked out. Dobie wanted the battalion to take shelter in the hospital grounds, but the orderlies asked him to leave because his presence would draw fire on to the hospital. At 6.30 in the evening the 1st Battalion had shot its bolt. They were exhausted and casualties had been extremely heavy. Heavy gunfire cut across every street and road junction. T Company was reduced to twenty-two men and the battalion had just 100 men left fit to fight.

Dobie had brought his men more or less to the same area that Fitch's 3rd Battalion had reached a few hours earlier and, like them, had found that the German forces had exerted too strong a hold on the routes to the road bridge. As it was, the two battalions were now both taking shelter in the houses and gardens to the west of the hospital, with the two battalion HQs unaware of each other's presence and individual companies split up and isolated from each other. But other reinforcements had been sent forward and neither the 1st nor the 3rd Battalion had yet given up the fight.

As far as the staff of the divisional and brigade HQs, still situated in Oosterbeek, were aware, Major General Urquhart and Brigadier Lathbury had disappeared, perhaps dead or captured. They had in fact left the 3rd Battalion HQ at about three o'clock on

Monday afternoon to make their own way back to their headquarters. Instead they had become trapped in the attic of a house in the streets close to the railway line west of the St Elisabeth Hospital. They had been out of contact for over a day. General Urquhart had left instructions that Brigadier Hicks, commanding officer of the 1st Airlanding Brigade, would be in command in the absence of both senior officers.

Hicks was struggling to make sense of the extremely confused situation, which was made worse by the very poor performance from the various radio sets in the extended divisional area. What he did know was that the position of the 2nd Battalion was precarious. They needed more men and ammunition, as well as rations. They were under almost constant fire, and casualties were eating into their limited numbers. The 1st and 3rd Battalions were facing a well-organized German defensive line set up to the west of the bridge, and so far they had not been able to join up with John Frost's men. If they were going to succeed they needed strengthening very quickly and Hicks proposed that units of the South Staffordshire Regiment, who had landed on Sunday and were holding the landing zones for the second drop, should abandon that task, form up and head to Arnhem. A section of 3 Platoon of Tom Carpenter's 9th Field Company was also detailed to spearhead the move by the South Staffordshires, because Hicks didn't know whether any other engineers had succeeded in reaching the bridge. Hicks also proposed that, as soon as the 4th Parachute Brigade arrived, which they were scheduled to do at 10.30 that morning, the 11th Battalion should be split from it and sent directly as a further reinforcement to the men holding on to the small perimeter north of the road bridge. The commander of the 4th Brigade, Brigadier Hackett, who had seniority over Hicks, was unhappy about this when he was told about the order, but that was for the future.

For the moment, at 9.30 that Monday morning, the 2nd Battalion of the South Staffordshires, with the section from Tom's 9th Field Regiment in the lead with B Company, set off for Arnhem. They were held up by snipers on the Utrechtsweg and had to make a detour to the southern route in the same way that the 1st and 3rd Battalions had done before them. As they made their way towards the St Elisabeth Hospital, they met jeeps carrying badly wounded men heading back towards Oosterbeek. The drivers told them that they would never make it to the bridge. Shortly after that, the front of the column was hit by machine-gun fire and mortar bombs, and the section of sappers took cover in a ditch. Sapper Cook was blinded when a mortar bomb landed on a Bren gun and its crew, and metal fragments struck him in the face. Concussed, he was taken into shelter by some Dutch civilians. The rest of the South Staffs Battalion pressed on, still under heavy fire, finally catching up with the remnants of the 1st and 3rd Battalions on the Klingelbeeksweg at seven in the evening.

* * *

Tom and the rest of the men at the bridge settled in for another night. Their questions about the whereabouts of the other units and the men of the second drop were left unanswered, but it was clear that there would be no more reinforcements until tomorrow, the third day of the operation. It was perhaps a good thing that they were unaware of how bad the 1st and 3rd Battalions' casualties were. Tom settled down in the smashed building, cradling his rifle, checking the sight lines over rubble-strewn streets. It would be a tense few hours before dawn.

15

THE SECOND LIFT

Monday, 18 September

Earlier that day, while the two battalions of the 1st Parachute Brigade were probing forward towards the bridge at Arnhem, both Ron Jordan and Pat Gorman woke to an early breakfast back in the UK. It was Monday, 18 September. They were both scheduled for an early take-off at 07.00. This second wave of gliders and parachute aircraft was to deliver the 4th Parachute Brigade, the rest of the 1st Airborne Division's guns and vehicles, and the remainder of the units attached to the division. Pat, a member of the 11th Battalion of the 4th Parachute Brigade, was due to take off in a Dakota from RAF Cottesmore in Rutland, while Ron, in one of the Royal Electrical and Mechanical Engineers (REME) workshop units attached to the Airborne Division, was going to be transported in a Horsa glider taking off from RAF Harwell in Berkshire.

Overnight the take-off time was delayed because of a forecast of poor visibility over southern England. Ron found this extremely exasperating. The *Daily Express* and *Daily Mirror* had made a big splash of the previous day's landings, making it sound, according to Ron, 'as though it all had worked out nicely', but he couldn't get over the feeling once again that this mission, like the many others he had prepared for, was going to be cancelled at the last minute. Ron had found the preceding weeks extremely frustrating. Four or five times he had experienced the build-up of tension as the date for an operation approached, only to be let down at the last minute. His small group of armourers and motor mechanics were becoming extremely bored and bolshie.

The week before, an ENSA party of entertainers had arrived at the camp for a concert. It was the same as always – a small troupe consisting of a comedian, some dancing girls and a speciality act, who was customarily jeered off the stage to get the dancing girls back on. Such was the extent of their frustration that the troops made an agreement amongst themselves that this time they would ignore the comedian and the girls and give rapturous applause to the speciality act, which in this instance was a man playing a violin with an old gramophone horn attached for amplification. 'You wouldn't credit it,' says Ron, in his Brummie accent, 'but you had no choice but to attend.' They remained stonily silent during the other acts and the violinist could not believe his ears at the cries of 'Encore! Encore!' every time he made to leave the stage, and so he continued to play until he broke down in tears. 'We were that brassed off and we were in an ugly mood.'

Now, however, the operation was on and after four hours' waiting for the weather to improve Ron was driven out to the runway to board the Horsa glider. The mist was clearing as the tug started up its engines and they took off shortly after 11.30. As they flew out over the North Sea, the weather cleared. Ron enjoyed flying, and the trip to Arnhem was nice and steady, with some anti-aircraft fire as they approached the coast but nothing, according to Ron, that was anything to worry about.

The briefing given to the REME units had been concise and easy to understand. It had made the whole operation seem extremely simple. The bridge was going to be captured on the Sunday, then the 4th Brigade would land on Monday and secure the high ground to the north to act as a cushion for any German attacks on the battalions holding the bridge. Then, of course, the Second Army would sweep through the airborne divisions and at this point Ron and the fellow members of his unit would re-form with those REME workshops that were following by land with the tanks and artillery. Ron's small force had been selected out of the main unit to land by glider and carry out repairs on the weapons and vehicles dropped with the 1st Airborne Division.

So the confidence of the troops in the Horsa was high. Ron had proved to be a good shot during his training and was assigned the unit's Bren gun, a light machine gun, while Ivor, the young lad, was the second man, responsible for changing the magazines and the barrel. Ron sat close to the front door of the glider with the gun held between his knees. Airborne troops expect to come under fire immediately, and on countless exercises Ron and the rest of the squad had practised the manoeuvre of exiting the aircraft and setting up a defensive position. When the glider came to a halt, the armourer sergeant major (ASM), the senior rank, would stand up as a signal to be ready to leave the glider, then he would open the door of the glider. Ron and his number two, Ivor, would stand up, leap out of the glider and set up the Bren gun so that they could provide covering fire. The rest of the troop would then exit, some to add weight to their fire-power while others unloaded the equipment and folding bicycles.

Over Oosterbeek, the glider pilot released the tow rope, and there was no sound but the swishing of the slipstream over the wings and fuselage of the glider. The Horsa swooped lower and lower, and Ron heard the speed brakes extend as they made their final approach. The ASM shouted out, 'Everybody set,' and the glider landed. The landing zone was a ploughed field, and the central nose wheel broke off and ripped open the fuselage along one side as the glider came to a grinding halt. The ASM sprang up and opened the door, Ron put his foot on the step, with Ivor behind him, and at that point the second pilot threw his rucksack back from the cockpit ready to get out. The straps of the rucksack caught on a catch and it fell short, trapping Ron's leg. He fell headfirst out of the glider and the Bren gun's barrel rammed into the black earth of a furrow. Gunshots were coming from the far side of the landing zone and bullets were zipping overhead. 'So of course the ASM came out after us and kicked me up the arse, the lads piling out after him on top of me. He said, "What the bloody hell are you playing at? Give us some covering fire." I told him the barrel was blocked. So Ivor went to get the spare barrel from the parts pannier, which was fixed under the wing, and he got hit by all the folding bikes that were being chucked out the door. We thought we would come out like John Wayne, but we looked more like Charlie Chaplin.'

The barrel of the Bren gun was changed over, but the firing from the edge of the landing zone hadn't escalated and there was no need for any covering fire. There was more danger from other gliders still coming in to land, and several times Ron threw himself flat as a Horsa filled the sky above him in its downward rush to earth.

Ron found that the folding bicycles were unmanageable in the ploughed field, so the REME unit plodded to their rendezvous, wheeling their bikes and carrying their equipment, which in Ron's case was the

Bren gun and several loaded spare magazines, as well as his Sten gun, pistol and pack.

They assembled at the railway station at Wolfheze, which had been turned into a medical centre to care for those injured during the landings. Some of these injuries were quite severe. Ron had passed a Hamilcar glider, the largest used, which had the cockpit raised above the fuselage, like a 747, so that it could carry a small tank or armoured car. This particular one had landed badly and the 18-pounder gun in the fuselage had broken loose, crushing the gun crew.

They waited at the rendezvous for an hour but the other members of their unit didn't show up, so finally they moved out, cycling along the Wolfhezenweg, passing the bodies of German and British soldiers where there had been an ambush the previous day. Ron noticed that the bodies of the British troops had posies of fresh flowers lying on them, but there were none for the German dead.

Finally, they reached the Hartenstein Hotel, liberated the previous day by the troops of the 3rd Battalion but now turned into the 1st Airborne's divisional HQ.

It was an uneventful journey for the REME unit. Apart from the casualties at the landing sight and the bodies on the road, they saw no evidence of the fighting that had taken place the previous day, nor of the desperate situation at the road bridge a few miles away. The Hartenstein Hotel was set in its own beautiful grounds, which merged into the woods to the south. It was set back from the road and faced an area of common grassland like a village green.

The HQ seemed quiet, but eventually the REME unit received orders to dig in on the far side of the green. Several of them had already searched the local houses nearby and requisitioned some garages containing workbenches, while the vehicle mechanics went on a search for any equipment or vehicles that they could also requisition. The local children were friendly, offering to bring them lemonade and apples. It was a peaceful scene.

They dug their slit trenches, trimmed them and made them as comfortable as they could. To Ron, it was just a summer's day, no different to a day in England on a training exercise. They took up a position in their trenches, fully expecting soon to be moved into Arnhem.

Pat Gorman had arrived at RAF Cottesmore early that morning from his holding camp in Melton Mowbray, but as for Ron, the flights were delayed by the weather and he waited several hours before he boarded the C-47. Pat did not think that the operation was going to be cancelled. He had been briefed that the 4th Parachute Brigade would be the follow-on forces to those who had landed on the Sunday. The operation had begun, so it was inevitable in his mind that he would also be going in. The wait was a strain, with little to do except smoke, check and re-check equipment, and make stilted conversation, about anything except the battle into which they were about to be dropped.

Pat's load was particularly heavy, with not only his personal weapons, a Colt 45 automatic pistol, grenades, knife and spare magazines for his gun, but a large container that held his PIAT projector. This was heavy, and was attached to his waist by a long webbing strap. Stepping out of the aircraft, he would hold the pack with his right hand, his left holding on to the frame of the door. As soon as his parachute opened, he would let go of the pack and it would hang a few feet below him, freeing both his hands for the parachute cords. When the time finally came for emplaning, the PIAT was so heavy that he had to be helped to climb the steps to the aircraft door. The take-off was smooth, and the flight uneventful as they joined up with the rest of the aircraft and gliders heading towards Holland. The German anti-aircraft batteries were waiting for them this time and shrapnel from a nearby shellburst hit Pat's C-47 as it crossed the Dutch coast. The dull crack of the explosion was quickly followed by a bang as the fragment of metal went through the tail fin. Then there was nothing for a while.

After another ten minutes there was more flak and the bursts became more frequent. So too did the sound of shrapnel hitting the fuselage and wings, like someone rapidly running a stick along some iron railings. The aircraft started to twist and turn and Pat saw the red light go on above the door, which signalled 'Stand by'. At this signal, all the para-troopers stood up in line and hooked their static lines up to a cable running the length of the fuselage. This line automatically released their parachutes as they stepped out of the aircraft. Then each man checked the lines and harness of the man in front, and an officer passed along them for a final inspection. The door by this time was opened by the dispatcher, who gave a last check, making sure nothing was caught, and if necessary was ready to push out anyone who might have second thoughts. But Pat and his comrades in the 11th Battalion were tough, deter-mined men and the dispatcher knew they would show no hesitation.

The slipstream and noise of the engines rushed into the confined space, and those standing near the door could see the earth below and other aircraft in the long stream of transports. The crack of the flak was louder, the plane jolted, then the green light went on and the first man stepped forward out of the door, the rest of them following one after another. Pat hoisted his pack with the PIAT projector until, with a final heave, he too stepped forward into a blast of noise and rushing air from the propeller, then silence. The parachute snapped open, but with the weight of all his equipment as well as the PIAT, Pat felt that he was falling like a rocket, far faster than he had done on exercises. He let the container go. As he fell he heard the sound of gunfire and bullets whistled past. This was not right. The second lift should be unopposed – unless something had gone wrong. He hit hard and was winded, but there were no bones broken.

Pat unclipped his parachute harness, then realized that there were a lot of bullets flying about, some at knee height. 'Jerry knew that, however fit you were, if you didn't have your legs you were useless.' He saw two or three other paratroopers hit as they landed, crumpling up on the ground, while some just landed in a heap and lay where they had fallen, their parachutes gusting in the wind. Pat had been briefed that he was to land in Drop Zone Y, the furthest one from Arnhem, on a big open space called Ginkel Heath, but he soon realized that he had been dropped somewhere else.

He looked around and saw other members of his platoon, and they made their way over to the side of the field. Lieutenant Wilfred Speke, in charge, called them together. Only fourteen had managed to survive the drop; others, Pat supposed, were lying on the field dead or wounded. The lieutenant worked out that they had been dropped in the wrong place, closer to Wolfheze, and so too it turned out had some others of B and HQ Companies of the 11th Battalion. The battalion was split before it had started, but their first task was to do something about the enemy firing at them. Gliders were beginning to land on the field next to theirs and they too would become targets.

The German soldiers had set themselves up on one side of the field, screened by some hedges, so the paratroopers split up and approached them from both flanks, opening fire when they were in range. It was not a very complicated action as far as Pat was concerned, and those Germans who were not killed or wounded immediately surrendered. To Pat they looked a sorry bunch, not like front-line soldiers, but apprehensive and subdued, anxious about how they would be treated. Two men were detailed to take them to the main landing zone on Ginkel Heath.

Lieutenant Speke had received a change of orders, and he formed up the platoon and told them that they were to head out to Arnhem straight away rather than trying to form up with the rest of the battalion.

They set out. Their intention was to take the lower route via Heelsum and along the southern edge of Oosterbeek, bypassing the Hartenstein Hotel completely. As far as Pat is concerned, it was a matter of 'get to Arnhem as quickly as possible'. The small party passed Heveadorp, and as they got closer to a crossroads Lieutenant Speke shouted for Pat to come forward. He had seen two vehicles in the distance coming towards them and, assuming that they were enemy armoured cars, ordered Pat to fire the PIAT. But they were two British jeeps with stretchers carrying wounded men, and in each one were two badly wounded paratroopers. As they drove past Pat's small party one of the drivers shouted out, 'Jerry's taking no prisoners!' The remark seemed odd to Pat, who, like everyone else he was with, had no intention of surrendering, but it confirmed what he already believed: that the fighting was going to be tough and without any mercy. The dead and wounded paratroopers on the drop zone they had just left were proof of that.

They continued on their march until, after another twenty minutes, the sound of Bren guns and the faster rattle of the German MG42 grew louder. The noise of fighting was coming from woods on their right. Lieutenant Speke halted the group, telling Pat and Jonty to remain on the road and keep a look out for enemy tanks or vehicles while he took the rest of them into the woods to intervene in the fighting. Pat did not think that this was what they should be doing. He had been told it was imperative that they get to Arnhem. Whether the lieutenant had been influenced by the remark of the jeep driver Pat couldn't tell, but into the woods Speke went, along with the other members of the platoon, to see what assistance he could give to the British troops fighting there.

Pat and Jonty waited, sheltering behind a tree, alert for any movement down the road. After some time the firing in the woods ceased, but the lieutenant and Pat's comrades from the company never reappeared. Pat now had to make a decision about what to do. He certainly wasn't going to go into the wood himself, armed only with a cumbersome PIAT and an automatic, but he also thought it was absurd to stay put. They had wasted over an hour and, whatever had happened to the rest of his comrades, it was clear that getting to the troops in Arnhem was a priority. These were their last orders.

They waited another ten minutes, then, shouldering the PIAT and the charges, Pat and Jonty moved forward. They remained alert, aware that there was no front line in the battle that they had literally dropped into, and that there might be enemy soldiers on the road ahead. Many ordinary soldiers would have been daunted by finding themselves alone, separated from their units behind enemy lines, with only a vague idea of what threats lay between them and their objective. Pat thinks that this is what he had been trained for. It was little different from the time that he had been dropped into occupied France on D-Day. His biggest problem was the PIAT. It was heavy, and in a situation like this you wanted a Sten gun not an anti-tank weapon. But they forged ahead, setting a steady pace, as though they were on a route march on manoeuvres.

As they went forward, the noise of battle grew louder. They could hear mortar fire and artillery as well as the sound of machine guns. Pat assumed they were getting near to their objective. He could see a thick cloud of smoke further along the curve of the river. They passed through the tunnels under the railway lines without any problems, but there were several jeeps carrying wounded speeding back along the road. They quickened their march, then saw 400 or 500 paras all trying to take cover from mortar bombs and machine-gun fire that seemed to be coming both from ahead and from the left-hand side of the road.

They had come up to the rear of the 2nd South Staffordshires, who had set off earlier that morning to assist John Frost's group at the bridge, but after several hours had managed only to reach this point in the route. A group of them were surrounding a house on the corner of the Klingelbeeksweg and bursts of machine-gun fire from the upper windows covered the road on either side of the house. It was impossible to advance further, and the German troops were successfully holding off the airborne troops that had been sent to deal with them.

A sergeant approached Pat and asked him what he could do with his PIAT.

'I can blow the wall up,' said Pat.

'Go on then, do it,' said the sergeant, and Pat crawled into position, with Jonty behind him. Pat had already cocked the spring that fired the charge, so it was merely a question of Jonty fusing one of the rounds and placing it in the barrel. The hollow warhead was designed to explode against the armour of tanks and generate shrapnel inside the crew compartment. Not certain how it would work against bricks and mortar, Pat crawled closer to ensure that he hit the wall square on, although he thought, 'It's not hard to hit a house.' He asked for some covering fire, then rose and pressed the trigger. He felt the hard punch on his shoulder as the spring recoiled, then there was a crash as the round hit the wall, blasting bricks into the air, and dust burst out of every door and window. Slates slid off the roof, then the wall of the house started to fall in, slowly at first but ending in a rush of broken bricks, plaster and joists. Seeing this, the paratroopers charged forward, firing as they ran, but the German troops had given up and came out of the house, their hands in the air.

With the Germans in the house out of action, the road was now slightly safer to use, so Pat and Jonty were able to continue their way forward, with the assistance of some of the South Staffordshire Regiment.

They were now caught up in the aftermath of the uncoordinated push forward by the 1st and 3rd Battalions. Pat and Jonty reached the junction where the Klingelbeeksweg and the Utrechtsweg merged. It was on a hill that rose up past the hospital, then the road split again, the Utrechtsweg continuing on the high ground past the municipal museum and going towards the old town of Arnhem, while a right fork – the Onderlangs – descended to join the Rijnkade running along the bank of the Rhine. Everywhere paratroopers were sheltering from the onslaught, crouched in the gardens and doorways of houses, huddled behind trees. There were dead and wounded everywhere. In all his twenty years Pat had seen nothing like the scene before him – not in the desert of North Africa, nor on the Greek island of Kos. He was gripped by a great fear – not only fear of his own death, but fear for everything he knew. Ahead rose

the bulk of the St Elisabeth Hospital, with paratroopers sheltering around its walls, rifle and
Sten-gun fire echoing down the road. Around the
hospital were the small terraced houses that stretched
down the hill and over towards the railway line. Black
smoke and yellow flame burst upwards from gardens
and alleyways as mortar bombs exploded, smashing
down the roofs and walls of the tidy two-storey
Dutch homes. It seemed impossible to move up the
narrow city street into Arnhem unscathed, and
the paratroops had come to a standstill.

The machine-gun fire and mortaring continued for
several hours. Pat and Jonty were at the point where
their lieutenant had been told to rendezvous with the
rest of the battalion. The two of them were all that
was left of the group that had set off, but Pat wanted
to join up with the 11th Battalion if he could. These
men had started to arrive after a delay at the
Hartenstein Hotel, where Brigadier Hackett had
questioned the orders from Brigadier Hicks that sent
the 11th to Arnhem. The situation at the road
junction was chaotic, however. Shells were landing
amongst the troops, bullets zipping through the air.
Units of the 1st and 3rd Battalions were separated
from their battalion HQs and there was almost no
communication with the divisional staff, now set up
in the Hartenstein Hotel several miles to the west.

Pat knew that he was now in the thick of it, but
darkness was falling. He decided to stay with the
South Staffordshires and sought shelter in an empty

house, one of the many that lined the road, bullet-scarred, doors smashed open, holes in their roofs and walls. Pat took it in turns with Jonty to keep watch and, despite the racket of machine-gun fire and mortar explosions, which did not let up, they each grabbed an hour of welcome rest. It wouldn't be long before they would be in action.

There was by now a considerable increase in the number of troops available to push forward to relieve John Frost's group at the bridge. Colonel Dobie of the 3rd Battalion was taking the lead in planning a move forward that would see the Staffords, supported by the 11th Battalion, advance on the higher road that led past the hospital and high ground of the museum, and the 1st Battalion advance along the Rijnkade on the bank of the river below them. It was extremely important that this advance started at night, because with daylight any troops on the embankment would be completely exposed to the German troops with their machine guns, mortars and artillery on the south bank of the river. The lower road to the bridge could quickly become a death trap.

The first assault was planned to start at nine o'clock that evening, but Hicks, in the divisional HQ, told Dobie to abandon it after he heard a rumour that the troops at the bridge had surrendered. He reversed this instruction at one o'clock on the Tuesday morning, so planning for the advance started again; but several valuable hours had been lost.

So the three men spent the night: Tom at the bridge, Pat on the outskirts of Arnhem and Ron in Oosterbeek. Pat and Tom were now deeply committed in the fight to hold on to the bridge at Arnhem. Ron, however, was still in relative peace, taking turns on watch in the slit trenches that he and his small unit had dug. He knew that things had gone seriously wrong. The events of the next day would confirm how bad they were.

16

THE BRIDGE ON TUESDAY

Tuesday, 19 September

The paratroopers holding the northern approach to the bridge had spent a tense, wary night, under constant random gunfire and mortar shelling. Tom Carpenter was hunkered down in amongst the rough fortifications of a house on the corner of Kadestraat and Marktplein. Around him were the other sappers of 2 Platoon and some paratroopers of A Company, 2nd Battalion. The house reeked of cordite and plaster dust. Looking out on to the square in front of them, they strained to see any enemy movements along the pavements, where shadows danced in the flickering red light from burning houses in the town. Machine-gun and sniper fire sent bullets smacking violently into the walls of the buildings all around the perimeter. Occasionally a grenade would explode and the rattle of automatic fire would echo from under the bridge as the German soldiers made short, sharp incursions. These were only designed to harass and wear out the defenders rather than to make serious inroads into the bridgehead.

Tom had been on the go for over thirty-eight hours and fatigue was becoming bone deep. He knew nothing about the vicious fighting that had been taking place in Oosterbeek and on the western approaches to Arnhem, although the noise of battle had reached them. Neither did Tom know a great deal about the situation in the small perimeter held by the 2nd Battalion and the other units that had made it to the bridge. Snipers made movement from building to building dangerous, and messengers brought only the most urgent of information from the brigade HQ building. Occasionally an officer would carry out a patrol, moving quietly from house to house to keep abreast of the situation, reporting back to Colonel Frost in his HQ about the latest casualties, stocks of ammunition and rations, which were getting very low. In the original dash to the bridge, the 2nd Battalion had been accompanied by three jeeps of the Royal Army Supply Corps towing trailers of ammunition. Some of this had been destroyed when a mortar bomb hit the jeep park. The rest had been distributed and now there was nothing left. Colonel Frost had ordered sniping to stop in order to save ammunition, but this aided the enemy. There was nothing to be done, though. Food and water were also very scarce and everyone would have paid a fortune for a decent mug of tea and a bacon sandwich.

The night wore on, and in the early hours of the morning Sapper Donoghue, guarding the entrance to the house with the Bren gun, saw in the half-light a figure in the street outside. Donoghue was set up inside the house some way from the door to gain a little cover from snipers, and as he saw the figure loom into the doorway he said, 'Who goes there?' He heard no reply, so put the butt to his shoulder and pressed the trigger. A short burst of bullets ripped into the body of the advancing man, who tumbled backwards. Tom and everyone in the house sprang into action as the noise of the Bren gun echoed around them. Grabbing Sten guns and rifles, they prepared to fight off an attack, but no more gunfire occurred. One of the paratroopers leaped out of the door and hauled the victim in. To the horror of Sapper Donoghue, the dead man was identified as Major David Wallis, second in command of the 2nd Battalion, who had been moving from house to house on a tour of inspection. No one blamed Donoghue. The major was known to speak quietly and anyway, as Tom said, 'It was a time when the next shape in a doorway was the enemy. It was that type of close-in sort of fighting, and a hand grenade has a very short fuse.'

Later that morning, a heavy 88mm anti-tank gun shell hit one of the buildings on the eastern side of the embankment, the explosion blowing off the corner of the building and taking part of the roof with it. The wounded from this blast were taken to the basement of the brigade HQ building, which was now serving as a first aid post. Conditions were primitive. The Royal Army Medical Corps units had not made it to the bridge, so the treatment of the wounded was in the hands of two medical officers and their orderlies, using the first aid kits that were supplied to every fourth man of an airborne unit. Morphine ampoules were scarce and so too was water.

The building that had been hit by the shell was part of a secondary school which was in the hands of the Royal Engineers under Captain Eric Mackay. They stayed in position and shortly afterwards heard a group of Germans having a casual conversation in the street outside. A section of enemy troops was setting up machine guns and seemed ignorant of the fact that the nearby building was still occupied by the British. Keeping extremely quiet, paratroopers positioned themselves by the windows with hand grenades primed and then, at a signal, lobbed them on to the machine-gun crews below. The blast and shrapnel created havoc amongst the German soldiers – the few that survived quickly retreated.

At the same time, other German units were trying to infiltrate the small British-held enclave from the north and from the east. Tom was ordered by a captain of A Company in the 2nd Battalion to gather up some PIAT rounds and follow him. Tom went through the building collecting some of the anti-tank rounds and picked up another two men for a second PIAT. Following the captain, he bent low to avoid sniper fire as he left the Kadestraat and dashed to the abandoned factory buildings to the east of the ramp. In front of them, about 25 yards away at a road junction, were two Mark IV German tanks, accompanied by an old French Renault tank, which had advanced from the east along the Westervoortsedijk, a road that ran parallel to the Rhine. The first of the Mark IVs was already taking aim at the school building held by the Royal Engineers. It fired with a loud crack and a blast of flame from the muzzle of the gun, and the shell hit the school at almost point-blank range.

The tanks weren't accompanied by infantry so were relatively vulnerable to a close-in attack, providing, that is, Tom and the rest of the group could remain unseen. In his training, he had learned how to thrust a Hawkins grenade on to the tracks of a tank that was close up. Fortunately, he didn't have to get that close with a PIAT, although he had trained only briefly on the anti-tank weapon. Tom thought that the Germans had realized that they were stronger in terms of firepower, so tanks were now being sent in in the belief that they were relatively safe. It was important that they were dealt with, because if the Germans could be held off for another few hours, the rest of the brigade could fight its way through to Arnhem and reinforce them, and then

XXX Corps would also show up south of the Rhine.

The small group of men ran from pillar to pillar under the bridge to find some cover. Then they heard a series of loud reports of a gun firing and the crash of exploding shells. It came from behind them, but they stuck to their task and kept moving ahead. Tom was glad that he had rounded up another PIAT crew, especially with three tanks to take on. 'It's a cumbersome bloody weapon. You get one shot away and then you have to reload it. If it has not recoiled properly, you have to take the end off and re-cock the spring manually. So you want another crew to step in and fire another one while you're reloading. The advantage of the PIAT is that it made a nice bang, so it doesn't make the crew of a tank feel very happy, especially if they can't see where the fire is coming from.' A good hit on the turret too should at least seriously injure them.

Stepping out, trying to keep calm while in the open, Tom fired a round from his PIAT, then stepped smartly back. After the explosion, the next two stepped out and fired, then a third round was fired at the old Renault. Tom is certain that one of the tanks was damaged – smoke was pouring out of it – but in any case they all quickly reversed and took cover behind a building. Tom and his mates weren't going tank-hunting; it would have been foolhardy and they were short of PIAT rounds anyway. It was time to get back to their own houses. The captain said, 'Back to your units, every man for himself.'

They turned and ran back, now facing fire from the south bank as they raced under the bridge, Tom running the gauntlet of machine-gun fire as fast as he could with the PIAT, shouting at his comrades as he tumbled into the building where his platoon was dug in. The first person he saw was Captain O'Callaghan, who yelled, furiously, 'Where the hell have you been?'

'Tank-hunting, sir!' he replied.

O'Callaghan's anger was not what it seemed. While Tom had been fighting the tanks, the Germans had moved up another huge piece of 105mm-calibre artillery and had started firing at the houses along the bridge embankment. It had found the range of the house on the Kadestraat and three sappers had been killed – Sapper Close, Sapper Russell and Sapper Rogers – while Corporal Evans had been badly wounded. O'Callaghan, who had seen his platoon avoid major casualties so far, was shaken by the three deaths and had believed that Tom was also one of the casualties.

The house they were in was hit several more times, and the row of buildings they were holding that faced out to Marktplein was now on fire. They had to move quickly or burn to death. It was easier said than done. The Germans fired tracer over the building, almost as though they were warning the defenders that they would be next, before directing the big gun at the house. It did not take many 105mm shells to bring down a house and it was already burning badly when

Tom returned. O'Callaghan pulled what was left of his platoon together and told them to prepare to move.

Tom barely waited for the order to go. In circumstances like that, the instinct for self-preservation is extremely strong, and he knew that the first one out of the building had a better chance of getting away with it, because as soon as the German machine gunners saw a movement they would get the spot in their sights, ready for other people to emerge. Tom ran quickly west to another house in Eusebiusplein, in the same row as the house they had first occupied on the Monday night. The rest of the platoon followed him.

They were like rats in a trap. There had been a marked change from the euphoria of the Sunday night when they had reached the bridge after what had been, in retrospect, a fairly serene airborne drop and a rapid advance to the main objective of the operation. Now the area was an inferno. Buildings were burning all around the bridgehead and mixed in with the explosions of mortars and grenades and the sound of small-arms fire were the crackle of flames and the crash of falling timbers.

Later that evening, at about seven o'clock, a Panther tank mounting an 88mm gun in its turret entered the road that led from Arnhem up to the bridge. It moved slowly, firing methodically at the houses on the western side of the ramp, blasting the façades. It pumped three rounds into the brigade headquarters, killing several defenders, but did not advance any further.

The defenders' situation was now extremely serious. They had little food, the water supply to some of the houses had been cut off, and they were so low on ammunition that many were using captured enemy weapons and bullets. The house in which Tom's platoon had taken shelter, No. 21 Eusebius-plein, was now a caricature of a dwelling, the interior totally gutted, slates smashed leaving the bare joists exposed on the roof, bullet holes in the walls, the doors ripped off and used to form defensive gun positions. Very soon this ruin also caught fire, and they knew they would have to move again. The Germans had started using phosphorous grenades to set light to the buildings and many of the defenders were splashed with the residue as they ignited, so that they glowed in the dark with a faint green hue. Tom caught some of the phosphorous on his legs; it penetrated his uniform and started to burn the skin, causing painful blisters. He could still walk, however, so formed up ready once more to lead the charge across the street to another place of safety. He hurled smoke grenades into the street to give some cover and then they charged out, weapons in hand, heading for some houses on the other side of Eusebiusplein, on Marktstraat and Hofstraat.

Halfway across the street, Tom and the first section of sappers ran into loose tram wires that were hang-ing down close to the ground. They were catapulted backwards into a heap on the road, while Captain O'Callaghan behind shouted out, 'No, no, go on, go on!' Too scared about their exposed position to see any humour in their situation, they picked themselves up and charged forward again, this time avoiding the wires. Entering the building they had picked out as their next refuge, they found to their astonishment that there was an old lady still living there. Tom had assumed that all the Dutch civilians had evacuated their houses on the first day. The old lady was bed-ridden, however, and her relatives had been unable to get to her in time. The whole area was in flames, and bullets and shells had been blasting the streets for over two days while she remained in her bedroom. They could do nothing for her but move her away from the windows. The house had a good field of fire towards the bridge ramp and the road under the bridge.

Tanks were moving up and down the approach roads, their engines roaring, the tracks clanking and squealing. The tank gunners were firing at almost point-blank range, their armour-piercing rounds sometimes penetrating the walls of the buildings without exploding. The platoon's PIAT had been lost in the building they had just left; it was lying some-where under ruins of the collapsed walls. The dead were piling up in the streets. Tom looked at his comrades. They were all covered in dust from blasted bricks and plaster, red-eyed from fatigue and smoke irritation, unshaven and filthy, concussed by the continuous explosions as their perimeter shrank under the onslaught of the 88mm tank shells. Fortunately, some PIAT gunners in brigade HQ were able to get some hits on the Panther tanks, as did a 6-pounder anti-tank gun, which was pulled courageously into the open by its crew. The tanks retreated, leaving behind one badly damaged Panther and some dead German soldiers.

Tom and the rest of the platoon held the house on the corner throughout Tuesday night. They could hold their own against infantry, but tanks were harder to defeat. Fortunately, these had retreated for the night, but the odd shell and mortar bomb still crashed into the area. Tom remembers that even in this desperate situation, as exhausted and tired as he and his comrades were, there was still a sense of optimism. They were convinced that Operation Market Garden was going to be a success and that they would be relieved by the advancing XXX Corps on their way from Nijmegen.

17

THE LAST CHANCE

Tuesday, 19 September

On the outskirts of Arnhem, at 2.30 in the morning, under cover of darkness the men of the 3rd Battalion slowly withdrew from the houses where they had taken shelter a few hours previously. They left the buildings one by one, under the command of a senior officer or NCO. They were moving independently to a building on the lower road by the bank of the Rhine that they called the Pavilion. From there they were going to move along the bank eastwards. They were making one last desperate effort to reach the men who were holding the northern end of the road bridge. As they made their way down the steep slope to their rendezvous, machine guns opened up, but the bullets went wide. They assembled successfully and set off. Tragically, their commanding officer, Colonel Fitch, didn't realize that behind him, at the road junction where Pat was hunkered down, were the 1st Battalion, most of the 2nd South Staffordshires and, further back down the road, the 11th Battalion of the 4th Parachute Brigade. These men were also planning to get to the bridge, and they would start advancing at four o'clock that morning.

It would clearly have been better if the attack could have been coordinated between all four commanding officers on the scene, because the obstacles that they had to overcome to reach their fellow paratroopers at the bridge were formidable. A German force of Panzer engineers, commanded by SS Captain Hans Möller, had occupied many of the houses on the Utrechtsweg 100 yards past the St Elisabeth Hospital. These houses were on the north side of the street, opposite a small park that housed a municipal museum. Their front doors opened on to the pavement and their upper windows offered a very good field of fire down the Utrechtsweg. German gun crews with 88mm artillery were in place in the area of high ground on the other side of the railway lines, to the north of the Utrechtsweg, and mortar platoons were positioned with them. The Utrechtsweg and the lower road that ran along the riverbank were overlooked by German 37mm and 20mm cannon situated in an old brickworks on the south bank. Machine-gun crews were stationed at several of the junctions along the Onderlangs, the riverbank road, all with direct lines of fire.

The commanders of the British battalions

preparing to advance had almost no knowledge of the strength or location of the German forces that they were about to take on. They had few options. The only routes available to them were the Utrechtsweg and the road by the river, and each of these was barely 30 yards wide. There was some cover from trees and dense undergrowth between the road and the water, but this petered out near the pontoon bridge.

The darkness favoured the 3rd Battalion at first. The German defenders could not see where the attack was coming from and their machine-gun posts were overrun, hit by Sten-gun fire and grenades. But as the leading men from the 3rd Battalion reached the small harbour near the pontoon bridge, they came under a concerted crossfire of machine-gun bullets. They crouched low, but then mortars started bursting amongst them. There was no way around this deadly killing ground. The battalion lost twelve men in the advance, and Colonel Fitch ordered his men to pull back to the Pavilion, their original start line, and there make an attempt to regroup.

As they did so they made contact with the leading sections of the 1st Battalion and the South Staffordshires. The combined advance of these two battalions had been planned to start at one o'clock in the morning, but it had been cancelled by a message from divisional HQ who were acting on a rumour that the forces at the bridge had been overrun. Four hours later the 1st Battalion received another signal reinstating the planned advance to the bridge, so the two battalions eventually crossed their start line at four o'clock.

It was Colonel Dobie's intention to move his battalion along the same route, the Onderlangs, that the 3rd Battalion had taken, while the South Staffordshires were going to push up the hill of the Utrechtseweg, and they would then be supported by the 11th Battalion following behind.

The 1st Battalion went forward in the face of intense fire from machine guns, mortars and artillery. There was now enough daylight for the enemy gun crews stationed over the river to get a clear sight of the advancing paratroopers. The war diary of Lieutenant Colonel Dobie also records that there were some tanks and armoured half-tracks on the high ground to their left. The battalion continued to press on under fire from both of these forces and in brutal hand-to-hand fighting cleared any German infantry positions on the road ahead with grenades, followed up by bayonet charges. The enemy soldiers ran, or were taken prisoner. The paratroopers succeeded in clearing the road as far as the small square next to the little harbour, which the 3rd Battalion had also reached a few hours before. Here the fighting became extremely intense as the 1st Battalion continued to press forward. Two tanks clanked into action, turning into the square, but men from R Company managed to get close enough to disable them with Gammon bombs.

Dobie's war diary adds that the position was desperate, as they were being fired on from houses on the high ground to their north, while anti-aircraft cannon and machine guns were targeting them from the other bank. Tracer bullets started to kill and maim the paratroops, who were bereft of cover and had to throw themselves flat to avoid the fire. They decided to make a frontal assault on the houses from which a lot of enemy fire was coming. If they could winkle out the Germans and occupy the buildings in their place they would gain some cover and be able to establish a strongpoint. But their numbers were now absurdly low. R Company had six men left, S Company had fifteen, T Company eight and the battalion HQ ten. T Company found it impossible to break away from their position while they were under fire, and the rest braved a barrage of hand grenades as they charged at the houses. The second in command forced an entry into one house, but there were only six men left to follow him in. They were cut off from the other paratroops, and Colonel Dobie was wounded and captured. SS troops and tanks reappeared, formed up outside the house and a tank fired a round into the building. When the paratroopers had stormed into the house they discovered that there were civilians sheltering there. There was nothing more that they could do in the circumstances, so they surrendered. The 1st Battalion had been wiped out. It was 7.30 in the morning. The first attempt that day to reach Tom and the rest of the men hanging on at the bridge had failed, at enormous cost, and one more hope had gone. It was now time for the second attempt, and Pat would experience how that ended.

The men of the South Staffordshire battalion started their advance up the Utrechtsweg at 4.30 in the morning. They pushed forward in the face of deadly machine-gun fire, the blast of mortar bombs bursting in the road ahead. Intense fire came from the houses along the road, and any movement along the Utrechtsweg was also a target for the German guns on the other side of the Rhine. After half an hour they came up against a strong German machine-gun post near the St Elisabeth Hospital. The men of D Company, which was in the lead, attacked it, killing the enemy soldiers by grenade and small-arms fire. Even this advance of a few hundred yards had taken its toll. The company had lost about 40 per cent of its men as casualties, including the commanding officer, Major John Phillip, and Lieutenant Erskine wounded, and Captain 'Oscar' Wyss and Lieutenant Roebuck killed.

The commanding officer of the South Staffordshires, Lieutenant Colonel Derek McCardie, ordered B Company to move forward into the lead. They advanced further and reached the building that housed the Municipal Museum. This was an elegant white mansion set in its own grounds on the right of the road, at the very crest of the hill. Beyond this the road narrowed, leading down past Arnhem railway station into the centre of town. B Company was not at full strength because the HQ troops and a platoon had not arrived at the landing zone. The advance to the museum had also seen men killed and wounded. The company stopped just west of the museum, while D Company moved up into the wooded part of the sloping museum grounds that looked out over the Rhine. A Company drove the Germans out of the houses on the north side of the road, installing three platoons in the terraced row, while the rest of the company set up firing positions in the museum itself.

The advance had seen a lot of men killed or wounded, but the Staffordshires had established a firm base along the main road into Arnhem and broken the back of the German defence along this line of advance. To take advantage of this, however, more reinforcements were needed, but the 11th Battalion, still in place to the rear of the Staffordshires by the hospital, planned to move north on to the railway line and then advance eastwards along it in an outflanking manoeuvre. The airborne troops of the Staffordshires in the museum and the adjacent houses waited for the 11th Battalion to form up. As they did so, the Germans intensified their mortar fire. They too understood the need to bring up reinforcements.

Pat Gorman and Jonty Bright had stood to at the start of the South Staffordshires' assault, but stayed with the group of soldiers at the junction of the Utrechtsweg and Klingelbeeksweg. It was a disorganized mixture of small units from the South Staffordshires and the 11th Battalion, unsure of what was happening but forced to take cover from the mortar and machine-gun fire directed at them from the area of high ground to their north-west.

The situation seemed confused to Pat. Not only were they under fire, and not able to form up effectively, but there was obviously a great deal of fighting going on further forward and any movement seemed slow. They had remained there for almost an hour when a call came down for PIAT gunners to move forward. Out of the hundred or so men there, Pat was the only one with a PIAT. 'It was pretty obvious – the bloody thing was on a strap across my back. So we went forward. I'm not going to pretend that I was happy about it.' They were told that two German tanks were advancing from the direction of Arnhem towards the paratroopers over the crest of the hill.

Pat and Jonty went up the Utrechtsweg, but they made slow progress. Mortars were landing in the trees to their right, but the incessant stream of machine-gun bullets, interspersed with tracer, that whistled overhead was the more worrying.

They ran at a crouch at first, but then were forced to their hands and knees to avoid the gunfire. All the while the cacophony of battle continued unabated, mixed with the cries of men in anger or great pain. It took over half an hour for them to move up the hill as far as the main entrance to the hospital. Bodies lay clumsily in the road, and men struggled back carrying the wounded. The PIAT seemed to weigh a ton and God knows how Jonty was managing with the pack of projectiles. Pat could see that there was heavy fighting over the brow of the hill: flashes of gunfire, explosions, smoke from grenades and mortar blasts hung in the air. It was less than twenty-four hours since he had been ordered to get to the 2nd Parachute Battalion at the bridge, and he was still a long way from it.

Ahead of them on the pavement was an officer, who Pat thought was a major. He was standing, looking not ahead but down through a clump of trees with a pair of binoculars at the road running by the side of the Rhine below. They made a quick dash to reach him. He turned and said, 'It's OK, there's no need to go any further. Stay here, lads – they've been turned back.' So they crouched down and Jonty looked at Pat with a resigned expression on his face.

At that moment there was a massive explosion and Pat saw a blinding flash. He felt his face distorted and the breath was knocked out of him. He sensed that he was flying across the road. For a moment he lost any awareness, and when he had gathered himself he realized that he was sitting on the road. His head was ringing and his ears seemed to be stuffed with cotton wool. A few yards away he saw the officer struggle to his feet. He walked unsteadily forwards and Pat saw that he had a massive wound in his stomach. Blood was pouring out over his smock and down his battledress. He fell to the ground again and Pat crawled to him. He thought he saw him say 'Mother', and then he died.

Pat turned away and looked for Jonty. He saw him on his hands and knees. There was blood everywhere. Pat could hear him as though from far away, shouting that he couldn't see. He was calling for Pat. There was a deep cut on Jonty's forehead and his face was covered in blood. Pat didn't know whether there was blood in his eyes or whether he had been blinded. He took him by the arm and they took shelter behind the low wall of a house on a side road. Shaken up as he was, Pat attempted to wipe the blood off Jonty's face with his yellow scarf and tried to put a dressing on the wound, but the bandages were quickly soaked in blood. There didn't seem to be much more he could do except give him some morphine, but that didn't seem the right thing. Then he saw a familiar figure. It was the battalion sergeant major, Sergeant Bancroft, and behind him was the 11th Battalion's commanding officer, Lieutenant Colonel George Lea.

The RSM was looking at Pat, with whom he was familiar from several run-ins in the past, and then approached him. 'How are you, Gorman?' he asked.

Pat was still shaken up, and he noticed that one of his legs was trembling uncontrollably, but he looked up at the sergeant major and replied, 'Not so bad, I think.' The sergeant major, somewhat solicitous for the first time in their relationship, told Pat that he would get better shortly.

Then the colonel came over and told Pat that he had a bicycle, and 'There's a couple of tanks in that small patch of woods. They're causing a bit of bother – you had better go and see what you can do.' It took a moment before Pat understood what the colonel was saying.

'My mate's blinded. What about him?' he asked.

'Oh, leave him with us. He will be all right' was the reply. Remembering this incident in later life, Pat recounts it with a wry sense of humour, but at the time he was horrified. 'Yes, but I need another man on the PIAT gun.'

'Well we haven't bloody well got one. Now get up there and do something about them,' and the officer waved his hand in the direction that had been taken by the battalion's A Company. Pat and the RSM looked at each other.

Pat had been given an order and he knew that he could do nothing but follow it. He got to his feet, scrambled together the PIAT, took the remaining rounds from Jonty and got on the bike. With a 'See you later' to his mate, he pedalled off.

The wooded area indicated by the colonel was back in a side street towards the railway line. As Pat, with some nervousness, approached he could hear the sound of small-arms fire. Ditching the bike, he crawled forward and saw that a group of about twenty paratroopers, a mixture of the 2nd South Staffordshires and the 11th Battalion, had taken cover in a house and back garden and were fighting some German troops ensconced in a house on the other side of the road. He couldn't see any tanks. Pat joined the small group of British soldiers. Three or four of them climbed over the garden fence and rushed forward to the next house, breaking into the cellar. The men were still intent on pressing forward, but had become trapped in the houses at the back of the hospital, pinned down by the Germans. It had taken them over an hour to move down the street. Pat suggested that he use one of his PIAT rounds. He put one in the launcher, then stepped into the hallway and fired at the wall of the opposite house. Once again, the impact was severe, with bricks and mortar flying, and the house trembled. The firing from it ceased and didn't resume. The paratroopers from next door stormed forward and found that the Germans had abandoned the position.

The road ahead was now clear and, keeping close to the fronts of the houses, they raced down the street until they came to the railway line, in a cutting, which was about 50 feet deep. Pat scrambled down it, across the rails and up the other side, while a machine gun fired bullets that ricocheted off the rails and the ballast. Pat couldn't see what or who was firing – he just ran up the embankment to cover. They were now in some streets behind the railway station, heading towards the prominent Eusebius Church, although

Pat had lost his bearings completely since his near miss with the mortar bomb. The men he was with, though, seemed to know the direction in which they should be heading. Pat tagged along, still encumbered with the PIAT projector and his one remaining round, and still deaf.

Sounds of heavy fighting continued to their right, and they had barely gone a few hundred yards when the front men of the group went to ground. They had seen enemy vehicles at a junction ahead and within a few minutes bullets from a German machine gun were whistling up the street. They took shelter inside another house, then sought a different way forward at the rear, but this was equally hazardous. Firing started up from the street they had just left and Pat realized that they were going to be cut off. They were beginning to run out of ammunition and had started to rummage through the pouches of any dead soldier they came across, British or German. Making their way round a corner, they smashed into another house, taking shelter in the cellar.

When the shooting seemed to have died away, Pat realized how exhausted he was. His hearing was still affected, but the shaking had stopped. He was with about eighteen other men, 'odds and sods' from the 3rd Battalion, the South Staffordshires and the 11th. They decided to stay where they were for the night. Boxes of fresh apples and pears were stacked up in the basement and they happily started eating them. They posted a lookout and took it in turns to grab some sleep, though the floor of the small Dutch house was cramped with so many men in it.

They were now close to the bridge, somewhere in the old part of Arnhem, closer than many of the units that had set out to bring much needed assistance to Tom and the others at the bridge. But there were just eighteen of them and they were at the end of their tether. They had no idea what had happened to the rest of the battalions.

18

A DIVISION DESTROYED

Tuesday, 19 September

Had Pat and the small group of men he was with known the fate of the rest of the 1st Airborne Division, their hearts would have sunk. The Germans had indeed brought up reinforcements to the Utrechtsweg, and a company of German infantry attacked from the south-east. This was knocked back, but more groups of infantry moved up and attacked the houses occupied by the South Staffs A Company.

A more serious development occurred around nine o'clock in the morning of this crucial day, when two self-propelled guns moved up from the east along the Utrechtsweg and started firing into the museum and the houses on the north side of the road. Despite receiving attacks by PIAT gunners, they stayed in the area, waiting for the PIAT ammunition to be exhausted. Soon the front of the museum was blown open and the houses from where A Company were firing were burning. At about 10.30 that morning a company of German infantry stormed the museum, and two Tiger tanks moved into action. The men of A Company were probably killed or taken prisoner shortly after this assault and the battalion HQ disappeared. The rest of the South Staffordshires retreated down the hill under heavy fire.

The commanding officer of the South Staffs, Colonel McCardie, expected the 11th Battalion to move up and reinforce his men as they held on to their strongpoints at the museum, but General Urquhart had finally returned to his divisional HQ at the Hartenstein Hotel and assessed the situation in the town. He took the view that the offensive along the central route into Arnhem had failed and he didn't want to commit the 11th Battalion, so ordered them not to take any action. This order was sent at nine in the morning, just when the German reinforcements were making their first counter-attacks against the two forward companies of the South Staffs.

Two hours later, Urquhart ordered the 11th Battalion to form up and move across the railway lines to capture an area of high ground to the north. The purpose of this was to prepare the way for the 4th Parachute Brigade, under Brigadier Hackett, to advance and move into Arnhem from the north.

By this time, the South Staffs' strongpoints at the museum had been overwhelmed and German tanks and infantry were advancing down the Utrechtsweg.

The 11th Battalion was in no shape to confront them and came under attack on their flank. At the same time, the battalion started to come under heavy mortar fire, and the Germans' methodical mortaring of area after area caused severe casualties. Lieutenant Colonel Lea, commanding the 11th Battalion, shortly after he had ordered Pat to seek out some tanks in a wooded area, was wounded and taken prisoner, and only 150 men of the battalion managed to escape death or capture.

Four battalions had been smashed against the defences that had been quickly thrown up by the 9th SS Panzer Division, reinforced by Tiger tanks that had rolled into Arnhem early that morning. A fifth of the strength of the entire Airborne Division had been lost on the streets of Arnhem in a few hours. Late in the afternoon, the survivors of the parachute battalions were streaming back towards Oosterbeek in an unorganized trek, confused and leaderless, pursued by the German Tiger tanks that they knew were behind them. So the German line had been pushed west, far past the house where Pat and his assorted comrades were resting up. They were in a very vulnerable position.

The 4th Parachute Brigade had landed on Monday and its commander, Brigadier Hackett, had been taken aback to be told by Brigadier Hicks that the 11th Battalion was to be sent directly to help the 1st and 3rd Battalions reach the bridge. He took his time going to the divisional HQ to discuss the current situation, but after he did so he agreed to modify his original plan to take up a blocking position north of Arnhem. Instead, his brigade would advance to an area of high ground north of Oosterbeek and from there move along the railway line to Arnhem and the road bridge. Hackett's forces were limited, however. He asked if he could take the King's Own Scottish Borderers, part of the 1st Airlanding Brigade, under his command to make up for losing his 11th Battalion. Brigadier Hicks agreed, but pointed out that the King's Own were still needed to guard the landing zone for the third lift, the Polish Parachute Brigade, which was expected on Tuesday afternoon.

By Tuesday morning Hackett was ready to move, and the 10th and 156th Parachute Battalions moved towards the high ground called the Koeppel. As the 156th Battalion reached the wooded area to the west of the Koeppel, they hit a strong German defensive line and were fired on by armoured cars, self-propelled guns and infantry. All the officers of the first two companies were hit and around half of the men became casualties. The 10th Battalion on the left flank had also advanced, but were stopped by the same German line, although they suffered fewer casualties.

Later that day, Urquhart told Hackett that the attempt to get to the bridge should be abandoned and that his troops should move south of the railway line to join forces with the rest of the division in Oosterbeek. Later still, Hackett was told that the

Airlanding Brigade was under attack and he decided to withdraw his troops. As the 10th Battalion pulled back, they realized that some German units had managed to get behind them. They moved back across the landing zone guarded by the King's Own, where, by cruel fate, part of the delayed drop by the Polish Brigade was just beginning. Their gliders came down into the middle of a confused battle between the 156th, 10th and Scottish Border Battalions and German armoured cars and infantry. Gliders were shot down, their occupants machine-gunned while they were still in the fuselage. Some Poles, emerging into a tumultuous firefight, returned fire at the first soldiers that they saw, sometimes hitting British para-troops. It was a chaotic situation, and the planned withdrawal turned into a rout as the British soldiers attempted to cross the railway in the quickest possible time. Units became split up and headed in the wrong direction.

That evening, in the woods south-east of Wolfheze where Hackett had assembled the remnants of his brigade before heading into Oosterbeek, the 10th Battalion had barely 250 officers and men; the 156th had 270. The King's Own Scottish Borderers had been similarly wiped out, losing two thirds of its men. That morning, General Urquhart, the commanding officer of the 1st Airborne Division, had seen four battalions that had landed on the first day smashed against a German line that had cut them off from the road bridge. By the end of the day the rest of the units of the follow-on forces from the 4th Parachute Brigade and the two Border battalions of the Airlanding Brigade had also been ripped apart. There was no possibility of relieving the men at the bridge. For everybody in Arnhem and Oosterbeek, it was a question of desperately hanging on, waiting for the advance of XXX Corps, which should be moving up from Nijmegen to relieve them.

The next morning, at daybreak, Pat and his companions, still sheltering in the house in Arnhem, could hear a considerable amount of fighting coming from the area around the bridge, and a cloud of smoke rose into the chilly morning air from the many burning buildings in the centre of Arnhem. The smell of charred wood and explosives was all-pervasive. Small-arms fire mingled with the crack of 88mm artillery and the detonations of shells. The sounds of battle were now a permanent accompaniment to Pat's life.

There was a brief discussion amongst them about whether to make another attempt on the bridge, but everyone felt that it was hopeless. They had not much ammunition between them, and they thought that they had little chance of getting through the German cordon around the bridgehead.

Some of the members of the 11th Battalion wanted to attempt a return to the divisional HQ. Pat thought that it was the best thing to do, but hadn't known that it was based in the Hartenstein Hotel. He also thought that the way that he had come, along the Utrechtsweg, was not the best way to get back to the rest of the division. The others agreed, but said that there was another route back to the Hartenstein, which was the way they had originally travelled to Arnhem.

They left the house and eased their way along the street, Pat a few yards behind the leaders with his PIAT armed with his last remaining round. As they moved from cover to cover along both sides of the road, clinging close to the houses, they stopped by the dead bodies of British or German soldiers to see if there were any rations or ammunition they could use. Some of the party were already armed with German sub-machine guns that they had picked up. Their Stens had either jammed or been lost, but the German 9mm ammunition was anyway perfectly compatible with the British Sten gun. Some dead German soldiers that Pat observed scattered along the road had armed themselves with captured Sten guns. The sideways mounting of the magazine allowed the gun to be fired from a prone position, unlike the German Schmeisser, and this gave better cover from enemy fire.

Their ammunition was low, and they were not eager for an encounter with the enemy. Their movement was slow as they took whatever cover they could at the sight of German troops. At one point they came up behind a self-propelled gun that had taken up station at a crossroads, and it took several hours for them to detour around what was clearly a strong German detachment making up a line running north to south. The Germans were forming up and preparing for the first assault on the remainder of the British troops gathering in Oosterbeek.

As Pat and his comrades advanced, they were moving into the rear of the German positions. They slowed even more, as the leading men were painstakingly negotiating each building, each corner and junction, any of which might harbour an enemy machine-gun post or conceal an armoured vehicle. The group moved sideways away from the road, keeping under cover of the forest. They continued like this for another hour, until they saw a building, a large house. To Pat's eyes it seemed like a farmhouse, not that badly damaged but deserted. They approached cautiously and two men made their way to the hedge around the building. They waved their comrades on and disappeared round the corner. As quietly as possible, the rest of them moved in, going through the gateway on to the gravel path. The front door was open and they poured through it, leaving a man on guard at the door, then down the stairs into the cellar. Here they had a shock. It was full of Dutch civilians from the farm, men, women and children who had taken shelter from the fighting and had no intention of going upstairs again. They cowered away from the troops who had invaded their house, but were slightly more relaxed when they understood that their visitors were British. The presence of soldiers could not have been welcome, but there was nothing they could do.

Pat and his comrades settled down, preparing to share out what rations they had and keep under cover. Rather than blunder about in the dark, it might be better to wait here until daylight.

They didn't have that option. To their consternation, and the alarm of the women, with a shouted '*Achtung!*' a German soldier appeared at the top of the steps, waving a stick grenade. The message was obvious. The women grabbed their children and started to scream. The British troops were paralysed. Nobody was prepared to fire under these circumstances, and the German soldier had shown that he preferred to take them prisoner rather than create needless carnage amongst unarmed civilians.

The Dutch went out of the cellar first and Pat followed last, having dumped his PIAT in the corner. The paratroopers were lined up outside the house, eighteen of them, with German soldiers, sub-machine guns at the ready, guarding them. Each man was called forward, frisked for any concealed weapons and his paybook was taken off him. Then, with their hands on their heads, they were split into two groups and marched off.

Pat trudged along. He remembered what the driver of the jeep had shouted out as he had set off towards the bridge on Monday evening: 'Jerry's taking no prisoners!' However, his anxiety about what might happen next was completely overshadowed by a sense of extreme disappointment. His head had fallen and he knew from the way that they were marching that the rest of his comrades felt the same. They had all embarked on this operation with such exceptional morale that it was extremely hard for Pat now to accept, not only that it had failed, but that he was a prisoner of war, disarmed and held at gunpoint.

The captured men walked silently, each one sunk into his own thoughts. After some time they approached a large house set back from the road in its own grounds. It had a drive about 50 yards long and at one side was a large double garage. Pat thought that it was an administration centre, as there were few guards to be seen and only a handful of soldiers in combat uniform. They were herded into one of the garages, where they found another group of POWs who had been captured earlier. There was now just one soldier with a Schmeisser sub-machine gun standing guard.

There was little communication between the prisoners, all of whom were equally depressed. After a few minutes, a German officer appeared round the corner of the garage and started talking to them. His command of English was very good and he spoke individually to the prisoners, asking them their names, where they were from and what their plans were. He was shaven, his battledress was clean and he stood erect with an air of self-confidence. Pat realized that they were an unwashed, scruffy shower compared to the way the officer was turned out.

He got little response to his questions, but his

charm and his well-spoken English removed some of the threat from their situation and the prisoners regained some humour. Several of them said that he should surrender to them – the war was nearly finished. Pat piped, 'You know that we will look after you.' The officer took this barracking with good humour. He asked a few more questions, then left them. They were no wiser as to their fate, but felt that they would not be shot out of hand.

They had been there perhaps an hour when they heard the sound of gunfire. They could identify the crack of small-arms fire and the quick rattle of a German machine gun. The Germans in the house reacted to the shooting as though a beehive had been hit. Suddenly there were men in uniform coming out on to the drive, and a vehicle with a machine gun mounted on it drove out of the gate, followed by other German soldiers. Their guards also disappeared.

The men in the garage looked at each other. The situation seemed absurd, but there was no one near them. They walked down the drive and immediately turned in the opposite direction to that taken by the guards. They broke into a run which became a mad scramble, and they kept going. At first Pat felt vulnerable, frightened that a shout of 'Halt' would be followed by a bullet ripping into his back, but he kept running.

They ran for half an hour before stopping, and then they started to become more cautious about their surroundings. They had been running downhill and Pat realized that they had been heading back into Arnhem. They could see the spires of the churches, and the bridge surrounded by heavy smoke. All of Arnhem seemed to be covered in a blue haze from burning buildings and gunfire.

Pat argued that, as it was getting darker, it made more sense to get to Oosterbeek via the lower route where there was more cover. The rest of the men agreed, so they made their way down to the river and along the bank of the Rhine, remarkably without any incident. They crossed under the railway line and started to meet some British troops who had established a perimeter on the eastern edge of Oosterbeek.

Pat had no idea what had happened to the paratroops around the road bridge in Arnhem, and no idea what had happened to the XXX Armoured Corps, who should by now have been charging up the road to relieve them. At least he had avoided becoming a prisoner of war and was enormously relieved to be back with the main body of the airborne troops. He was still suffering the effects of the shellburst, and the situation was desperate, but he was free, and able to fight again.

19

OOSTERBEEK: THE LAST STAND

Tuesday, 19–Wednesday, 20 September

Ron Jordan woke to stand to at 5 a.m. on the morning of Tuesday, 19 September. He still anticipated that his unit of the Royal Electrical and Mechanical Engineers would form up and move with their equipment to Arnhem, in accordance with the briefing he had been given in the UK. He was completely unaware of just how badly those plans had fallen apart.

It seemed odd to him that the first thing that he was asked to do was to go and inspect a Vickers machine gun at the divisional HQ a few hundred yards away in the Hartenstein Hotel. It was a puzzling request. From his experience there was very little that could go wrong with a Vickers machine gun, and it would have made more sense if the machine gun had been brought to the REME workshop that they had established in a requisitioned garage rather than for him to go to inspect it. What use was it at the divisional HQ? But he was in no position to question what he was told to do, so went with his assistant, Craftsman Ivor Brewster, to inspect it.

When Ron arrived he saw a machine gun that had obviously been well cared for. It was polished and clean, and it gleamed in the sun. It was in far better condition than anything he was used to dealing with, although he judged it to be of First World War vintage. It had been, so he was told, removed from the front steps of the Tafelberg Hotel, which had been the German Field Marshal Model's HQ in Oosterbeek. The Vickers was kept on display wherever Model was, so that despatch riders and anyone else would know where to report. It seemed a far-fetched story to Ron, and he had no idea where the Tafelberg Hotel was, although he was told that it was now seeing service as a casualty station. The gun had obviously been maintained as a display piece and had hardly ever been used, but he was asked to check it out. It hadn't been converted from the .303 British calibre, so he dismantled it, rebuilt it and fired a round into a slit trench. It was in perfect working condition.

They left the Vickers and decided to go into the divisional HQ at the Hartenstein Hotel to make a cup of tea. There was, according to Ron, an enormous amount of activity in the building, with staff officers dashing around. While they were using Ivor's little spirit stove to boil some water, General Urquhart came in. He had just returned from his entrapment in the western edge of Arnhem near the St Elisabeth Hospital and he had, of course, been missing from the divisional HQ since a few hours after the landings on the 17th. On his return the activity amongst the senior staff increased considerably while Urquhart familiarized himself with the situation around the perimeter at Oosterbeek. He got as much information as there was about what was happening at the bridge and was brought up to date with the efforts of various units to break through to relieve the 2nd Battalion there. It was at this point that he ordered the 11th Battalion to break off from this attack and prepare to move north to assist the rest of the 4th Brigade under Brigadier Hackett in their planned move into Arnhem along a route north of the railway line.

Ron and his 'oppo' Ivor were in complete ignorance of any of these movements by other units. Still in the dark about why they were not moving forward to Arnhem, they were beginning to feel impatient at their idleness. The feeling did not last long. Ron heard the sound of aircraft engines in the distance and identified them not as transport planes, but as faster fighters. He assumed that a patrol of RAF Spitfires or Typhoons was approaching. He was wrong. They were German Messerschmitt 109s, intent on carrying out a strafing attack on the divisional HQ. As the three aircraft flew low over the tops of the trees, gun flashes started winking on the leading edge of their wings. Ron was in the flight-path and the houses near him started to get hit by the cannon shells, slates flying off the roofs and chimney-pots shattering. He was dimly aware of people running in all directions, with shouts of 'Take cover', as he went flying into his slit trench. His Bren gun could be mounted on a tripod to fire against aircraft, but Ron did not have one with him. In any case it wasn't much use in a trench. He leaned back, rested the Bren on the lip of the trench and blasted off a magazine at one of the German fighters as it flew low over his head. He thought he saw bits fly off it, but the Messerschmitt continued on its way. Another one made a pass and Ron went on firing, but all the air-craft, apparently unscathed, flew off, leaving several casualties in the grounds of the Hartenstein.

The silence that followed the departure of the planes was quickly followed by the sharp bang of a mortar bomb exploding. It landed close to Ron and its blast hit two officers from the Royal Army Service Corps who had been walking along a path. Ron went to help them, calling for a stretcher, but when he reached them he found that there was nothing he could do. They were both dead from the explosion, although he could not see a mark on them. The Dutch owner of a nearby house came out and gave him some blankets to cover the bodies, but no sooner had he done that than a mortar barrage started in earnest.

It was now that Ron understood that the operation had gone seriously wrong. Market Garden had not been the seamless success that was planned. Ron's REME detachment was not meant to be in the front line, but clearly it was. The mortars fell on the nearby houses and on the woods surrounding the Hartenstein Hotel. It was an accurate barrage and the enemy had plenty of ammunition.

After half an hour the bombardment slackened and a runner came up with orders for Ron and others in his unit to move down to the south of the divisional HQ. Tennis courts in the grounds were being used as a prisoner-of-war compound and men were needed to dig more slit trenches there. Ron loaded up his bike with panniers of full magazines for his Bren gun, but by the time he started on his move, the mortaring had intensified once again. He ran as fast as he could to where he had been ordered to take up position. The REME troops had to cross the Utrechtsweg to do so, but bullets were being fired down the road. They waited, then made a dash for it, and as they got to the other side of the road a major waving a pistol intercepted them. 'Right, you men, get down to the crossroads,' he said, pointing with his pistol to the Utrechtsweg from where the gunfire was coming.

Ron made his way to the crossroads with the Stationsweg, which was a few hundred yards to the east of the Hartenstein Hotel. There he found himself part of an ad hoc force put together from some of the 11th Battalion, who had made their way back from the battle in Arnhem, some Service Corps men and glider pilots under the command of Major John Royle from the Glider Pilot Regiment.

There were two hotels at the crossroads, the Schoonoord and the Vreewijk, both of which had been taken over to create temporary positions for field ambulances. They were now functioning as first aid posts and dozens of wounded soldiers, both British and German, were receiving treatment in them. They were about to become part of the front line on the perimeter of Oosterbeek. Some men from the South Staffordshire Regiment, retreating from the battle at Arnhem, had stopped there, as had some gunners from the 2nd Airlanding Anti-Tank Battery, who set up their 6-pounder anti-tank guns to cover the approach from the east. German troops and tanks had moved westwards from Arnhem, but had infiltrated Oosterbeek via side roads to the north of the Utrechtsweg. Two of these tanks, Panzer IVs, now edged gingerly into sight from a side road off the Stationsweg. Both were halted by shells fired from the anti-tank guns, and they retreated. No more tanks appeared. Ron started digging in on the western side of the road, opposite the Schoonoord Hotel.

No sooner had the men finished their slit trenches than the drone of more aircraft engines was heard. These were not fighters but heavier, slower C-47 transports and converted four-engined Stirling bombers loaded with panniers of ammunition, medicine and rations – a load that amounted to a total of 390 tons of supplies. These drops were vital, because the paratroops carried only the minimum field rations and ammunition for two days, and the plan for Operation Market had envisaged that the airborne troops would be resupplied every day from the air. There were now around 164 aircraft heading for the designated drop zones around Oosterbeek. They were escorted by fighters to protect them from enemy aircraft, but it was the situation on the ground that presented a more immediate, and unaccounted for, danger. Anti-aircraft artillery, 88mm- and 37mm-calibre guns, had been moved into the area all around Oosterbeek by the 9th SS units, as had some rapid-firing 20mm cannons.

The freighters flew in low, at about 900 feet, and were an easy target. Ron lay in his slit trench as the shrapnel from the exploding anti-aircraft shells scattered all around in a metallic rainstorm. It was as bad as anything he remembered from *Ark Royal*. Looking up, the troops saw several C-47 aircraft in flames; in one, a crewman still stood in the doorway unloading the panniers. Others crashed near the surrounding villages, and one Stirling attempted to ditch in the Rhine, but turned over as it hit the water. Thirteen aircraft in total were shot down – a high casualty rate.

To compound the disaster, the previously designated drop zones for the supplies were not in British hands. The divisional headquarters had tried to send a signal asking for a change of coordinates, but it was never received back in the UK. The surprised German infantry moving in on the Oosterbeek perimeter scooped up ammunition, morphine, water, food, cigarettes and the emergency rations that were desperately needed by the British soldiers.

The Oosterbeek perimeter was forming around a very small enclave. The western limit was the high ground above the Heveadorp ferry, and the southern edge was the north bank of the Rhine. Originally, General Urquhart had hoped to establish the eastern edge along the railway line at the north of the rail bridge, but there was some strong German pressure on the south-eastern edge of the area, where the Royal Artillery had positioned their 75mm-gun batteries. The northern edge was along a line to the north of the Utrechtsweg, and here the 9th Field Company set up some defences based on a large building known as Sonnenberg House. Various units made up of those battalions that had guarded the landing zones, glider pilots and various divisional units, like the REME troops and engineers, were used to help fill in gaps in the line.

The crossroads where Ron was stationed was on the eastern side, north of the gun positions, and the enemy was moving into Oosterbeek warily in this area. The streets were narrow and the houses close together. Ron had managed to get back to the REME depot at the Hartenstein and collected as many of the spare magazines for the Bren gun as he could. At the junction he could hear more gunfire from the east and saw two German infantrymen slowly approaching down the road, moving carefully from tree to tree. It was surprising that they had reached this far and he assumed that they were the advance guard of a scouting party. He enquired of the major whether he should let them have a burst from the Bren, but Royle said no – he wanted to capture them to obtain some information about the approaching German forces. He told Ron to concentrate on the road behind the two and make sure that no other enemy soldiers followed them. If he saw any, he was to open fire. The two German soldiers continued to advance, and the major detailed a small group to charge at them when they came abreast of their position.

Unfortunately for the major's plan, he had positioned a paratrooper from the 11th Battalion further up the road as an advance lookout, and no sooner had the two German SS soldiers got level with him than he fired off a shot, killing the first one. The second dived back for cover and managed to crawl away. That was the only action that Ron saw that afternoon, and as the day wore on he asked to go back to his unit to see if there was anything he could do as an armourer.

Major Royle let him go, so he returned to the REME HQ, where he was presented with another oddity. A Russian-built Thompson sub-machine gun with a circular magazine had been seized from the German captain of a boat that had been trying to navigate the Rhine earlier that morning. The captain had been forced to put in at the ferry crossing below Westerbouwing. Ron found several bandoliers of ammunition that would fit the .45in-calibre chamber and he loaded the big round magazine with them. It was heavy, with a limited range of about 50 yards, but the bullets had a lot of stopping power and Ron was already thinking that things might be desperate quite soon.

By the late afternoon of that Tuesday a variety of German units were advancing towards Oosterbeek. From the east, the 9th SS *Kampfgruppe*, under Lieutenant Colonel Spindler, started moving westwards from the outskirts of Arnhem, where they had inflicted a crushing defeat on the paratroopers attempting to reinforce the men at the bridge. Six or seven German battalions were advancing from the west as part of *Kampfgruppe* Von Tettau and this was moving on a wide front that included the drop zone of Ginkel Heath to the north and the towns of Heelsum and Renkum to the south. Captain Sepp Krafft's unit, which had been instrumental in holding the very first advance to the road bridge on the 17th, had been added to Spindler's command and was moving in from the north, mopping up the rest of Hackett's 4th Parachute Brigade as it retreated under fire back over the railway line into the Oosterbeek enclave. Urquhart realized that Hackett was not going to be able to break through to Arnhem and, given that the thrust along the Utrechtsweg had also failed to reach John Frost's forces, he hoped that the perimeter around Oosterbeek might still be useful to create a bridgehead for the arrival of XXX Corps. There was still a strongly held belief throughout the airborne divisions that they would soon be relieved by the arrival of the British armoured columns.

The situation on the ground at Arnhem and Oosterbeek was still fluid. No one knew the strength of the forces that were retreating from the western edge of Arnhem in dribs and drabs, or how severe the losses had been in Hackett's retreat across the railway. The light infantry with their 75mm guns were still stationed on the low land to the west of the old church in Oosterbeek, and their commanding officer was sweeping up the troops retreating along the road and placing them in defensive positions. The 9th SS was already starting to probe forward along the two main routes, the southern one along Benedendorpsweg and the central route along the Utrechtsweg, but the eastern part of Oosterbeek, with its narrow streets and tightly packed buildings, was not held securely by either the airborne troops or the Spindler *Kampfgruppe*. The German units were wary of a rapid advance through such a dense built-up area and for the moment the southern road was more favoured in the eyes of their commanders. On this route their flanks were protected by their own forces stationed on the south bank of the Rhine to their left and on the higher ground to their right.

The Germans moved forward more decisively on

the morning of Wednesday the 20th, with self-propelled guns and tanks protected by infantry, and with fire support from some mortar battalions to their rear. While their flanks were secure, the area into which they were moving was defended by the remnants of units cut up by the fighting on Tuesday. They had been beefed up with anti-tank guns and some Vickers machine guns, and totalled about 450 men, with some sixty or so glider pilots. They were placed on a line defending the 75mm guns of the Light Artillery dug in on the polder. These men were still able to fight once they were reorganized and succeeded in defeating the first German attack, knocking out several tanks in the process.

As a result, the German units, under the command of SS Lieutenant Harder and SS Captain Klaus von Alworden, shifted their line of attack to the houses on the north of the road, attempting to outflank the anti-tank guns by moving down a side street. Two 6-pounder guns held them off, and the gunner in charge, Lance Sergeant John Baskeyfield, knocked out two tanks and two self-propelled guns, finally firing a gun single-handed at the last SP before being killed himself. He was awarded the VC for his action, but it did not stop the men of the 11th Battalion in the surrounding houses from coming under attack from flamethrowers and tanks. They were forced to retreat, leaving the houses in flames.

At the same time, German infantry crossed over the railway embankment. They were badly shot up by machine-gun fire, but there was an acute danger that the German manoeuvre was working and that the anti-tank guns and some of the South Staffordshire men would be cut off by tanks moving down Acacialaan. The airborne men, now under the command of Major Richard Lonsdale, second in command of the 11th Battalion, retreated to the Oosterbeek church under heavy German mortar fire. Despite more casualties, they were able to form another line, and with the 75mm guns of the Light Infantry held the Germans yet again, and continued to do so for the next two days.

The Utrechtsweg also offered a line of advance into Oosterbeek, but here the Germans found it heavier going after their advance guard was defeated. Their progress was painstakingly slow, with every house, garden and street fought over. *Kampfgruppe* Spindler was handicapped by the arrival of fresh troops with no previous battle experience. It took them some days to settle into their new units. Meanwhile, the airborne troops were fighting hard over every house and Lieutenant Colonel Walther Harzer, in charge of the 9th SS Division, decided to form small groups of assault troops backed up with self-propelled guns. Even with these new formations, the advance for the Germans was a slow one, with the British anti-tank artillery and PIAT crews showing great bravery and skill. German crews of the armoured vehicles were very cautious about moving forwards if the presence of a PIAT or anti-tank gun was suspected.

On Wednesday Ron once more stood to at 5 a.m. He had explained to the armourer sergeant major that he had been ordered to return to the crossroads the next morning. By now they had used all their water supply and had nothing with which to make a cup of tea, so Ron and Ivor headed for the divisional HQ at the Hartenstein Hotel to forage for some breakfast before making their way to their position on the perimeter.

Halfway to the hotel, a barrage of incoming mortar bombs opened up. They both dived for a slit trench. The bombardment was devastating. The REME stores were hit and the portable lathes, special tools and motorcycles were all destroyed in a series of explosions. Ron saw an ammunition store and petrol dump hit by a mortar, creating a massive explosion that sent a great column of black smoke into the air, providing an aiming point for more mortar bombs. It was a calculated and precise bombardment. Ron realized that the mortar crews knew what they were doing. The line of falling bombs would move forward like a curtain of rain, then stop. The mortar crews would allow just enough time for people to leave their slit trenches to assist the wounded, or begin a move to a new position, then they would start firing again, the bombs falling on anyone who hadn't remained under cover. The psychological effect was intense; to Ron's mind it was far, far worse than anything he had experienced on *Ark Royal* or in the Blitz. These mortar barrages continued for two hours every morning, becoming known as 'the morning hate'. They took a relentless toll of casualties.

Later that day, more German troops supported by self-propelled guns advanced along the Utrechtsweg to the crossroads. There was more heavy mortar fire, and one of the self-propelled guns fired four shots into the Schoonoord hotel, killing some of the casualties. An anti-tank gun fired at the self-propelled guns, but with no success. They refused to budge, and the crossroads and the hotels fell into German hands. There were similar advances all along the eastern perimeter, and Ron's ad hoc unit, still under the command of Major Royle, was ordered to move southwards to recapture the Tafelberg Hotel, which had, like the crossroads, fallen to the Germans. Its top floors overlooked the grounds of the Hartenstein, and the divisional officers wanted it recaptured.

The Tafelberg was located down a narrow, tree-lined road and they set out in single file, cutting through some shrubbery towards the hotel. The major was in the lead and Ron brought up the rear with his Bren gun. They were going to formulate a plan of attack once the major had a chance to assess the state of the enemy forces.

They had gone barely 300 yards when a shot rang out. Major Royle fell, lifeless, with a bullet between his eyes. A sniper had shot him. The men dived for cover and slowly crawled back to regroup. The shot had come from a building down from the crossroads, one of a row of four houses. Ron wasn't sure which one the sniper was hiding in, so they decided to occupy and clear all four of them one at a time. They moved sideways under the cover of some bushes, then rushed at the first house, Ron firing into the windows with his Bren while two others rushed up and threw grenades through the windows. They cleared the ground floor, then moved up to the bedrooms, firing through the ceilings to kill anyone taking shelter. It was empty, so they prepared to move on to the next house.

Someone suggested to Ivor, Ron's mate, that he should go up to the attic to keep a look out for any enemy troops coming down the road while they launched their next attack. Ivor climbed the stairs while Ron and the rest of the men gathered around the door of the house they had just secured in order to coordinate their next assault. As they stood there, a four-barrelled mortar fired and the bombs crashed on to the house. Doors were blasted out and, with a massive crash, the roof collapsed in a cloud of dust, with tiles flying through the air. A fire started and everyone thought that Ivor was dead. It was hard to believe that anyone at the top of the building could have survived the explosion. They were just about to clear the next house for some shelter, however, when Ivor appeared round the corner, covered in pale plaster dust and black ashes. He had miraculously survived the mortars, but had been forced to find his way down to the ground through a metal chute that had been used to empty the ashes from the fireplaces into a dustbin. He seemed unhurt, although quite badly dazed.

Before they could storm into the next house, a staff sergeant ran up to them and said that he had been sent by divisional HQ to take over command. He was not interested in the sniper, telling them instead to press on to the Tafelberg, their original objective. They approached the former hotel without any more casualties, but they found that German troops surrounded it and rows of wounded men on stretchers were lined up in the driveway. A direct attack seemed impossible.

They withdrew, but shortly afterwards more orders were received to bypass the Tafelberg and move down to join up with some other members of the 1st Battalion. Their instructions were to dig in, then occupy a row of houses, retreating to the trenches if it proved impossible to hold the buildings. Here Ron remained, separate from the rest of his REME unit, under the command of a sergeant glider pilot. The optimism of the morning had completely evaporated.

20

THE ROAD TO NIJMEGEN

Monday, 18–Wednesday, 20 September

The fighting had become bloodier in Arnhem on Monday and Tuesday, and the situation increasingly desperate. Tom and the rest of the men at the bridge were barely hanging on amongst the rubble of the smashed buildings. Pat was using all his skills to make it back to the safety of the airborne units, and Ron was dug in at Oosterbeek, facing a developing German offensive. From now on, all that would keep hope alive was the promise of rescue by the British Army XXX Corps and their Guards Armoured Division, who were advancing along the road through Eindhoven and Nijmegen. Their arrival would not only bring ammunition, food and medical assistance, it would set the seal of success on the biggest and boldest airborne operation in history. They had 65 miles to travel and they had set off on Sunday, as the gliders and transports bound for Arnhem had flown overhead. The Irish Guards, the spearhead of the advance, had not made it to Eindhoven by Sunday night, however, and it was on the Monday morning that they once more started their advance along the road to Eindhoven, just 5 miles away. Progress was rapidly halted again, however, by the presence of a single self-propelled gun, which was firing down the road at their leading troop of Sherman tanks.

Responsibility for the road's defence fell between two different German divisions but, even so, the enemy had established a strongpoint at the village of Aalst, south of Eindhoven. Here some self-propelled 88mm anti-tank guns and eleven 75mm artillery pieces were disposed to form a screen along the southern side of the village. The leading Irish Guards tanks made contact with them around midday. The German gunners were handicapped by having nothing with which to tow their artillery, so the guns had been manhandled into position. As a result, they were more exposed than they should have been and the guns became easy targets once they were spotted. But the advance was halted. Other squadrons of tanks tried to bypass the German guns, but off the main road heavy tanks tended to get bogged down and the tank crews found it hard negotiating the small bridges over ditches and dykes.

On the other side of the town, the US 506th Parachute Infantry Regiment, who had landed on Sunday, also restarted their forward movement into

Eindhoven. It was a cautious progress, with scouting parties moving ahead of the main platoons. There were enemy snipers in the trees and buildings on both sides of the road. Once they had worked their way into the outskirts of Eindhoven, the parachute infantry met even deadlier fire. Heavy machine guns and 88mm guns were lodged in buildings at various road junctions covering the main entrance into the town. Outflanking these enemy strongpoints took more time, and cost more dead and wounded, but they succeeded, killing or capturing 300 German soldiers. By five o'clock that evening Eindhoven was free of German occupation – the first Dutch city to be liberated. Jubilant civilians poured into the streets, blocking the path of the Guards' Sherman tanks.

Armoured cars of the Household Cavalry had managed to drive into Eindhoven at around two o'clock, but it took another five hours before the Irish Guards negotiated the route through the town. It was not until seven o'clock that they were clear once more to press on to Son, where the sappers could start work on building a Bailey bridge over the Wilhelmina Canal to replace the one demolished by the Germans the day before. The sappers worked through the night, doubling up the prefabricated sections so that the bridge would support the 30-ton weight of a Sherman tank. It was an impressive effort on the part of the engineers. By first light next morning the bridge had been completed, and the Household Cavalry led the Grenadier Guards over it and on to the road to Veghel. The Guards Armoured Division drove forward at a cracking pace on a road now free of enemy forces and defended by the US 101st Airborne Division. In just two hours the leading vehicles had joined up with General James Gavin's 82nd Airborne Division at Grave, the southern point of the 82nd's large perimeter.

For all their speed up the road towards Nijmegen, XXX Corps was now a day and a half behind schedule. Major General Allan Adair, commander of the Guards Division, had been told in his orders that the huge road bridge over the River Waal at Nijmegen would be in Allied hands, so they would be able to sweep over it on their way to Arnhem. The road and the rail bridge were, however, still firmly controlled by German forces and the 82nd Division had lost many men trying to capture them.

Their first attempts to take the southern ends of the bridges had met some opposition and a more concerted effort began again on Monday morning, when the 1st Battalion of the 508th Regiment tried to break through the German defences. They proved to be still too strong and had, moreover, been reinforced by artillery on the north side of the river. The battalion managed to advance to a junction about 200 yards from the start of the road bridge, but it was impossible to move any further and stay alive. It would need more than a battalion to seize the bridge now.

The 82nd Division was facing multiple threats, however, and German tanks and infantry had moved into the forests near to its drop zones, so Gavin decided to call off the assault on the bridge to secure these areas. A second airlift was due that morning. The 1st Battalion withdrew and marched 8 miles back to the Groesbeek Heights. There they braved a fusillade of 20mm cannon shells and small-arms fire from German troops in order to clear the drop zone, killing fifty enemy soldiers and capturing another 150. The fighting was continuing on the edges of the drop zone as the first gliders landed, their take-off delayed fortuitously by bad weather in the UK. Some of the troops and glider pilots were hit, but overall the drop was successful. The 82nd had been reinforced with another 1,800 men, eight anti-tank guns, thirty-six howitzers, 200 jeeps and 120 trailers, and the later drop of supplies got more than three-quarters of its loads on target.

When the second drop was completed, General Browning, whose HQ was close to that of the 82nd Division, asked Gavin to come up with another plan to take the bridges. In response, Gavin proposed making a frontal assault on both the road and the rail bridges, which were just over half a mile apart along the riverbank, with a single battalion from the 504th Regiment, while the whole of the 508th Regiment would mount simultaneous assaults from either flank. Yet after listening to this, General Browning had second thoughts, saying that the retention of the high ground – that is, the Groesbeek Heights south of Nijmegen – was of greater importance. Browning's headquarters had landed in the same drop zones as those of the 82nd Airborne and in doing so had made use of thirty-six gliders and their tugs which could have carried another battalion of troops. Yet Browning seems to have played almost no role in the mission other than to repeat his questionable instructions to Gavin about the strategic importance of the Groesbeek Heights. So another effort to secure the bridges was abandoned. Whether this would have succeeded better than the previous one is hard to say. The Germans had managed to build a pontoon bridge over the Rhine upstream of the bridge at Arnhem, which was still blocked by Colonel John Frost's small band of men, and reinforcements of men and tanks from the 10th SS Panzer Division were using this to head south to strengthen the German hold on Nijmegen.

So when the leading armoured cars of the Household Cavalry arrived at Grave on the Tuesday, both General Gavin and General Browning were there to meet them. The Grenadier and Coldstream Guards Regiments who were following were a significant boost to the 82nd Division's forces. The Coldstream were detached and put under Gavin's command, and he now felt much more confident about holding off any further German incursions into his area of responsibility. The Grenadiers could now, with the 2nd Battalion of the 505th Parachute Infantry Regiment, take on the task of rushing the bridges they desperately needed to cross to get to Arnhem.

First, however, they had to make a detour to use the only bridge left standing over the Maas-Waal Canal and they were not in place to start their attack on the main bridges at Nijmegen until three o'clock that afternoon. The effort did not go well. The attack on the railway bridge was carried out by Sherman tanks of the Grenadier Guards with the American paratroopers riding on their hulls. The lead tank was hit by artillery and knocked out, and the advance shuddered to a halt. Similarly, a log barricade had been put up by the Germans on the approach to the road bridge and the position was covered by arcs of fire from self-propelled 88mm guns. The leading tank of the 2nd Battalion of the Grenadiers was hit and its commander killed, and another three tanks fell victim to shellfire in quick succession.

The Allied force was facing a tough, experienced enemy, who had set up covering fire on all the approach roads and fortified every square. The fighting continued, but the British and Americans were suffering serious casualties. Tanks and armoured vehicles were abandoned, smoking or damaged, while dead bodies lay desolate in the roads. There were soon 150 men missing or dead, while another 600 wounded were rushed for treatment in the liberated Nijmegen hospital. That night the Germans set fire to every fifth house around the approaches to both bridges so that the leaping flames would illuminate any surprise attack. As the acrid smoke, tinted orange by the blazing homes, climbed into the sky, it seemed that the operation had become badly derailed. The bridges over the Waal at Nijmegen were the only route to Arnhem and the besieged British airborne troops – but they were still in German hands.

There were now four generals in Nijmegen, Browning and Gavin having been joined by General Horrocks of XXX Corps and Major General Adair of the Guards Armoured Division. The problem was simple – it was one that John Frost had understood when he was first told the tasks of his battalion in Arnhem. It requires overwhelming firepower to defeat an enemy blocking a very narrow line of advance across a bridge. There was the added complication that, as soon as it appeared to the enemy that the bridge might be lost, they would detonate the demolition charges. It was General Gavin who came up with a plan that might solve both problems. It would require exceptional bravery on the part of those called on to carry it out. Gavin proposed that some of his men cross the Waal by boat a mile downstream of the railway bridge and coordinate a rear assault on the northern end of the bridges, to be carried out simultaneously with a direct attack from the Grenadier Guards on the southern end.

There were, however, no rivercraft in the Nijmegen perimeter. XXX Corps did have some in its supply train in the rear, but they were flimsy canvas assault boats, propelled with wooden paddles, and there were just thirty-three of them. It would take time for the lorries carrying the boats to travel up the congested highway, which was being used by the whole of XXX Corps to move forward. Moreover, there was a permanent threat to the route from German forces. On Tuesday night, a German bomber force had hit Eindhoven. As many as 3,000 civilians had been killed or wounded in the raid. Supplies had been destroyed, ammunition stores exploded and parts of Eindhoven were in flames. Rubble blocked parts of the route through the town.

German forces had also made a determined effort to destroy the newly built Bailey bridge over the canal at Son, which was now the only route over the Wilhelmina Canal. If the Germans succeeded in cutting this, then the whole route to Nijmegen and thence hopefully to Arnhem would be blocked. Two attacks were attempted by the Germans, from the east and the west, and it was incredibly good luck for the 101st Division that these attacks were not better coordinated. The first attack came from the west, where the German 107th Panzer Brigade moved forward from the village of Best and were confronted by the 1st and 2nd Battalions of the 506th Regiment. The fighting continued for several hours until the 15th/19th Hussars arrived with six Churchill tanks and a flamethrower mounted on a Challenger tank. Those present say that even at the sound of the approaching armour the Germans' fire began to falter and the Hussars broke the back of the Panzer brigade with their assault. Over 1,100 prisoners were captured. While this battle went on, the Son bridge was closed to traffic, so the journey of the lorries carrying the assault boats from the rear areas at Eindhoven was halting and painfully slow.

In Nijmegen they had yet to realize how painfully slow it was. There was still a lot to do in preparation for the combined assault on the bridges and the river crossing. The previous efforts to take the bridges had demonstrated one thing. The approach to the road bridge was overlooked by the tower of a medieval strongpoint known as the Valkhof and this, and the park surrounding it, had to be cleared of any enemy troops and secured before a frontal assault had any chance of success.

On the Wednesday morning the Grenadier Guards and infantry from the 505th Parachute Regiment approached the road from the western part of Nijmegen, seeking cover in the narrow streets of the old town. The Grenadiers used their firepower to break their way through the German perimeter, advancing slowly against strongly defended machine-gun posts and strongpoints in the houses around the southern end of the bridge. It was slow progress. They reached the Valkhof, the King's Company of the Grenadier Guards finally taking it that afternoon at around three o'clock. The US paratroopers fought their way in on the right of the Grenadiers, leaping from rooftop to rooftop across the old, tightly packed buildings, so avoiding the stream of bullets that the carefully sited machine guns poured down the streets at knee height. Allied troops were now close to the southern end of the bridge, dominating the approach road and the lower ground on the riverbank. Still the Germans did not set off their demolition charges.

Further west, the Irish Guards and the 505th Regiment infantry started to move through the western suburbs of Nijmegen, intending to reach the riverbank and secure it in preparation for the crossing. The site that General Gavin had selected for the men of the 504th Regiment to embark in the assault boats was close to a power station roughly half a mile west of the railway bridge. Two squadrons of Irish Guards tanks were in position along the bank of the river, ready to open fire on any German defences on the north bank during the crossing. The infantrymen were in position at midday. The prospect before them was bleak.

The River Waal is fast-flowing, and more than 400 yards wide at this point. It was daylight, so the men knew that they would be perfect and defenceless targets as they struggled to control their boats on the water. Nobody could pretend that it was anything other than a desperate, potentially suicidal gamble. They waited and waited. Still the boats didn't arrive. General Gavin found the situation more than his patience could bear. He knew that delay was un-settling for his men. The longer they had to contemplate the dangers in front of them, the harder it would be to find the resolve and courage they needed to carry out their mission. He was also aware that just a few miles away the 1st Airborne troops in Arnhem were desperately waiting to be relieved by XXX Corps. He didn't know what their situation was, but he could imagine that, like him, they were overstretched, short of supplies and fighting a determined enemy.

The assault boats and their crew of engineers finally arrived at 2.30. They were quickly taken to the riverbank. Two crossings were needed, given the small number of boats available. The first would take A and B Companies of the 3rd Battalion of the 504th across the river, then the final company of the 3rd Battalion and one of the 1st Battalion would follow.

The unlucky first wave of paratroopers stumbled down the bank to climb into the fragile boats. An airstrike by Typhoons had rocketed and machine-gunned the Germans on the opposite bank and the Irish Guards had added their firepower to this bombardment. A smokescreen had also been laid down, but it was to no avail. At the very start some boats capsized, and some of the paratroopers were unable to control their boats in the fast eddying current. Some of the soldiers used their rifle butts as paddles to gain some extra speed and control, but when the first boats were in midstream the German defenders opened up with everything they had. Machine-gun bullets, mortar and artillery shells started pouring down on to the exposed boats. Fountains of water were blasted out of the river while the dead and wounded collapsed over their paddles or toppled over the side. Some boats were ripped to shreds by cannon fire and sank, leaving their occupants struggling with their heavy equipment in the rapid current. Just half the boats that set out reached the other side.

Scrambling out, the US troops faced a high dyke, over which they had to charge to confront the enemy on the flat land behind. It was like going over the top in the trenches of the First World War. Angry and frightened, with adrenaline coursing through their veins, they scrambled up and over, hurtling themselves at the enemy in their slit trenches and machine-gun posts. It was a ruthless battle of hand-to-hand fighting using bayonets and grenades. The Germans were overwhelmed. Meanwhile, the boats that had survived had returned to the south bank to bring over more men.

After an hour's fighting the US infantry were approaching the northern end of the railway bridge, and the German defenders now realized that they were lost. They started to pour back over the bridge to avoid being cut off, but they were cut down in a deadly crossfire from the US infantry on the north and the Irish Guards on the south bank. There are reports that the bodies of 267 dead German soldiers lay crumpled on the railway tracks after the battle.

The men of the 504th Regiment charged on and reached the German position at the north end of the road bridge. The paratroopers of the 505th Regiment and the Grenadier Guards had pressed forward, firing on the remaining SS troops who maintained a toehold on the southern road bridge. They retreated, and four Sherman tanks of the Grenadier Guards advanced across it. With them was Captain Terry Jones, a Royal Engineer, who quickly cut any visible wires leading to demolition charges and declared the bridge safe. As he did so, German snipers, ensconced high in the girders of the huge suspending arch, fired on him. If the Germans were going to blow the bridge, now was the time to do it. The leading tanks continued on the advance. It was a long way down and everyone, in the tanks and on the shores, held their breath, anticipating a series of huge explosions and the collapse of the great span into the dark water below. Nothing happened.

The tanks rolled across and met up with the men from the 504th Regiment on the other side. As they continued up the road, the first two tanks were hit by anti-tank shell fired from two German guns. The remaining tanks charged on, rolling over the enemy guns and their crews before they could reload. It was seven o'clock in the evening on Wednesday, 20 September, and finally the bridge was in Allied hands. It was four days since the first landings at Arnhem, and two days later than XXX Corps had been scheduled to arrive at Nijmegen.

The Allies, in particular the tank crews on the bridge, had been extremely lucky that the bridge was still intact. General Model had delayed destroying any of the bridges over the Waal because he knew that he would need them for a counter-attack against the Allies. But the commanding officer of the 10th SS Panzer Division, Brigadier Heinz Harmel, had exercised his own initiative when he saw that the road bridge was lost. In his command post at the village of Lent, a mile from the bridge, he saw the tanks start to cross the river and ordered his engineer to press the plunger to initiate the detonation sequence. Nothing happened. The wires may have broken, or Captain Jones of the Royal Engineers may have successfully isolated the charges. In any event, Harmel would also have sent to their deaths eighty-one of his own men hiding in various parts of the structure. The Royal Engineers winkled these men out as they clambered over the bridge dismantling the dynamite charges set by the German demolition men.

Brigadier Harmel had to abandon his command post very quickly afterwards, because the infantry of the 504th Regiment continued their advance until they surrounded the village. They were joined by the troop of tanks that had crossed the bridge, then by another two companies of the Irish Guards, but instead of moving rapidly forward towards Arnhem, they halted and waited for the rest of their armoured groups. Colonel Reuben Tucker, CO of the 504th Regiment, and the rest of the men in his regiment who had carried out the audacious and heroic crossing of the Waal could not believe what was happening. That the tanks of the Guards Armoured Division were not speeding up the road to Arnhem made a mockery of their sacrifice. They were airborne soldiers and knew without needing it explained that the units that had captured the northern end of the Arnhem road bridge were down to their last few bullets. But XXX Corps had stopped. The last great obstacle to the advance on Arnhem had been overcome by the remarkable audacity and courage of the men of the US 504th Regiment; the enemy was disorganized and in retreat. Now was the time to advance. But for whatever reason, the Guards Division stayed put and again rested overnight. It was a grave miscalculation, and the men in Arnhem were doomed.

21

THE BRIDGE ALONE

Wednesday, 20–Thursday, 21 September

Tom Carpenter and the platoon of the 9th Field Company Royal Engineers saw the dawn of their third day in the slowly shrinking perimeter around the entrance to the bridge over the Rhine. They had had no sleep. Water and food was now almost gone, although some of what rations they did have were being shared with the old lady in the second-floor bedroom. Members of the platoon would occasionally visit her to see that she was all right.

Once more, there was an attack by the enemy. Tom had lost count of the number of times that they had opened fire on German soldiers flitting from ruined building to ruined building across rubble-strewn streets. In the half-light they saw German infantry further up the road, keeping close to the buildings for cover. They advanced to the doorway of a nearby house and threw in what one of the sappers recognized as a demolition charge. The explosion that followed blew dust and smoke out of the ground-floor windows, and there was a tumbling crash as the floors and interior walls collapsed. A few rounds from the sappers' firing positions made the Germans quickly retreat, but it was clear that the noose was tightening. Their position was not ideal. The platoon was now reduced to just fourteen men and they had lost a lot of ground. Tom sat for most of the morning at a firing position on the first floor, looking out over Marktplein and the approach to the bridge. He couldn't see the battalion or brigade headquarters from this viewpoint. These were situated just around a bend in the road about 60 yards away, but he could tell from the smoke and flames coming from that direction that the buildings were on fire.

The crews of the German tanks and armoured cars that were constantly attacking the paratroopers were now much bolder, racing past the houses with their main guns firing. They could have taken their time, because the sappers no longer had any weapons with which to take them on, and the force was facing a near complete lack of anti-tank shells and PIAT rounds. Two anti-tank guns were still available, but the British positions had shifted so much that it was impossible to man them without the crews coming under sniper fire. The 2nd Battalion's mortar platoon had suffered heavy casualties and the commanding officer of the platoon, Lieutenant Reg Woods, and the sergeant, Maurice Lajikoff, were both killed in an attack early that morning. Every unit in the perimeter was desperately short of ammunition. Tom's platoon now had fifteen rounds of .303in cartridges per man, plus three full magazines for the Bren gun. This, according to Captain O'Callaghan, was slightly better than the other airborne troops, whose supplies were even lower. There were three full belts of ammunition left for the battalion's Vickers machine gun stationed at their HQ. Otherwise, that was it.

That morning the Germans sent a strong force of infantry into the area under the bridge where it crossed the Rijnkade. They were determined and managed to clear the last defenders from the ruins of the old factory and warehouse that stood on either side. This was part of a plan to place demolition charges in the pillars that supported the ramp, and also into the big brick pier that held the large girders of the bridge proper. The original charges had been disarmed by a team from the Royal Engineers on the first day.

The Germans succeeded in placing the charges and the troop of their infantry withdrew. When they had done so, a party of Royal Engineers from the 1st Parachute Squadron, supported by some men from A Company of the 2nd Battalion, rushed out to remove the detonators. While the engineers worked feverishly away, the paratroopers held off the Germans, but they came under heavy fire and

Captain Grayburn of A Company was hit by rifle fire. They retreated under fire, but the engineers then thought that another rush forward to remove the demolition charges altogether would be more secure. The Germans were expecting them this time and a tank had moved forward to cover the large supporting pier. When the engineers and the men of A Company made their second charge they ran straight into a stream of bullets from the tank's machine gun. Captain Grayburn, his arm in a sling and his head bandaged from his previous wounds, was killed instantly. The Victoria Cross he received posthumously for this action was the only one awarded to any of the men who were under siege at the bridge.

Back at Tom's position in the Hofstraat, on the western side of the perimeter, their house was being pounded with artillery shells in a bombardment that saw twenty-eight of the 88mm rounds from either a tank or an artillery piece striking the building. One of these crashed into the old Dutch lady's bedroom and exploded, killing her. The sappers found her frail body lying amongst her bedclothes, covered in plaster and the remnants of her smashed bedframe. There was little time for any sentimentality about her death. The building was rapidly becoming a heap of rubble, although it wasn't yet on fire, and every one of them knew that their situation was very bleak.

* * *

At around 1.30 in the afternoon, a hundred yards east from Tom's position, Colonel John Frost was wounded by shrapnel from a mortar round and was taken on a stretcher to the basement of the brigade HQ for medical treatment. He was injured severely enough to hand over command of the diminishing British troops to Major Gough of the Reconnaissance Squadron. As Frost recalled, 'I wasn't really able to control things. Freddy came along and I told him to carry on. Not that there were any orders much to give by then.'

This was a fair assessment of the situation. The force at the bridge had lost the ability to defend their perimeter. The firepower of the enemy was so great that any movement between buildings or different positions was now lethal. The German tanks and artillery faced almost no opposition and could destroy individual houses whenever they so desired.

The most important bastion on the eastern perimeter was the school building that overlooked the road on the embankment leading to the bridge. It was still defended by a group of Royal Engineers and some of C Company of the 3rd Battalion. There were about thirty men in total, armed with small arms and a Bren gun, and they had been able to hold out since Sunday with the protection provided by the mortar platoons and the anti-tank guns. Anti-tank raids with PIAT projectors similar to that carried out by Tom on Tuesday morning had also helped to keep the enemy at bay. Tom's raid, in fact, had driven off three tanks that were opening fire on the school and the other houses on the eastern perimeter. The availability of that defence had now gone, and the school building started to receive hits from large-calibre shells. It caught fire. It had to be evacuated, but several wounded men were being treated in the basement. A rear guard was set up to cover the retreat and the evacuation of the casualties to the main aid post in the brigade HQ. Eight or so men too injured to walk were carried on mattresses or doors. As the first party left the building, machine-gun fire and mortars hit them, killing three of the wounded. As soon as men got outside the building they were targeted; it seemed that no one would be able to run the gauntlet of the German fire and survive. The building was still burning and shells were destroying the upper floors.

The officer in charge of the men occupying the building, Major Peter Lewis, was himself one of the wounded. Lying on a mattress, he suggested that it was time to surrender. Some of the men wanted to escape, while others were prepared to stay with the wounded and be taken prisoner. Those who made a run for it left the building and rushed desperately for the HQ building, but were cut down as they crossed the exposed embankment and roadway. After everyone who wanted to leave had done so, a sapper was sent to the top of the embankment with a white towel tied to his rifle, but he was shot in the legs by a German firing a machine gun. This was the last shot, however, and the Germans closed in to take their prisoners and check the wounded.

Further to the west of the perimeter, where Tom's platoon was grimly ensconced, they were also coming under fire but had no wounded to worry about. Their position was also precarious. At around five o'clock that day Captain O'Callaghan told Tom and the rest of the sappers to get out of the building and dig slit trenches in the garden. The building was falling around them and they would either die in a shell blast or be buried under the collapsing walls. Tom took a leap out of a first-floor window into the rubble surrounding the house and started to excavate a slit trench and a firing position. As he did so, a souvenir that he had taken from one of the buildings they had occupied the previous day fell from under his parachute smock. He had snatched it from the wall when he had first spotted it. It was a crucifix, carved from ivory and mounted in a polished mahogany case. Tom left it on the rubble while he continued to dig.

A German fighter aircraft flew over, one of several that had appeared that day. In the chaos of the fighting and the incessant noise of gunfire and explosions, it was impossible to tell whether they were strafing the British positions or just observing the situation of their own forces on the ground and providing air cover for the German troops. Their presence highlighted a surprising lack of air support from the US

2nd Tactical Air Force, which had been so important to the Allies in the break-out from Normandy. Typhoons armed with ground-attack rockets could have added enormously to the defence of the men in the Arnhem bridgehead. As it was, the weather at their forward airfields in Belgium and France was reported to be too poor for flying.

But as Tom was digging in, a great cheer went up when the pilot of a Focke-Wulf 190, flying low over their heads, failed to spot the hazard of the spire of St Walburgis Church and hit the cross at the top of the spire with his left wing. The aircraft tumbled out of control and crashed into the ornamental lakes along the Eusebius Binnensingel.

This small moment of celebration was quickly over for the sappers in the garden of No. 29. No sooner had they dug some trenches than they started to receive incoming mortar shells and the garden itself became a death trap.

Each exploding mortar bomb rearranged the rubble, blasting pieces into the air, creating clouds of pulverized brick dust, and the sappers could do nothing but shelter, crouching as low as they could get at the bottom of the shallow trenches. This was the toughest moment of all, as they lay powerless, anticipating the next explosion. Tom was very frightened now and it was only his training that helped him control the panic and despair that threatened to take over. As the explosions rose to a crescendo, Captain O'Callaghan ordered his men to move before they were all killed. Tom, lying in his trench, heard the shout, 'We're pulling out.'

He forced his unwilling body to rise up and get ready to jump out of the slit trench. He climbed out, keeping low but ready to run, when he noticed that the crucifix was still lying undamaged by the side of the trench. He turned in mid stride, leaning sideways to pick it up and shove it back inside his tunic.

As he did so he heard an explosion behind him and felt a massive blow to his back. He was hit with the force of a hurtled house brick, which knocked him over. He lay stunned, and found he couldn't move. His legs and arms wouldn't respond to any instructions from his brain. He lay face down on rubble and dust and realized that there was blood on his cheek and neck, dripping down and soaking into the dust by his eyes. He has no idea how long he lay there, but he heard gunfire above his head. It was Corporal Alex Lancaster, firing single rounds from his Sten gun, while the platoon sergeant, Sonny Gibbons, was stuffing a field dressing into a deep wound in Tom's back. They picked him up and half dragged him with them as they stumbled across the rubble to a low building in the Hofstraat.

Other members of the platoon in the cover of the building were firing at some German troops pursuing them as the two men, with Tom between them, fell through the doorway of their new refuge. Tom was lowered behind the shelter of some racks and cabinets. He said that he was desperate for some

water. There was none – the platoon was now completely out of any water or rations. The building they
were occupying was a fruit and vegetable warehouse,
so one of the sappers found some tomatoes and gave
them to Tom to help quench his thirst.

Self-propelled guns and tanks were now firing at
the buildings that were still occupied by the airborne
troops at almost point-blank range. Captain
O'Callaghan rounded up a party of sappers and
mounted a raid on a nearby German machine-gun
post, killing the detachment of five soldiers with it.
They captured the machine gun and 1,000 rounds of
ammunition, and took the rifles of the men they had
killed. They cut the webbing harness off the bodies
and ransacked their ammo pouches for another 500
rounds of rifle ammunition.

While Tom's comrades were slaughtering enemy
troops for their ammunition, just a few hundred yards
away a truce was arranged with the German troops.
The brigade headquarters had been largely immune
from shellfire up until now, because it was set back
from the surrounding houses, but with the eastern
side of the bridge ramp evacuated by the British,
German tanks could now easily approach the big
double-fronted villa. It was already on fire and the
medical officers told Lieutenant Colonel Frost that
there were so many wounded in the basement
that there was no time to evacuate them all. They
would die in the fire if something wasn't done. Some

of the German prisoners were sent out with a white flag to arrange a truce and an evacuation of the wounded. The rest of the men defending the building were ordered to abandon it and attempt to make it back to the main divisional force.

There was no shooting for two hours while the wounded soldiers, both British and German, were carried out from the basement of the house on Eusebius Binnensingel, while flames and smoke poured from the upper storeys. The Germans used this ceasefire to visit other parts of the perimeter, with German officers approaching men in slit trenches, offering them cigarettes and suggesting they surrender.

The battle could not last much longer, but still the British did not stop fighting. There was now only one building left standing, and Captain O'Callaghan was ordered to bring his sappers to join the rest of the greatly diminished force near the battalion HQ.

While this dangerous and fraught move was planned, Tom was carried towards the door of the warehouse that was nearest to the Hofstraat. He was going to have to make a dash for it across the narrow road into the grounds of what had once been a staid, grand bourgeois Dutch merchant's house but was now the last refuge of some hungry, desperate British para-troopers. Overcoming the pain in his back, he forced his limbs into some movement and hobbled across the open ground supported by two of his comrades. The garden was an area of about 40 yards by 40 yards with buildings on all sides, all of them reduced to burning shells. Slit trenches had been dug close to the walls and some of the lower brickwork had been removed to give a limited field of fire along the street. The captured German machine gun was dragged into place and was fired by Lance Corporal Johnson, with short bursts of rounds helping to keep the German infantry at bay.

But they were surrounded. Tom heard the voices of German officers giving orders, and he could hear their mortars, so close they must have been firing almost vertically.

Tom was becoming very light-headed, suffering not only from loss of blood and the effects of the morphine that had been injected into him, but from the accumulated lack of sleep, water and food. He believed that he could hear the shrieks of large-calibre shells flying overhead and that these must be from the heavy guns of XXX Corps approaching along the road from Nijmegen. A large explosion nearby jolted him awake and the walls of the slit trench started falling in. A mortar had landed very close. One of the men in the trench had received a hit and was slumped in the corner, motionless.

At around twelve o'clock, in the darkness of Wednesday night, the few officers that were left, Major Gough and Captain O'Callaghan, with Captain Drake, the second in command of A Company, decided that they would leave the wounded and, with the rest of the able-bodied men, make a break for the main British positions. Only the fit and fast would be able to make it. They split up into parties of ten and hoped that the night would help them to evade the encircling German troops. O'Callaghan had been injured himself by this time, receiving a shrapnel wound to the head that had rendered him unconscious for around thirty minutes. He decided to go ahead with the break-out, however, and started negotiating the dark, flame-lit shadows of the ruins around the bridge, trying to move quietly, leading a group of five or six sappers and some infantry from the remains of the battalion force. After twenty minutes of climbing the piles of rubble, sneaking past German rifle positions and mortar crews, seeking cover from every pool of blackness and fragment of wall, he collapsed once more from the wound in his head and was left by the others where he lay.

Tom Carpenter lay in the slit trench in the garden, alternating between dreams of safety, a soft bunk and a mug of hot, sweet tea, and moments of detached lucidity, staring up at the smoke-blackened night sky, feeling the rough earth against his face, desperately thirsty, with a raging pain in his back. He went over the events of the last few days in his head. What had happened to XXX Corps? He had seen his comrades maimed and killed at the clog factory on Monday, and again every day as the German tanks and artillery had destroyed their fragile firing posts and defences. There had been ten sappers left in the garden prior to the break-out. As well as Captain O'Callaghan there was Sergeant Gibbons, Corporal Lancaster, Sergeant Cawood and Sappers Turner, Cottle, Tunningly, Donoghue and Fox. Where were they now? Where were the others who had left Oosterbeek with him?

It was a fearful night. At some point in the early morning he realized that his companion in the slit trench had died. Tom found it hard to accept that he would not see his parents or his brothers and sisters again, but he thought that he too would soon join his comrades in death.

When next he regained consciousness it was light and there were voices nearby. Bursts of machine-gun fire sounded from outside the walls. Faces were looking down at him, and Tom realized they were German soldiers. One was holding a rifle with a bayonet pointing at him and Tom thought that it would be easy for the man to finish him off. There was nothing he would be able to do. But the soldier shouted something to other men whom Tom couldn't see and then he was hauled out, to his considerable pain, and laid on a stretcher. He was carried across the broken, rubble-strewn grounds and laid on the back of a jeep. A German soldier thrust a cigarette in his mouth. As the jeep drove off, Tom lay there, helpless, heading into captivity.

22

THE MEAT-GRINDER

Thursday, 21–Monday, 25 September

Ron had remained posted in slit trenches in the south-eastern part of the perimeter at Oosterbeek, defending it against enemy incursions. Some of the glider pilots were used as emergency units to reinforce areas that were coming under strong attack, and Ron was also called on to take part in these 'firefighting' parties. His part of the Oosterbeek perimeter was also under constant threat from tanks and self-propelled guns that had established an enclave just to the east of his slit trenches. These had shot up and set fire to houses along the Klingelbeeksweg and around the junction with a road leading north to the Tafelberg. Lieutenant Colonel 'Sheriff' Thompson of the Royal Artillery had set up some 6-pounder anti-tank guns to defend his 75mm-gun positions, and these held off the German armour, but they occasionally made some forays with infantry into the area where Ron was stationed with a mixed force of glider pilots and other units. His Bren-gun fire could cut down the infantry, while some of the more active glider pilots would move out on a tank hunt with PIATS and Gammon bombs. In between these attacks there were constant mortar barrages.

Ron put up with dirt, the stink of cordite, sleeplessness and lack of water. 'In battle you go into a higher state of awareness,' he told me. 'Like a wild animal, every little noise has a meaning that has to be checked. You become so hypersensitive with looking, listening, firing quickly, watching out for things, it wears you out. I knew somebody who was so tired he fell asleep in the slit trench while we were engaging the enemy.' He was exhausted, and they were all suffering from thirst. It would have been easy for the Germans to overrun their position in the next few days, but they didn't. The British were saved to an extent by the arrival, a day late, of the Polish Parachute Brigade, which landed at five o'clock on Thursday, 21 September.

The Polish Independent Parachute Brigade, commanded by Major General Stanislaw Sosabowski, should have landed on the third day, Tuesday the 19th, but poor weather over their airfields had disrupted their plans. The glider element of the brigade, carrying anti-tank guns and jeeps, did land on Tuesday, in the landing zone defended by the King's Own Scottish Borderers, but both the Polish and British units became engulfed in the German attack

Above: Field Marshall Montgomery, in his black beret, the architect of Market Garden, looks at the plans with General Horrocks *(on the left)*, the commander of XXX Corps, and Prince Bernhard, king of the Netherlands.

Above: Major General Urquhart, commander of the 1st Airborne Division, stands in the grounds of the Hartenstein Hotel in Oosterbeek, where he established his HQ. He lost contact with his divisional staff for a crucial two days during the battle.

Below left and right: Field Marshal Walter Model *(centre left, with monocle)* fled from the Hartenstein Hotel when the British troops landed, but quickly organized a counter-attack. He ordered Brigadier Harmel *(below right, with field glasses)*, to take the 9th SS Division south and defend the bridge at Nijmegen, buying his troops in Arnhem valuable time.

Left: Lieutenant Colonel John Frost, wearing his parachute helmet, was the commander of the 2nd Battalion. He was one of the most experienced airborne officers and the only battalion commander to reach the bridge, where he was wounded in the closing days of the battle.

The airborne troops retreated to Oosterbeek, where they put together some ad hoc groups to form a perimeter. They dug in amongst the trees and hedges, armed with rifles and Sten guns *(above)*, and some three-inch mortars *(below)*, but ammunition was scarce.

The 9th SS Division had been reinforced, but the new men were untrained in tank warfare and their advance towards Oosterbeek was tentative. They set out from Arnhem *(above)*, but as they moved along Utrechtsweg, accurate anti-tank fire from British units pinned them down *(below)*, and they started to lose significant numbers of armoured vehicles.

The situation inside the perimeter at Oosterbeek grew worse. Lack of food, water and sleep affected everyone. The mortar barrage from German units was incessant, and men were confined to their muddy slit trenches, or seeking shelter in shell holes. *(Left and below)* Ron Jordan and a group of glider pilots occupied trenches on the eastern edge. Casualties *(bottom)* were taken to the cellars of the Hartenstein Hotel, where conditions were horrific.

Sherman tanks of the Guards Armoured Division finally crossed the bridge at Nijmegen *(top)* but inexplicably waited until the next day before advancing the last few miles to Arnhem.

The Oosterbeek perimeter shrank. The remaining anti-tank units held off German tanks with their last few shells *(above)*, but nowhere was safe. An airborne soldier in a slit trench by the Hartenstein Hotel *(left)* watches helplessly after an enemy barrage sets fire to a jeep.

Operation Market Garden brought devastation not only to Oosterbeek and Arnhem, but towns like Nijmegen *(above)*. Fire and artillery shells destroyed thousands of homes.

After seven days the 1st Airborne was told to organize a retreat across the river. But the residents of Arnhem had nowhere to go, and they came out of their cellars *(below)* to survey the wreckage.

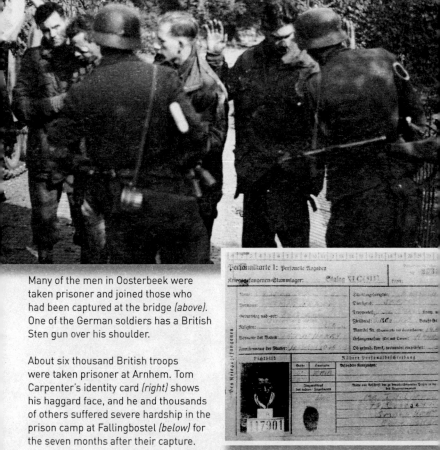

Many of the men in Oosterbeek were taken prisoner and joined those who had been captured at the bridge *(above)*. One of the German soldiers has a British Sten gun over his shoulder.

About six thousand British troops were taken prisoner at Arnhem. Tom Carpenter's identity card *(right)* shows his haggard face, and he and thousands of others suffered severe hardship in the prison camp at Fallingbostel *(below)* for the seven months after their capture.

Tom Carpenter *(above left)*, Ron Jordan *(above right)* and Pat Gorman *(inset)* have made regular visits to Arnhem for many years, where they meet up with other veterans. Their Dutch hosts treat them with enormous respect and hospitality, but the ranked graves of the cemetery at Oosterbeek are a sombre reminder of the many young men who were killed in just a few days in the battle for the bridge at Arnhem.

against the 4th Parachute Brigade, so the Poles were absorbed into the forces defending Oosterbeek.

It wasn't until Thursday that the weather was judged good enough to drop the rest of the Polish Brigade – the paratroopers – and even then, because of poor weather forecasts over Belgium and Holland, coded radio messages were sent to the C-47 aircraft to turn back. Only some of the flight crews correctly interpreted these signals, however, and 1,000 paratroopers continued and made the drop.

Originally, the planned drop zone was south of the road bridge, next to the road to Nijmegen, but on Wednesday the drop zone had been moved westwards near to Driel, a small town on the southern side of the Rhine on the road to the Heveadorp ferry. This drop zone was selected in the belief that the ferry landing at Westerbouwing was still in British hands. By the time the Polish paratroopers had landed, this was no longer the case. Their presence did, however, cause the Germans to shift much of their armour and men from the assault on the eastern flank of Oosterbeek to take on the new threat. But the Polish forces could do nothing and waited at Driel for the arrival of the British armoured units, all the while suffering shelling and sniping from the enemy who were attempting to surround the town.

Ron Jordan stood to on the Friday morning in the smashed house in which his small ad hoc unit had sheltered for the night, prepared to take up his place in his slit trench. The trenches were better protection against the daily mortaring, which would start, he was sure, very shortly. The houses offered better observation and firing positions against enemy incursions, so one person always stayed in the house during the mortaring in case there was a concerted move forward during a lull in the bombardment. It was a cat-and-mouse game to some extent. Any movement – a bush swaying, or the flicker of a shadow in the house opposite – immediately drew Ron's attention, although ammunition was so scarce that nobody fired until three or four of the enemy were clear targets.

The trick, according to Ron, was to draw the enemy on and let him reveal his hand before taking action. He knew that the situation with ammunition was such that it would be hard for his small group of men to resist an all-out charge by German troops. This was the reason that he kept the Thompson carbine with him. It would be the last desperate attempt to stop them being overwhelmed, the fifty rounds of 45-calibre bullets the one thing that might prevent him from being taken prisoner.

That Friday the mortars started early. He was engulfed in a mad world of explosions, falling shrapnel and blasted earth that continued for what seemed a lifetime. When it ceased, the sounds of wounded men screaming and the cries of 'Stretcher-bearer' were heard from all over the perimeter. Ivor, Ron's mate, had remained in the REME slit trenches near the tennis courts and later that day Ron was told that he had been severely wounded by a mortar bomb exploding next to him. He had lost part of his hip and had been taken to the casualty station in the cellar of the Hartenstein.

The idea of Ivor being badly hurt disturbed Ron. Ever since they had first teamed up in Africa, he had expected Ivor to come through any scrape with his usual bull-in-a-china-shop ebullience, as he had after the mortar had hit the houses they were trying to clear a few days earlier. It was touch and go whether he would come out of this one. The men who had taken him to the casualty station reported that he had been taken care of by the medics, patched up and seemed to be settled.

There was no time to brood, and once more the day settled down to more intermittent mortaring, artillery and sniper fire, and the constant watch for any movement of the enemy in the opposite houses.

Later that day a runner arrived with orders for some of the defenders to report back to the Hartenstein at the double because there was a report that the line had been breached to the north. Ron and three others of his small group went, moving north as quickly as the threat of snipers would allow. He joined a group of around thirty in the grounds of the now shattered hotel, waiting for orders, when once more the mortars started. Caught in the open, without any slit trenches to get into, the men fell to the ground, some already dead or injured. A shouted order to 'Get back to your units' was all that Ron needed. He made a dash for some trees and crouched down by one of the trunks, then in a slight easing of the bombardment moved forward again.

The explosion was not close enough to deafen him, but he felt the heat and the blast, and a sharp pain in his leg. He lay on the ground for a few minutes, collecting his thoughts and trying to feel mentally where he was injured. The pain seemed to come from along his left leg. He knew that there was blood seeping into his battledress, but it didn't seem that any bones were broken. Rising painfully to his feet, he made his way back to the Hartenstein Hotel.

He hobbled down the cellar steps into the casualty station and was confronted with a horrifying scene. It was like something out of Victorian times. The casualty station was dimly lit, with the wounded packed in so tightly that there was barely room to move about. There were cries of pain from many of the patients and the smell of stale sweat, blood and suppurating flesh was almost overpowering. In front of him, slumped in a chair, was an unconscious glider pilot with blood pouring out of numerous wounds. The medical orderly told Ron to ignore him – he was beyond help. Examining Ron's leg he said that it had been deeply penetrated by several pieces of shrapnel, but no bones were broken and no major arteries cut. However, in the conditions in which he was working, the orderly wasn't interested in probing for the pieces. He dusted the wounds with some antiseptic powder and dressed them with bandages taken from Ron's own first aid kit. Ron was told that there was nothing more to be done, and he needed no more encouragement to get back to his slit trench on the perimeter. The glider pilot had clearly died, with his head hanging back, and the basement seemed like purgatory, with more wounded being brought in even as he left. He was glad to get out into the open air once more.

Ron hobbled back to his group's position, but the thought of leaving Ivor in the hellhole that he had just left made him uncomfortable. He spoke to the sergeant and, as evening approached, he was allowed to leave to take some water to Ivor and see how he was managing. Once more he made his way back along the road of shattered, blasted houses, moving as fast as he could between the shelter of the buildings, until he could walk across the grounds to the casualty station, passing some members of the Ordnance Corps who had dug in and were brewing up. It took him a while to find Ivor in the crowded, dark basement, but he walked through the ranks of wounded, calling out 'Ivor, Ivor.' Some of the casualties were groaning, muttering to themselves; others were unconscious; but everywhere was the rank smell of blood and fear.

He found his mate in a small alcove, lying on a stretcher, his face pale under the grime. He was sweating profusely, and shivering with shock. He was in great pain. 'Christ, it hurts,' he said.

Ron leaned down, took his canteen from its

webbing straps and poured a little water between Ivor's parched lips. 'I thought I'd come and see how you are,' he said.

'I'm finished, Ron.'

'Now then, lad, don't say things like that,' replied Ron. 'You'll be out of here in a few days.'

Ivor grabbed his hand. 'I don't want to be a cripple, Ron,' he said. 'I don't want to be useless like this.'

'Nonsense, lad, you'll be all right when you get back to Blighty.'

Then Ron's blood froze as Ivor tried to struggle up and fixed his grasp tight around Ron's wrist. 'Kill me, Ron! Please! Put a bullet in me, for God's sake. I can't go home like this! Be a mate!'

Ron recoiled. 'No, son! I can't do that. Don't be stupid. You'll be all right, I'm telling you!'

Ivor gripped harder. 'Ron, please! I'm begging you!'

'I can't, I can't, mate!' He was angry.

Ivor's head sank back and tears poured from under his closed eyelids. Ron released his hand, spoke a few more incoherent words of encouragement, then left him and stumbled out of the basement. As he came out on to the hotel's veranda he wished that a sniper's bullet would tear the life out of him. In all his wartime service, in the Fleet Air Arm, in Arnhem and in the grim events that were to follow, he never experienced a deeper sense of despair. It was irrational, but it was as though he had abandoned his comrade in his most grievous need, and the furiously mixed emotions of anger and sadness that he experienced as he walked back to his post have never left him. He never saw Ivor again. He was taken by the Germans not to the St Elisabeth Hospital but to St Joseph's Infirmary in Arnhem, where he died a few weeks later of blood poisoning.

Ron went back to the perimeter and took up his turn to keep watch in the small group of men under the command of a staff sergeant glider pilot. The whole area inside the divisional perimeter was now a complete shambles, strewn with rubble from demolished houses, debris and felled branches, as well as many burned-out vehicles. Nothing on wheels could move, and the presence of snipers made even short journeys within the perimeter dangerous. The weather, which had been so fair and sunny at the beginning of the week, had now turned overcast and rainy. Water dripped from trees and from the eaves of broken houses; it collected in the bottom of slit trenches, and mingled with brick dust and blasted mortar to become a paste that clung to boots and uniforms. Food was becoming extremely scarce. Their rations had long been exhausted, as had the rations that had been stripped from the dead. Fruit and vegetables from the Dutch civilians had also run out, and men were beginning to become weak and listless.

On Friday, General Urquhart had sent his chief of staff and the CO of the Royal Engineers across the Rhine to make contact with the Polish Parachute troops who had landed on Thursday morning. From there they were going to make contact with the advance units of the British Second Army. None of the bridges over the Rhine was in British hands, and the only crossing point, where roads crossed the low flood plain and reached the banks of the river, was at the ferry at Heveadorp. The northern bank of this crossing had been within the perimeter held by the airborne forces, but it had been lost earlier. The ferry was a dumb barge, large enough to carry vehicles, which was pulled back and forth across the river by a cable. The landing stages on both sides of the river were overlooked by high ground on the north bank, the bluff known as Westerbouwing, which in peaceful times had been the site of a restaurant and was a popular summertime resort. This key point had been defended by a company of the 1st Border Regiment, but they had been attacked on Wednesday morning by a German unit from the Luftwaffe training school, boosted by four French light tanks captured in 1940.

The German assault had been a direct one and they experienced heavy casualties, but finally overwhelmed the defenders to take the surviving British troops prisoner. The ferry itself had been defended by a platoon from Tom Carpenter's 9th Field Company, but they also had to retreat in the face of an attack from German infantry. One sapper, however, remained. Lance Sergeant Hugh Lake kept himself hidden below the riverbank, ready to fire a charge and sever the cable if the enemy approached and tried to use the ferry. Unfortunately, his brave efforts to keep watch on the ferry were of little use to the rest of the British troops. An effort to recapture the Westerbouwing on Thursday was repulsed, and Lance Sergeant Lake eventually made his way back to the 9th Field Company by travelling along the bank of the Rhine.

After the ferry was lost, other sappers from the 9th had tried further along the banks to string a cable across the river to form some sort of crossing. The current was too swift, however, and the plaited telephone cables snagged on rocks and broke. They also tried to build rafts from some of the jeep trailers, but these were impossible to navigate in the current. By Saturday morning a few Polish officers had been brought across from the other bank in collapsible rubber reconnaissance boats, able to carry just one or two passengers at a time. Crossing the river was only possible at night, because in daylight hours the Germans stationed on the high ground at Westerbouwing could call down mortars, and their machine guns covered an arc of fire for 700 yards along both banks.

The situation regarding the Polish paratroopers was now at a stalemate. They were ensconced on the south side of the Rhine but had no means of crossing the river and assisting in the defence of the perimeter around Oosterbeek. They were joined late on Friday by the first units of the British Second Army – some

Sherman tanks from the Royal Dragoon Guards and infantry with Bren-gun carriers from the 5th Duke of Cornwall's Light Infantry. These were the advance guard of a division from XXX Corps, who were approaching along roads from Nijmegen.

Yet despite all these forces now assembling, only fifty-three Polish paratroops had managed to cross the Rhine by daylight on Saturday. The Polish commander, General Sosabowski, sent an urgent request to the British divisions at Nijmegen for more suitable boats and was promised twelve that could carry sixteen men each. Another attempt to cross the river was planned for Saturday night.

Ron knew nothing of this, but he and an Australian glider pilot were ordered on Saturday evening to escort a Polish liaison officer down to a rendezvous on the lower road. From there the officer was going to be guided to the crossing point on the Rhine. Ron wasn't very happy about this, because his wounded leg was not improving and he couldn't move that fast. He was in no position to refuse, however, so, choosing to take the Thompson sub-machine gun, he met the glider pilot and the Polish officer by the Hartenstein's tennis courts. Ron's task was to protect the officer from British as well as German troops. The Polish Officer's English wasn't very good and the officers in divisional HQ were worried that his attempt to respond to that day's password, 'Gracie Fields', wouldn't convince any British soldiers that he wasn't German. In the circumstances, the British troops were prone to shoot first and ask questions afterwards.

They had to make their way down a series of paths and bridleways through the woods south of the Hartenstein Hotel. Fallen branches and twigs blocked all of them, and Ron was alarmed by the noise that the Polish officer was making as he clambered over them. It seemed to him that the Pole did not realize how close they were to German positions, or how tenuous the perimeter was. During the day's fighting, the Germans would often make incursions and occupy a house or a copse without being noticed, and any movement this close to the front line had to be circumspect in case they stumbled on the enemy.

It then turned out that the glider pilot was not sure where exactly on the lower road they were heading. When the Polish officer realized this he started loudly complaining and Ron told him to shut up and keep quiet. The Polish officer started muttering to himself, and the glider pilot told Ron to keep quiet and stop interfering. Tempers were running high, but they pressed on, still making far too much noise for Ron's liking.

It seemed to him that they had negotiated their way through the woods for over an hour when eventually they came to a road. There was no one to whom they could hand over the officer, as there should have been. The Australian, sure that he had arrived at the appointed place for the rendezvous, wanted to remain where they were and wait, but the Polish officer was now out of patience with his companions. He said that they were useless and that he would continue his journey by himself and could as easily find his own way. Ron's orders had been to accompany the liaison officer until he was safely handed over to a sapper who would lead him to the crossing, but both Ron and the Australian pilot were so sick of him that they were happy to see him go. He disappeared into the darkness and they turned and retraced their path, Ron feeling extremely uncomfortable, with pains shooting through his legs. He now assumes that the officer eventually made his way to the river, but the crossing that had been planned was beset by further problems and relationships between the Polish Parachute Brigade and the British staff were as fraught as that between Ron and the officer he had escorted that night.

The boats to ferry the Polish brigade across the river arrived late and were smaller than anticipated. They could carry only twelve men, not sixteen, but a worse handicap was that there were no crews to operate them. The Poles had not been trained in their use, nor had they any experience of water crossings. They manoeuvred the boats into the river, dragging them across ditches and dykes from the roadway where they had been unloaded from their transports, under constant fire from the German guns on the north bank of the Rhine. The crossings actually started at around 3 a.m., when there were only a few hours of darkness left. Because of all the delays and difficulties, just 153 Poles reached the northern bank before the boats became too vulnerable to enemy fire.

These men were absorbed into the British positions but could not affect the outcome of the battle. The Germans were bringing more artillery and tanks into the fray, and the perimeter started to shrink under their gunfire. By Sunday, the area held by the British was just over 900 yards across from east to west, although they still held a stretch of the riverbank. The Light Artillery, still in place in the south-east by the old church of Oosterbeek, was able to hold off some of the assaults on the inside of the perimeter, and some anti-tank units were effective against incursions by tanks and self-propelled guns, which would often move down Weverstraat from the Utrechtsweg. Ammunition for these guns was also running low. In addition, there were some 3in mortars located close to the old church, and some Vickers machine guns that covered the approach to the south-east and remained a powerful weapon against infantry. Some units of XXX Corps artillery that had advanced up the road from Nijmegen were able to lay fire on to German units threatening the perimeter, and this helped to break up many of the attacks. The noose, however, was tightening.

Pat Gorman had been sent to the southern edge of the perimeter after his arrival back at the divisional HQ and was stationed there throughout the siege. He alternated between manning a slit trench on the eastern side of the old church, close to the light artillery gun positions, and assisting in the casualty station that had been set up in the rectory of the church 50 yards to the west.

Like all the other casualty stations in Oosterbeek, it was overcrowded and the staff were struggling to help the wounded. They had no proper medical supplies, equipment, clean water or food. A Dutch civilian, Kate ter Horst, had stayed in the rectory with her husband and children, and she was doing what she could to treat the injured and comfort the dying. Pat helped to carry out the dead and dug graves for them in the garden of the house, because he was one of the few able-bodied people left. It was a disturbing experience. He remembers to this day an incident on Saturday night. He had entered the house to remove a body when, as he was passing down the rows of patients, a hand grabbed at his in the darkness and held on tightly. The wounded man said nothing and Pat remained where he was for twenty minutes or so, until he felt the grip slacken, and he knew that the soldier, whoever he was, had died.

As the days continued it became harder to find space in the garden for the graves, and harder for Pat and the others to dig them as they became weaker from lack of food. They dug away at the soft, sandy soil, going down for just a few feet before covering the dead soldier with earth and hammering in a rough wooden cross.

Pat could not understand why the Germans didn't

advance. Manning the slit trench along with a glider pilot, all they had between them was one magazine for their Sten gun and a hand grenade. In his opinion, they could have been overwhelmed quite easily. It was hard for the British to appreciate that their enemy also had his weaknesses and that the battle was beginning to slow him down too. The officers of the various German units encircling the Oosterbeek perimeter were experienced and battle-hardened, but their troops were an ad hoc force that had been rapidly drawn together from a variety of units. They had paid a price for their inexperience in the initial assault, with heavy losses, and they were not eager to repeat the bitter hand-to-hand fighting that they had encountered against Colonel Frost's force at the road bridge.

While Pat and the other British soldiers waited, expecting a sudden onslaught at any moment, the Germans were content to rely on their superiority in artillery and armour. Early in the morning of Sunday, the 24th, a battalion of forty-five Tiger tanks arrived on an armoured train. Thirty were sent south over the Arnhem road bridge to prevent XXX Corps approaching from Nijmegen; the other fifteen were sent to boost Spindler's 9th SS on the eastern perimeter of Oosterbeek. The Germans had already lost a considerable number of tanks in the streets of Oosterbeek. This was due to a combination of very effective anti-tank fire and inexperience on the part of the German units in deploying tanks in built-up areas. The new Tiger tanks were sent into action with a proper infantry escort, and their 88mm guns started to demolish the houses where the British had set up strongpoints. A group of these tanks advanced down Weverstraat, a favoured approach that would provide them with ample cover and bring them out at the bottom of the Oosterbeek perimeter. But the tracks of the massive armoured vehicles, weighing 50-odd tons, ripped up the cobbled streets and they sank below the level of the kerb into soft, sandy soil. The narrow streets limited the manoeuvrability of the gun-turrets, as well as the area of vision of the tank commander and his gunner. As they reached the bottom of the street, the leading Tiger tank was hit by a mortar bomb from the section by the church and its fuel tanks ignited. Shrapnel flew into the air and the tank crew scrambled out of the hatches as flames spread over the hull.

Along with the introduction of more powerful tanks, troops using flamethrowers were brought into action – a close-quarter weapon with dreadful effects. It was impossible to withstand these jets of fire, which caused horrible injuries. The perimeter shrank slightly on the eastern side.

Casualties were increasing and the senior medical officer, Colonel Graeme Warrack, realized that if the battle went on for much longer many wounded soldiers would die from lack of treatment. The Hartenstein Hotel and Kate ter Horst's house were regimental aidposts where the injured received basic first aid. Amputations and other surgical treatment were carried out at main dressing stations. These were at the two hotels on the crossroads, the Schoonoord and Vreewijk, and at the Tafelberg Hotel. These were all on the perimeter and had been taken over by the Germans, but were treated as though they were in a sort of no man's land. Fighting took place around them and occasionally they were struck by shells, but German and British medical officers worked in them side by side treating the wounded who were brought in. The dressing stations were isolated, however, and the casualties in them were also suffering because of the shortage of medical supplies. Warrack approached General Urquhart on that Sunday morning and asked him for permission to seek a truce with the Germans. He wanted to transfer the wounded out of the perimeter to the St Elisabeth Hospital, where he hoped they would receive better care.

Urquhart gave Warrack permission to do what he could and he went first to the Schoonoord, where he spoke to the senior German medical officer, who then took him to meet General Bittrich. A truce was arranged, and at three o'clock in the afternoon casualties were evacuated from the main dressing stations and walking wounded were allowed to leave from the perimeter. The more seriously hurt were driven to hospitals in Apeldoorn to the north, while the others made their way to the St Elisabeth Hospital. The route here, back along the Utrechtsweg, passed the still-smouldering wrecks of burned-out vehicles, uprooted trees, blasted houses and shops, and bodies scattered around – the debris of the fighting that had stretched along this road since the landings just a week ago. The Dutch inhabitants of this small town had seen their world wrenched violently off its axis, plunged into bloody chaos. There was scarcely a house that was not damaged; hundreds had been reduced to rubble. Through them now marched a couple of hundred weary, unshaven, bandaged airborne soldiers, some moving painfully, helped on by their comrades. It was remarkable that such a humanitarian gesture could be arranged between two forces who had fought such a deadly battle for the last week, but apart from a few minor incidents the truce held and the wounded were treated well by their German captors.

The truce also signified a change in attitude by General Urquhart and the other senior officers in the divisional HQ, whether they admitted it to themselves or not. For the past week, the expected imminent arrival of the British forces advancing from Nijmegen had mitigated the seemingly hopeless situation, but now, clearly, they would not be arriving quickly enough to save the wounded. When and how they would come to relieve the troops in the perimeter was not a question that had a ready answer any more.

Troops on the ground, however, had still not given in. After the truce ended later that Sunday, shrapnel from a mortar hit another of Ron's small band. He could not move and blood was pouring from a wound in his back. It would have been easier to carry him to the Tafelberg Hotel nearby, where he would have received better treatment. It was in German hands, but the protocol that had been established was that the wounded could be left in the road outside the building and the orderlies inside would come out to pick them up. Neither side would open fire while this was going on.

The paratrooper who had been hit, however, was certain that relief was on the way and was vehemently opposed to being handed over to the Germans. He insisted that his comrades take him to the Hartenstein aid post instead. So they patched him up and gave him some morphine, while Ron and one of his companions rather unwillingly set off to fetch a stretcher from the divisional HQ.

The orderly searched around the rows of wounded, until turning to Ron he said, 'This one's gone. Take him outside and put him on the pile, then take the stretcher, but bring it back, mind.'

Ron and his mate carried the dead man outside and tried to lift the corpse on to a pile by the door. He had been dead for some time. Rigor mortis had set in and, as they lifted the body, Ron at the feet and his mate at the head, large pieces of dried blood and flesh stuck to the canvas fabric. It was ghastly, but Ron was immune to anything now, he had become so used to seeing dead and wounded.

Before they had time to make their way back, the

sergeant major rushed out of the divisional HQ and shouted, 'You two come with me. We are about to be attacked!' Ron and his mate rushed forward and were told to set up a guard on the rear door. The sergeant major was going to take up a position at the front of the building and unless he gave the all clear they were to fire on any vehicle that appeared.

The orders seemed clear, so they went into the doorway, working out how to achieve a field of fire whilst keeping some cover. Ron noticed that the interior was a shambles, with papers, bandoliers and haversacks littering the floor. It was obvious that a sniper had been targeting the door, for the plaster on the walls and ceilings had been gouged out by bullets and pieces of it hung down or lay crumbled in the passageway. Shreds of torn lace curtain hung in the smashed windows of the glass doors.

They waited tensely until, without any warning, a jeep came round the corner of the building. In the instant before he squeezed the trigger of his sub-machine gun, Ron realized that both the men in it were wearing berets. The driver and his passenger were climbing out when he shouted out the password, 'Mae. Who goes there?'

The correct response should have been 'West', but both dived for cover under the jeep. Ron knew instinctively that they were not enemy soldiers and shouted, 'Come out of there, you stupid buggers.'

Out from under the jeep crawled the driver and Brigadier Hicks, commanding officer of the 1st

Airlanding Brigade. He was furious and told the sergeant major to get rid of them, then stormed into the building. Ron and his mate returned to their unit, where they found that they had taken so long to return that the wounded man, now in great pain, had been persuaded to go to the Tafelberg and had been safely handed over.

Why the sergeant major had believed that there was about to be an attack on the divisional HQ Ron never discovered, and would never have expected to be told, but he believes that Brigadier Hicks was lucky not to have fallen victim to friendly fire that evening.

There was a reason for Hicks's urgent arrival at the Hartenstein, however. A decision had been taken earlier that day at a meeting on the other side of the river that a battalion of the 4th Dorsetshire Regiment, from the 43rd Division in XXX Corps, would, along with the remainder of the Polish Parachute Brigade, make a crossing that night to assist the beleaguered 1st Airborne Division, or what was left of it.

23

FOR YOU, THE WAR IS OVER

Thursday, 21–Monday, 25 September

Tom Carpenter was hoisted at gunpoint out of his slit trench and strapped on to a stretcher laid across the bonnet of a captured jeep. The bridge was now securely in German hands. Along with several other wounded prisoners, Tom was driven to a German command post. An SS officer in an immaculate uniform, with jackboots polished to a mirror-like shine, approached him. He handed Tom a tin of English chocolate taken from one of the many supply panniers that had dropped into German hands and said, 'This will be of use to you in the coming days. It's been a good fight, but for you, the war is over.'

Two German soldiers, walking wounded, got into the back of the jeep and they then drove to the St Elisabeth Hospital, which was staffed by Dutch,

British and German medics, who were treating patients regardless of their nationality or military status. Tom was laid, still on his stretcher, between a German soldier and a Dutch woman, and a Dutch nurse gave him a drink of coffee. It was the first hot drink he had had in almost thirty hours and, although it was German 'ersatz' coffee made out of roasted acorns, it tasted like nectar.

After an hour a British orderly came up to Tom and asked how long it was since his wound had been treated. Nothing had been done, of course, since his comrade Corporal Lancaster had stuffed a field dressing into it immediately after he was hit by the shrapnel, but there was no time for the orderly to do very much because Tom was going to be moved. The orderly didn't even take off Tom's uniform, which was beginning to stiffen up like a board with congealed blood; he merely opened up the parachute smock and battledress that Corporal Lancaster had slashed from neck to waist and covered the original dressing with another clean bandage.

Then Tom was helped outside and loaded into an ambulance. He found he was with three other British wounded and four Germans on stretchers. One of the stretcher cases was a young German with a stomach wound, and they started talking, the German showing Tom photos of his girlfriend and his family, and explaining to him that he had been a casualty before, in Russia. It occurred to Tom that a day or so previously they could have been looking at each other down the sights of their guns, and that Tom might be responsible for the German's gaping wound. The way they were talking now, even with difficulty, made it hard to think about that.

Tom was in pain, but he was also very worried. He couldn't see out of the enclosed ambulance and had no idea where he was going. He still believed that XXX Corps was just across the Rhine and that any move in the direction of Germany was going to prevent his being quickly released. While these scattered and anxious thoughts were going through his mind, the ambulance stopped abruptly and they heard the driver and guard slam open the doors. Some aircraft were flying low overhead and the driver clearly thought that they were going to be attacked. There was no gunfire, however, and after ten minutes the two men came back and the rear doors were opened. The wounded Germans on the stretchers were given some food. The young lad who had struck up a conversation with Tom now started talking to the guard and it quickly became an argument, with the rest of his companions joining in. The guard finally gave in and went away, returning with food for Tom and the other British soldiers. They found that they had been given a chunk of black bread and a greyish substance that had the texture of cheese but tasted of fish. Tom found it revolting and stuffed it in his pocket.

They travelled on, every jolt of the badly sprung ambulance sending sharp pains through Tom's back. After another hour, the ambulance stopped and the doors opened to reveal a building with lots of soldiers and medical staff milling around. The Germans on the stretchers were lifted out and said their goodbyes with handshakes and smiles. These were the last friendly gestures Tom was to see for some time. He recalls that the further he got from the front line, the worse his treatment became. He had hoped that he too would be allowed out of the ambulance and finally get some medical treatment, but the doors were closed and they drove on.

When it stopped next, the open doors revealed a very different scene. The ambulance was parked by a railway siding with a waiting train of cattle trucks. There was a large number of wounded British soldiers and a lot of German guards, who looked very threatening. With much shouting and pushing the prisoners were loaded into the wagons. Every one of them was wounded, some severely. There were smashed limbs, and head and trunk wounds, but there was just the bare board of the railway wagon to lie on. About fifty men were loaded into each wagon, then the guards slammed the sliding doors shut, leaving them in the gloom as they struggled to find space and ease the pain in their damaged bodies. They lay there for several hours while the guards laughed and gossiped outside. The pain became worse for everybody, and the men were forced to relieve themselves in a corner of the wagon. Most of them had been given no food or water for over a day, and the more able-bodied started to hammer and bang on the doors, but there was no response.

Eventually there was a violent jolt as the wagons were coupled up, and slowly they heard the wheels screech as they started rolling over the rails. The motion lulled Tom into a reverie about the events of the last few days, and how his life had changed so drastically in such a short time. A few days ago he had been on leave, drinking a pint in a pub in England; now he was lying in a filthy railway wagon, hungry, thirsty, covered in dirt and dried blood, a wounded prisoner of war. He had no idea what had happened to his comrades in 2 Platoon, nor of the fate of the 9th Company.

The train journey continued into the night, broken when they came to a halt to the sound of anti-aircraft guns firing and bombs exploding. After an hour the train moved again, proceeding slowly, as though it were feeling its way. The journey went on for hours; the next day dawned and still there was no end to their pain, no water, no food.

Later that next day they again ground to a screeching stop and at last the doors were flung open. Painfully, with guards shouting at them, they slowly struggled to their feet, helping each other out of the wagons on to the siding, which was in the station of a large town. A crowd of civilians had been assembled to witness their arrival and Tom believed that they were ready to jeer and hurl abuse at them. But many who saw the bloody state of the prisoners, and the painful way they tried to lower themselves to the ground, moved forward to help them. Two of the prisoners – Tom had no idea who they were – had died in the night.

Slowly the guards pushed them into line and ordered them to march off. They had still had no water or food for over two days. They were nearing total exhaustion, with a considerable number of men in shock because of the loss of blood. Many of their wounds had started to become infected. After half a mile they entered the gates of a civilian hospital, where, finally, they were given a medical examination.

The staff probed Tom's wound for the piece of shrapnel using 18-inch metal rods. There was no anaesthetic. It was an extremely painful operation, and it proved unsuccessful. After the effort was abandoned, his wound was dressed again and he was given a bowl of barley soup – his first hot meal for six days. Then he was taken to a ward and given a bed, with sheets, where he was allowed to sleep. In the middle of the night, however, he was woken and shepherded with a lot of shouting from the guards into an air-raid shelter. The sound of anti-aircraft fire and the constant thump of bombs exploding made Tom realize that heading into the heartland of Germany was not only taking him further than ever from freedom, but might also be taking him into danger.

The next morning they were once more on the move, making slow and painful progress. The prisoners, still in their bloodstained uniforms, wounded and roughly bandaged, hobbled along for an hour, covering barely a mile before they were ordered off the road and into a field. The guards withdrew and stood around the edges. Alarm sped through the assembled soldiers. They stayed there for some time, all the while thinking that they would shortly be machine-gunned down. They were not in a condition to do anything about it. Then a car arrived and a civilian got out, walked towards them and started looking closely at some of the wounded prisoners. They had a rash that was caused by exposure to gunpowder, but the guards had thought that it might be typhus. The civilian visitor, a doctor, drove away again and their march resumed. It was a clear, sunny day and in the sky above Tom could see the vapour trails of large numbers of American B-17 bombers on their way to targets deep in Germany.

They arrived at a narrow-gauge railway that took them through small villages and fields before passing through a large war cemetery. Tom assumed it could only have been from the First World War – it seemed to stretch on for ever. Finally they stopped and were put out at a small prisoner-of-war camp, with wooden huts surrounded by barbed wire. The huts were divided into rooms, each with twenty bunks, and Tom was put in one of them. There was neither mattress nor bedclothes, and when the shutters were closed the room was pitch dark. He lay there, his back twisted in pain, his wound now leaking, the wartime crepe bandages with which the German hospital had covered it completely sodden. He was close to despair.

They all wondered when they would get some food and water, but in a few hours a guard appeared. He had two loaves of black bread and two tins of small fish in oil. The prisoners had nothing with which to eat it. They couldn't even cut up the bread. Then Tom remembered that he had a short hacksaw blade that he had sewn into the epaulette of his battledress. Along with a map on a silk handkerchief and a compass disguised as a brass button, it had been part of his escape equipment. This was all he had and his captors were not going to supply anything else. Tom realized that the situation was unlikely to improve; even the smallest utensil would have enormous value. After the small pieces of bread and fish had been hungrily eaten, one of the fish tins was licked clean and stowed in Tom's tunic. It was bound to come in useful! He didn't eat all his bread either. He was developing a habit that was to continue for years – hoarding a small piece of food in the conviction that sooner or later that was all he would have to survive on.

His journey hadn't ended at that small camp a few miles from the German town of Kassel, however. After two days, with Tom's wound getting ever more painful, they were formed up again and the guards marched them outside the camp to two railway carriages with prominent red crosses painted on the outsides. This time they had seats, even if they were wooden. They were hooked up to another train and set off on a slow, erratic progress across northern Germany.

The area was under constant attack from the air, and as the carriages made their jerky way through goods yards and junctions they heard the noise of overhead planes and the explosions of bombs. Coming to a sudden halt in a marshalling yard, the guards evacuated the train, leaving the British prisoners locked in the carriages. They heard the rattle of cannon fire and the roar of low-flying aircraft, and they all instinctively ducked, trying to make themselves as small as possible, as though they were back in their slit trenches in Arnhem.

Many of the prisoners were furious that the guards had abandoned them and started hurling abuse at the Germans when they returned to the carriages. The guard commander ordered his troops to unsling their rifles and threatened to open fire if the prisoners didn't keep quiet. It was a tense moment, exacerbated when the guard commander discovered that the prisoners had rifled his pack while he was seeking shelter and taken his cigarettes. He drew his pistol and Tom thought that he would shoot someone in the head, but despite their experiences of the past few days, or perhaps because of them, the British airborne prisoners refused to be cowed. Extremely angry to be left as targets in the middle of a goods yard, but powerless, they chose ridicule and started singing a popular song, 'Oh Mr Porter, what can I do, I wanted to go to Birmingham but they put me off at

Crewe.' The guards did not know how to respond, but understood instinctively that their behaviour was making them ridiculous. The weapons were put away, while the train jerked forward on its way.

Now the prisoners were buoyed by their own show of spirit and kept singing for another hour, until the train pulled into another siding. Here they were told to get out and were marched again towards a vast area of huts and barbed wire, with searchlights probing the darkness. Their induction was something that they were now used to. They were exhausted, hungry and thirsty, but made to stand in the cold air while their guards counted and re-counted them; then they were marched to another compound where they were counted again before being shown their huts. These were a dreadful sight, filthy and cramped with narrow bunks in three tiers.

They were in Stalag XIB, in Fallingbostel. It contained Russian, Yugoslav, Polish, Dutch and French prisoners of war, and was heavily overcrowded. There were 25,000 inmates, and each hut designed for 200 prisoners was now crammed with 400. Tom had to find his way to a narrow wooden bunk at the bottom of the tier. There was no bedding. The lights went out and within a few minutes he heard his companions muttering and cursing, saying that they were being eaten alive. Tom too was beginning to feel itching all over his body. Lice were coming out of the woodwork.

He felt that he had entered purgatory.

24

XXX CORPS: THE LAST MILES

Thursday, 21–Sunday, 24 September

Whatever the reasons for the refusal of General Horrocks to send the Guards Armoured Division on a rapid drive to Arnhem after they had crossed the Waal at Nijmegen, overnight the Germans seized the chance to strengthen their blocking line. When the Irish Guards' Sherman tanks had rolled into Lent, all that stood between them and the bridge at Arnhem were a few infantry pickets. In the nineteen hours that it took for orders for the advance to be given, the Germans managed to cobble together a defensive line that blocked the road south of the village of Elst. The Sherman tanks didn't cross the start line until 12.30 p.m. on Thursday, when three squadrons of tanks, accompanied by five platoons of infantry riding at the rear, set out. They had travelled a few miles when they met the first

German position, made up of some self-propelled 88mm guns and Panzer Mark IVs.

The tanks of the Irish Guards were in single file on a road that ran high above the low, flat polder; they looked like ducks in a fairground shooting gallery. As the first three Shermans were hit, the column ground to a halt. The tanks were on fire and only some of their crews managed to escape. The infantry leaped from the hulls of the rear squadron of tanks and took shelter in the low ground on either side of the road, in ditches and dykes, but there they started to get hit by mortar bombs and shells. Welsh Guards tried to out-flank the German position, knocking out three Panzer tanks in the process, but they too were effectively blocked from advancing up the road. The Irish Guards had problems with their radios and couldn't get in touch with RAF Typhoons to call down rocket strikes. Their other problem was that the accompanying infantry was too small a force and too lightly armed to outflank the German position.

Horrocks had ordered one of his two infantry divisions, the 43rd, to move forward, but they had been slow in doing so. The unit charged with making their way to Arnhem, the 214th Infantry Brigade, had taken their time as they moved along the line of advance from the original start line at the Albert Canal. At Eindhoven they had taken a wrong turning and got lost in the maze of the huge Philips factory there.

In Nijmegen they had again been delayed and part of the brigade, the 7th Somerset Light Infantry, had headed mistakenly towards the road bridge instead of the railway bridge, which they were meant to cross so that they could move out on a route using side roads that would enable them to outflank the German blocking position. The Somerset Light Infantry should have carried out this manoeuvre on Thursday afternoon, but in the confusion they did not start out until Friday morning. Shortly before them, two troops of the Household Cavalry's armoured reconnaissance vehicles also set out, heading for the HQ of the Polish paratroopers in Driel. Driving along the narrow side roads, protected by a blanket of early-morning mist, the armoured cars found their way without any interference. Their arrival coincided with that of two messengers from Urquhart on the other side of the river – Lieutenant Colonel Charles Mackenzie, his senior staff officer, and the commanding officer of the Royal Engineers, Lieutenant Colonel Eddie Myers, who had the job of arranging for the Polish troops and their supplies to be ferried across the river. Although the appearance of the Household Cavalry made it seem that XXX Corps had finally arrived, no other forces materialized during the day. Mackenzie and Myers must have drawn their own conclusions from this, despite the assurances they received from General Browning when they visited his headquarters at Nijmegen the next day.

The 7th Somerset Light Infantry had not been as fortunate as the Household Cavalry. As they got close to the village of Oosterhout, north-west of the railway bridge, they were fired on by anti-tank guns. Like the Irish Guards, they were strung out on a road raised above the low surrounding countryside and could not turn round or head off the road into cover. Various efforts to cut through the ditches and dykes around the village failed, and finally Brigadier Hubert Essame, commander of the 214th Infantry Brigade, ordered a frontal assault on the village. With a heavy bombardment from artillery mortars and two troops of tanks, the Somerset Light Infantry stormed the village, where among the resulting ruins they found three Panzer Mark IV tanks, a self-propelled gun and 130 SS men who were no longer willing to keep fighting. They had been delayed, unnecessarily, for several hours, but with the way open, the 5th Duke of Cornwall's Light Infantry mounted up on the tanks of the Dragoon Guards and their own armoured cars and made the rest of the journey to Driel in just over half an hour. Lieutenant Colonel George Taylor, commanding officer of the Duke of Cornwall's Light Infantry, wanted to move east to the southern end of the road bridge, but Mackenzie advised against it. He did not believe that any of the 1st Airborne troops were still fighting there.

The Duke of Cornwall's Light Infantry could do nothing now but wait. They had arrived at five o'clock in the afternoon and over the next few hours more units from the 43rd Division appeared. The Somersets reached them, then at around eight in the evening came the 1st Worcestershire Regiment, bringing their DUKW amphibious lorries with them. Although these seemed at first an ideal solution to the problem of crossing the river, they were very difficult to manoeuvre around the narrow roads of the local countryside and were almost uncontrollable on rough ground.

While the Polish paratroopers and the 43rd Division waited on the southern bank of the Rhine, Model ordered his troops to mount a counter-attack on what he rightly saw as XXX Corps' weakest link. German units under General Student attempted to cut the corridor at Veghel and Uden, towns between Eindhoven and Nijmegen. Small units of the US 101st Airborne Division defended both towns. At Veghel the 501st Regiment fought off the attack, then the German tanks moved north to cut the road to Uden. Here they succeeded, leaving along the road a convoy of supply lorries burning fiercely, with the dead bodies of drivers and guards lying by their sides. The fight for Veghel absorbed several Allied units heading towards Nijmegen and grew fiercer when another German battle group attacked from the west. The fighting for the defence of Veghel went on all day, but throughout this time the road to Uden remained closed and XXX Corps' long artery, through which flowed food, ammunition, fuel and reinforcements to the front, was cut.

The Grenadier Guards and Coldstream Guards, who had fought their way up the road to Nijmegen, were now ordered to turn round and head back to free Uden and force a way through to Veghel again. On the Saturday afternoon, they joined forces with the 506th Infantry. The road had been closed for over twenty-four hours and General Horrocks could be in no doubt about the vulnerability of his long supply chain. It was cut again on Sunday, by five tanks and around 200 infantry at a point south of Veghel, as well as a force of extremely determined SS troops. It proved very difficult to dislodge them, and once more units were forced to reverse direction and head south to take on the enemy. By Sunday evening the whole of the Allied force in the long salient was engaged in some way with enemy forces.

Lieutenant General Horrocks had travelled to Driel to form some idea of the situation and to see what could be done to assist the 1st Airborne Division. They would either need major reinforcements or they would need to retreat across the river. The Polish General Sosabowski was in favour of a major divisional effort to cross the river, perhaps a few miles further downstream to relieve the pressure on the Oosterbeek perimeter. Horrocks suggested that he agreed, but wanted to send a battalion across that night to take supplies and provide rapid reinforcements.

The troops selected were a battalion of the 4th

Dorsetshire Regiment from the 43rd Division. That Sunday their commanding officer, Lieutenant Colonel George Tilly, and his staff officers went up the church tower at Driel to look at the lie of the land. They saw how exposed they would be as they approached the riverbank, and how difficult the landing would be on the steep slope of the Westerbouwing on the other side. They had definitely drawn the short straw.

The crossing started late because of difficulties getting the boats down to the bank from the road. Each boat needed two sappers to paddle it and could carry ten soldiers with their supplies for several days. The first boat crossed at one o'clock in the morning. Artillery fire from the XXX Armoured Corps was intended to suppress the German defences, but the shelling set alight some buildings in Heveadorp that lit up the river. The Germans opened fire with machine guns, and men were hit and some boats started to sink. Only two companies of the 4th Dorsets crossed before the operation was cancelled. The men that did manage to land did so scattered all along the length of the river and were never able to form up as complete companies. The attempt to reinforce the 1st Airborne was a failure.

25

THE LAST DAY

Monday, 25 September

On the morning of Monday, 25 September, Tom Carpenter was at the start of the long journey to a prisoner-of-war camp, and Ron Jordan and Pat Gorman were holding on in their slit trenches at Oosterbeek, under regular mortar and artillery fire. The abortive crossing by the 4th Dorsetshire Regiment had passed unnoticed by them and the majority of the men in the Oosterbeek perimeter. Efforts to send troops across the river on the previous two nights had, however, been obvious to the Germans and they now tried to cut off the British from the northern bank of the Rhine.

The 9th SS made two attacks on the slit trenches and strongpoints in the ruined houses just above the Benedendorpsweg, which led to the church and the Royal Artillery positions. They managed to get as far as the first line of the 75mm guns of the Light Regiment, whose crews were getting extremely low on ammunition. The first attack was stopped by very accurate shells fired by the 64th Regiment from south of the river, but when this barrage stopped the German advance, spearheaded by several Tiger tanks, resumed. By now some of the gunners had managed to manoeuvre a 6-pounder anti-tank gun into position and they disabled one of the Tiger tanks. Elsewhere, attacks were made on the northern part of the perimeter, which again were held back by strong machine-gun fire.

Tanks and infantry also took advantage of gaps that were developing all around the perimeter under the onslaught of mortar and infantry attacks and they made incursions into the heart of the Oosterbeek pocket. A group of German soldiers took over some houses on the western perimeter in the Van Lennepweg near the Hartenstein and they were able to ambush anybody moving towards the divisional HQ. Groups of glider pilots attacked them and, after a fight with hand grenades and bayonet charges, succeeded in regaining control of the houses. This respite did not last long. A Tiger tank and three self-propelled guns loomed into view and moved up as far as the tactical HQ of Brigadier Hicks's 1st Airlanding Brigade. A 6-pounder anti-tank gun was manhandled into position and fired three rounds into the tank, which was put out of action. The self-propelled guns retreated, but a machine-gun post in a wood nearby was able to spray the rear lawn of the Hartenstein with bullets with impunity.

Pat Gorman's duties alternated between resting in the church, working in the casualty station at the Rectory and standing to in a slit trench to the east of the church. There was considerable action in this area all morning. Lieutenant John Widdicombe of the Light Regiment Royal Artillery, with a captain from the Polish forces, took a machine gun to the top of the church tower to fire on the German infantry advancing with the tanks and self-propelled guns. The Germans had lost a lot of their armour at the start of the siege because their advance was not co-ordinated properly with infantry and they were vulnerable to attacks by PIATs and Gammon bombs. They were now much better organized, but if their accompanying infantry could be cut down the tank crews would be unwilling to press home their attack on their own; however the two British officers were eventually shelled out of the tower. The fire directed at them brought down the tiles of the church roof in a shattering cascade; to some resting inside it seemed like an omen.

The most critical losses that day were at the other side of the church from Pat's slit trench, where the 1st and 2nd Batteries of 75mm guns were set up. The area where the 1st Battery was established was overrun by three Tiger tanks, and the 2nd Battery area, to the west of this, was overrun when tanks got in amongst the guns and the gun crews had to retreat quickly, which they did under heavy sniper fire. The situation looked extremely serious. The regimental HQ was now surrounded and Pat, firing single shots from his slit trench at slowly advancing German infantry, expected the worst. To his surprise, the Germans seemed content with their gains. Their shelling and mortaring quietened down – no doubt, Pat assumed, because there was a real danger that their shells would fall on the German troops that were now deep inside the perimeter. So the tumult of the morning changed into an uneasy quiet.

As the day progressed, bringing a lull in the fighting, Ron became obsessed with the need to find water. It was extremely scarce. The mains water to the town had been cut off by the Germans and anything that had remained in the Dutch houses had gone. The canteens of the British troops had been emptied days earlier. It was raining again now, but the small amounts that could be collected in mess tins merely emphasized how long it had been since they had had a proper, refreshing drink of water. Everyone was now longing for something to quench their thirst. The fear and adrenaline of fighting kept hunger pangs at bay, but everyone was suffering from parched mouths and cracked, peeling lips.

Ron remembered that there was an old horse-drawn fire engine near the Hartenstein Hotel. He had passed it as he moved down to the crossroads a few days earlier. Would there, he wondered, be some water left in the old appliance? He was so desperate that he thought it was worth a chance, so, collecting some canteens from his mates in the slit trenches, he and another soldier made their way to the fire station. They dodged and ducked into cover every few minutes, avoiding any open ground as it was increasingly likely to be a killing zone for a sniper or machine-gun post. They had just passed the divisional HQ when an officer in the Royal Artillery, making his own cautious journey, asked them where they were going. They explained their mission, but he shook his head and said, 'You'd better get back to your unit. We're pulling out tonight.' Ron was stunned. He had assumed, like all his mates, that he was going to be in Oosterbeek until they were relieved. The sergeant in charge of their small fire group was equally disbelieving when they returned, without any water, but, as Ron pointed out, he hadn't been to divisional HQ that day yet for the latest briefing, so should cut along there as soon as he could.

When the sergeant returned he confirmed the news and added that the evacuation was going to be carried out by units. Ron and another member of the REME in that set of trenches should go back to their maintenance base, which had been established behind the tennis courts in the grounds of the Hartenstein.

It is unclear when the decision was made to bring the men of the 1st Airborne Division back across the Rhine. Some unit accounts suggest that it was decided on the morning of Sunday, the 24th, when plans to send reinforcements across the Rhine were being whittled down from a division- to a battalion-sized force of the 4th Dorsets. Other accounts written subsequently suggest that the debacle of their crossing was the final event that convinced General Horrocks that a withdrawal was the only course of action open to the British.

Whenever the decision was made, Lieutenant Colonel Myers, commanding officer of the Royal Engineers in the division, arrived at the Hartenstein at around six o'clock on that Monday morning. He was wet and exhausted from his river crossing the night before, which had taken him hundreds of yards downstream, forcing him to work his way back along the riverbank into the British perimeter. He carried with him a letter from Major General Ivor Thomas, in charge of the 43rd Division, and he handed this to General Urquhart.

Urquhart read that the plan to reinforce the bridge-head over the Rhine had been abandoned and that arrangements should be made for the 1st Airborne troops to retreat across the Rhine whenever he and Thomas decided. Urquhart spent a couple of hours pondering the question. The mortars were now falling as part of the German's daily bombardment. News of the various incursions from German armour and troops convinced Urquhart that he had to get his men out as soon as possible. It could not have taken him very long to decide; he had been sending signals to XXX Corps HQ about the desperate nature of his position for days.

More difficult were the timing and the manner of the withdrawal. Troops are at their most vulnerable during a retreat, particularly when they are in close contact with the enemy. They lose any advantages provided by their prepared defensive positions, and are liable to be cut down in the open as they form up and prepare to move. General Urquhart remembered from his training as a young officer how the British had withdrawn from a bridgehead at Gallipoli on the Turkish coast in the First World War. One of the key tactics was to keep up the semblance of a well-maintained defensive position while the bridgehead was hollowed out. The evacuation would of necessity have to take place under the cover of darkness. Small pockets of troops would need to keep up their firing to distract the Germans, and radio traffic would need to be continued as normal. Inevitably, some men would have to remain behind. So too would most of the wounded and some medical staff. General Urquhart also wanted the gunners in XXX Corps to mount an artillery bombardment, which would encourage the Germans to keep their heads down and prevent them from moving into action should they suspect what was going on.

There was inevitably going to be a lot of activity on the banks of the river, as two engineer companies, the 260th (Wessex) Field Company and the 23rd Canadian Field Company, manhandled their boats on to the southern bank of the Rhine and moved across the river to embark the airborne troops. Urquhart hoped that the Germans would interpret this activity not as a withdrawal, but as another attempt to reinforce the bridgehead. It was inevitably going to be a dangerous manoeuvre. Urquhart later wrote that the cost in lives of pulling out his division through a riverside bottleneck, which was now reduced to just 600 or 700 yards, might be very high indeed.

He called a planning meeting at around 10.30 in the morning and announced his decision to what remained of his staff officers. The sounds of fighting could be heard from all around the perimeter. There was nothing to say but discuss the details. One final thing that Urquhart insisted on was that the news of the evacuation should be kept secret until it was absolutely essential to let the men know. He believed that their ability to keep fighting might be compromised by the information, and there was also the danger that someone captured by the Germans might inadvertently let the news slip out. Many men, like Ron, were however in ad hoc formations, separated from their units, and were never told about the planned evacuation.

Back in the REME workshop trenches, Ron found that plans were well advanced for the pull-out. One of his mates, Bernard Cubberley, was wrapping strips of material torn from an old tent around his boots and he offered some to Ron. Bernard had been deafened by the explosion from a mortar and shouted to Ron to make sure that anything that might make a noise was wrapped in fabric. The REME workshop contingent was assigned to No. 2 party, under Armament Sergeant Major 'Matty' Reid, and Ron was going to take the route down to the river on the western side of the perimeter. He was put on alert twice after that when he was assembled with some other men and could hear an attack starting on the western side. He was sure that they were going to be directed to move out to fill a gap, but each time the firing petered out. The second time a few mortars landed amongst them, killing three or four men, and orders came to get back to the slit trenches.

Both outbreaks of shooting that Ron heard were firefights between German troops and a group of sappers from the 9th Field Company, whose job it was to mark a path down to the riverbank with long lines of tape. The CO of the 9th, Major Jack Winchester, had set off with three of his men to make the journey from divisional HQ down to the riverbank, skirting hedges, crossing fields and ditches for over a mile. There were two routes to be marked and Winchester had the western one, which was just upriver from the ferry. They tried to work in silence, because this route passed in places within 40 yards of enemy strongpoints. Twice their movement started a response from the enemy, but Winchester and his men melted away while other airborne troops nearby returned the fire.

Other sappers, in the company of some glider pilots, were marking out the second route, which ran west of the church and Kate ter Horst's house. They did not arouse the attention of any German soldiers here. The Royal Engineers were going to have sixteen assault boats at each site, and the Canadians were providing twenty storm boats, which could carry fourteen people each and which were powered by outboard motors. There would be fourteen of these opposite the church and six at the crossing closer to the ferry. Major Winchester hoped that when the evacuation was in full swing the artillery fire from the guns in XXX Corps would mask the sounds of columns of soldiers making their way down to the river.

At 22.00 hours the first parties of men were arriving at the riverbank. The shelling from XXX Corps was intense, directed at the enemy positions around the British perimeter, and two aircraft batteries stationed on the southern bank fired streams of red tracer bullets as a guide to the boats now starting to make their way to the far bank. Initially, just as Urquhart had hoped, the Germans did believe that this was the start of another attempt to reinforce the Airborne Division and started to lay fierce, merciless mortar fire along the riverbank. Many of the rivercraft were hit. Soldiers dropped into the river, some wounded, some already dead, but the British and Canadian sappers crewing the boats continued unflinchingly into this deadly fire, while the waiting men took what shelter they could in the muddy flood plain.

Ron's unit started out on its escape route an hour or so after the bombardment began. They lined up, each holding on to the rear flap on the parachute smock of the man in front, like a crocodile of children. It was raining and the wind was gusting, blowing the trees wildly; the night was split open by the flashes of exploding shells as the men stumbled forward, the sergeant in the lead trying to keep track of the guiding tapes. They had been moving forward for just ten minutes when a German machine gun opened up from close by. Bullets whipped through the leaves and branches of a hedge by their side, and they inched forward as the machine-gun crew fired randomly for several minutes, then stopped. They continued for about another 100 yards before another machine gun started firing. They all hit the ground. The bullets were coming from directly in front of them, the machine gunner firing straight ahead up the road. Ron could see the gun flashes as he lay flat, in the rain, seeking whatever meagre shelter he could find in the kerb of the road. Two more short bursts rang out, bullets whiffling close over his head, then there was a loud explosion and a bigger flash and the firing stopped. One of the sergeants had crawled forward with a grenade and hurled it at the machine-gun post, killing both of the gun's crew. With the machine gun silenced, Sergeant Major Reid now stood up in the middle of the road and called the men to re-form. The soldier in front of Ron made no move to get up. Ron grabbed his foot and shook it. There was no resistance and Ron realized he was dead, killed by a bullet from the machine gun. Ron had escaped unhurt, but to his consternation there was another dead body behind him and, on examination, he discovered that both the dead men were from the Border Regiment.

There was nothing they could do for their dead comrades, so they went on, Ron's wounded leg now starting to throb painfully. They were moving slowly, very cautiously, because within the space of ten minutes they had been fired on by two different groups of Germans. Ron knew that they were very close to the enemy lines and he was tense, desperate not to give away their position. He remembered how he had escorted the Polish officer through this same stretch of woods and isolated houses, straining not to make a noise while the officer urged them on. He thanked God the Pole was not with them now. Ron might have shot him himself.

The column came to a halt again. He could not believe it, and thought, 'Oh Christ, not another one.' They stopped for what seemed an age, and some of the men began muttering, asking what the hold-up was? The reply came back that the sergeant in the lead had lost the trail.

There was nothing to be done. They pressed on in the general direction of the river, then came to a clearing in the trees. It would be fatal to try to cross any open ground; the only way to negotiate it was by following the line of trees around its edge. Carefully, they started to move from tree to tree as the rain dripped down from the branches and the bandages on their feet became sodden and thick with mud. After a few minutes Ron saw a shape on the rough grass ahead of him. It was the body of a German soldier. He was on his knees, slumped forward over a pannier of supplies that had been dropped on one of the re-supply missions. His helmet had rolled forward and his head lay in the open pannier. Ron saw his blond hair wet in the rain. He had been shot as he searched for cigarettes or chocolate amongst the contents, and had been dead for several days.

Down at the bank of the Rhine, groups of men were gradually being taken across the river, but the current was strong and the arrival of the boats was becoming intermittent. Machine guns were firing into the water from the high land on the Westerbouwing, as well as mortars landing in the water and on the banks. Several soldiers who fancied their chances decided to swim across, but the current took them rapidly downstream. The sappers in charge of loading up the boats began to wonder how long they could keep going. Many of the outboard motors were running out of fuel and the soldiers were urged to use their rifles to paddle the 20-foot-long craft through the swirling water. Major Winchester was on the riverbank acting as a beach master, controlling the embarkation; he wrote subsequently that there was no panic – men waited patiently for their turn to board. At about midnight he saw General Urquhart board a boat and cross safely. Still men appeared out of the dark, but the boats were beaching irregularly along a wide stretch of the riverbank and men waded through the water to reach them. By one o'clock in the morning he was becoming exhausted, so he took the opportunity to board a boat. Gunfire hit the water a few yards away as the boat crossed and he reached the far bank unscathed, but wet through and numb with fatigue.

Ron's party was still negotiating a meadow, skirting the edge in single file. He knew that their progress needed to be faster. This was not a planned embarkation with an adjutant ticking off units on a clipboard as men boarded a gangplank. This was a retreat, a rushed evacuation through a half-open door that could be slammed shut at any minute. But they dared not make any noise. They cleared the meadow and on their right saw a ruined farmhouse. Only one wall was still standing and the ruins were smoking, as though it had only recently received a direct hit. Ron was asked to cover the building while the group he was with each took it in turns to run past the gated entrance to the destroyed building. There was no gunfire or movement from inside the ruins, so Ron went forward.

The stretch of road they were on seemed to have several farm buildings along the right-hand side and they passed each one in the same way, Ron covering the entrances as each man ran across them. They were then held up for what seemed a very long time, crouched in the shelter of a hedge. Ron moved up to the front of the line. Lance Corporal Jack Grafham had brought them to a halt because he could see the silhouette of what he thought was a tank positioned further along the lane. It didn't move and Ron thought it looked more like a concrete pillbox, but as far as he knew nothing like that had ever been built around Arnhem. After staring for so long at something in the darkness, he knew that the mind could start playing tricks, but it was foolish to run any risk. After twenty minutes, Ron suggested that they try to detour around it. The lance corporal agreed, so they slowly backtracked and turned into the last entrance they had just crossed. They moved back on their original line of advance. There was no sign of life from the tank or pillbox or whatever it was.

After another 100 yards they broke out on to the lower road, the Benedendorpsweg, which had been the designated start line for the very first troops to move down to the river, and the small party made its way past another row of seemingly empty houses, with roofs caved in and gaping holes in their walls. Pieces of rubble and slates littered the road. They were close to the flat flood plain that leads down to the river-bank and Ron saw that there was a junction ahead, and that the side road ought to take them down to where they could reach the river. Once there, it would be a simple task to find the embarkation point.

At the start of the side road were two white gates with a low building set back from them. Ron knelt and covered the entrance with his machine gun as the rest of the squad moved quickly across it. As Sapper Cubberley made his dash there was a gunshot and he went down into the road. Ron crawled forward to him and grabbed his shoulders, pulling him on to a patch of grass. The forward men, including Lance Corporal Grafham, came back. Ron was turning round, swinging the machine gun, desperate to see where the shot had come from, when he was caught in a deafening blast. He saw nothing but bright red flashes and lost consciousness.

When he came round a machine gun was blasting away just a few feet from his head, so close that every shot rang in his ears as if he were being hit with a hammer. The sound of two more grenades came from inside the building, and Ron saw the figure of a German soldier crawling towards him. The German grabbed his ankle, and Ron felt a jolt of pain shoot up his leg so excruciating he screamed, then he lost consciousness again.

He came to once more to find himself being carried in a tarpaulin, with one of his comrades at each corner. His whole body was in agony. Every jolt sent waves of pain through his body and his leg felt as if it were on fire. Another pain in his back stabbed him with extra energy every time he drew breath. His mouth was full of blood, which was dripping down his chin. Still stunned by the explosion, he felt no fear, but knew that his life was probably ending. He neither knew nor cared where his mates were carrying him and it crossed his mind that they might have thought he was already dead. The situation became clearer when he was lowered painfully to the ground. He and his mates were being guarded by two German soldiers, sub-machine guns at the ready. They had been taken prisoner.

At eleven o'clock that night Pat Gorman left the Rectory and took up his position in the slit trench with the glider pilot with whom he normally shared it. He had ignored, as much as he could, the start of the artillery bombardment earlier that night, assuming that another attempt was being made to bring troops across the river from the south. German mortar fire seemed to be concentrated on the riverbank, although shells were landing inside the perimeter further north.

He remained in the trench, taking it in turns with the glider pilot to keep watch in the night for any sign of movement, knowing that there were enemy soldiers almost surrounding them barely 200 yards away. What Pat would have done if they had suspected an attack was hard to imagine. Between them, they were down to a handful of bullets for their Sten gun. The rain continued, it was cold, and gunfire and the flash of exploding shells split the darkness.

Keeping watch at night was tiring, and normally they would be relieved after three hours. Pat waited and waited, but no relief came. As the darkness lifted slightly, the glider pilot looked at his watch and said that they had been there for over four hours. Other men in slit trenches next to theirs were also concerned.

Telling Pat to keep watch, the glider pilot and a rifleman from another trench went back to the church to find out what had happened to their relief.

They found that the church was empty. They crossed over to the Rectory where there were just the wounded men and medical staff, who told the glider pilot that all the troops had been evacuated that night. The two men returned to their trenches.

Pat recalls that the glider pilot seemed stunned, disbelieving, but Pat, exhausted, felt nothing in particular. After all that had happened to him, it was just one more piece of bad news. He realized that they had been kept in position deliberately as an involuntary rearguard. It was what he had come to expect.

The glider pilot was concerned about what to do. 'We can't defend this place. I don't know what the hell we can do.'

They had been sitting in the bottom of the trench while they talked. There was nothing to guard any more. It was getting lighter, and Pat looked up as a shadow seemed to cross the trench.

'You don't have to worry any more,' he told the glider pilot.

Looking down into the trench were six German

soldiers, their guns pointing at Pat and his companion. They climbed out. All around them, in the cold morning air, were German soldiers and dirty, dispirited British airborne troops climbing out of trenches and putting their hands above their heads.

26

A BRUTAL JOURNEY

September 1944

Ron didn't know how severe his wounds were. In addition to those in his right leg caused by shrapnel from a mortar round, the grenade that had exploded next to him on the night of the evacuation had damaged his ankle and foot, grenade fragments had torn his back open and injured his right arm, and there was blood coming out of his mouth. His ankle was causing him the most pain, but he was more alarmed by the blood pouring from his mouth. The medical orderly who treated him realized that this was caused not by any internal injury but by Ron biting the inside of his mouth when he was flung into the air by the blast of the grenade. He staunched the blood with a thick pad and dressed the rest of the wounds as best he could. Ron was relieved, but his wounds prevented him from walking. He also could not use his right arm or lie on his back. But he was alive at least.

His mate from the REME, Private Bernard Cubberley, was less fortunate, with a large open wound in his chest; he was in such pain that he was often delirious between periods of unconsciousness. Ron lay on the road, talking to his comrade, hoping that the sound of his voice would be of some comfort. Vehicles were driving past and German soldiers were standing around, their machine guns held loosely down in front of them. He could hear their conversations, and orders, but there was no gun-fire and Ron was aware of birds singing. The fighting had finished.

Both he and Cubberley were loaded on to a small, 15cwt truck, with a wooden frame added to it for four stretchers at the back. The bottom two positions were already taken by two wounded Germans, so Ron and Cubberley were on the top of what proved to be a very ramshackle structure. Every time the lorry turned a corner, Ron thought that all four of them were going to be tossed into the road. He hung on as best he could, trying to keep his mate secure as well.

The road they were travelling on was full of refugees, pushing prams and wagons or carrying bundles of possessions or small children. The lorry weaved its way through, but Ron, lying half on his side, saw a plane approaching. The only ones that he had seen throughout the battle were German fighters or Allied freighters on their re-supply drops. Now that the battle had ended, a Typhoon ground-attack aircraft appeared to be zooming into the attack. No sooner had Ron noticed than so did the German driver and guard, who was sitting on the back with his peaked forage cap turned back to front. The lorry swayed to a stop and both of them leaped off and ran for the side of the road. Ron watched, helpless, as the Typhoon, its huge air intake like an open maw, banked low and headed towards him. Ron cursed and prayed in equal measure, but the pilot turned the aircraft again at the last minute and it flew to the side; Ron could see the pilot staring at him from the cockpit. The wings of the Typhoon waggled as it roared off, keeping low.

The driver and guard climbed back aboard the lorry and it started off again with a grinding of gears. They had gone no more than a couple of miles when Ron once more heard the drone of an aircraft above the noise of the engine. Once more the lorry stopped and the two Germans fled into the fields. Ron was less alarmed this time, but was filled once more with fear when another Typhoon roared very low over the lorry and, as the civilian refugees screamed and flung themselves headlong, it turned very tightly, headed down the road again and fired two of its rockets from under its wings. For one fearful moment he thought that he was the target and that after all the events of the last week he was going to be killed by his own air force. As the rockets blasted on their course above him, he felt that he was once again in the midst of a deadly mortar barrage. They were not aimed at him, however; they exploded some way down the road ahead and that was the last of the attack. As the lorry staggered on, Ron saw a column of oily smoke drifting in the wind. They got to a crossroads where the target of the Typhoon's rockets, a Tiger tank, was burning briskly and Ron once more tasted the smell of burned metal and flesh. He thought that if it wasn't for the refugees, this second Typhoon might have machine-gunned them, as they had no Red Cross signs on the lorry to identify them.

It took a long while to negotiate the crossroads, with the refugees trying to gather their belongings, which had been scattered all over the road as they fled from the attack, while the blazing tank was still slewed across the road. Finally they came to a building like a church hall, where Ron and his companions on the truck were unloaded. On one side of the building was a pile of civilian bicycles, in a huge jumbled heap, and next to it was a line of dead men covered by tarpaulins. From the row of boots that stuck out under the edge, Ron thought that they were all German.

He eventually found himself alone, lying on the floor with some German walking wounded, who were gradually being looked at by a medical orderly. Despite their injuries they seemed cheerful, no doubt because the fighting was over for the moment, and many of them had chocolate and cigarettes that had been intended for the airborne troops. Ron was given a cigarette and offered some chocolate by one of the wounded Germans, but the orderly waved him away, saying that he was to have nothing to eat. All that he wanted was a drink. Both he and Bernard were given an injection through their uniforms, which was extremely painful and seemed to Ron to have no effect. Bernard was taken away, and Ron was carried to another building where he was laid on a mattress in a room on the second floor of the building, where there were two rows of wounded British prisoners. A guard marched back and forth down the middle of the room, but Ron thought that, as everyone there was injured, it was hardly necessary for him to be there. He was told that he had arrived too late for the ration of stew, but this was the first mattress he had seen since he left England and he sank into an utterly exhausted sleep.

Next morning he was woken by a small, pretty Dutch girl in a nurse's uniform. She put her fingers to her lips and, reaching into her tunic, gave him a hard-boiled egg, already shelled. He was so parched he could not chew it, so he swallowed it in two pieces, which nearly choked him. The Dutch nurse then went along the rows of wounded men, giving each of them the same thing. Ron became grateful for this act of charity later, because the guard discovered that one of the prisoners was missing. During the night a man from the Border Regiment had slipped out of a window and down a drainpipe. Ron admired the man's pluck, especially as he had one arm in a sling, and it seemed that he had got away. The guards were extremely angry, however, and in the fruitless search for the escapee, breakfast never arrived.

Ron was then moved downstairs, loaded on another lorry with several other wounded and driven to a barracks in Apeldoorn. Here captured members of the Royal Army Medical Corps were running a makeshift operating theatre and Ron's wounds were finally examined. Those in his back, arm and leg had all bled profusely – his parachute smock and blouse were thick with dried blood – but these wounds were not deep and nothing vital had been damaged. The most serious injury was to his foot and ankle, through which shrapnel had passed, shattering bones and tendons. Ron's boot and sock had to be carefully cut away before the doctors could re-set the bones and strap them up. There was no anaesthetic, although fortunately they did have some supplies of morphine. Finally he was given a cut-down German boot that left his broken ankle free.

After resting for a few days, the next stage of Ron's journey to prison camp saw him put on a train, like Tom, at Apeldoorn station. The train was delayed by a strike of Dutch railway workers, who were refusing to operate it, and when it did finally arrive the prisoners were badly overcrowded. There wasn't enough room for everyone to sit, but the airborne prisoners made way for the badly wounded. Ron was allowed to lie down; so too was Regimental Sergeant

Major Gay of the 156th Battalion, who had caught a burst of bullets from a German heavy machine gun through both legs. He was in constant pain. One of the prisoners was a young soldier from the 10th Battalion, who had moved through Ron's position on the Utrechtsweg on Wednesday, and he talked to the hungry soldiers in the packed wagon about his life in the Yorkshire Dales and his favourite sandwich – fresh white bread with cheese and strawberry jam. Talk of food became the most popular way of passing the time over the next few months.

When the wagon doors were slid shut, a young subaltern from the Royal Engineers stood up and announced that it was their duty to escape. He explained that it would be easier to escape in Holland than in Germany, so they should make the attempt as soon as possible. He asked for volunteers. Ron was pleased that he was clearly incapable of making any effort to escape, because he thought that the chances of success were slim, but six others were prepared to do so. The subaltern's plan was that, when the train slowed down a bit, they should force open the door and jump, scattering as far away from the railway line as possible. Two guards were housed in a little box on the end of each wagon, but if the prisoners waited for a bend they might get away unseen.

The subaltern managed to undo the clasp and slid the doors open a few inches. The six volunteers were lined up as though they were going to parachute from an aeroplane. The train slowed and the wagons tilted, for a long bend, and the subaltern slid the door open a little more. The first man to jump must have tripped or fallen, because there was a terrible shriek from him. The rest of the volunteers followed quickly and the prisoners shut the door. The subaltern's hopes of escaping unseen were in vain, however. The train screeched to a halt and the guards dismounted. Everyone had to get out, and Ron and the badly wounded RSM were helped out on to the tracks, where they lay, shivering. A group of guards had walked down the line to where someone was lying, then a shot rang out. They were not satisfied and the German guard commander, an old veteran, an ex-submariner from the First World War, walked up and down the line of prisoners threatening to shoot every seventh man if the escaped men weren't recaptured. It was, fortunately, an empty threat. The guard commander was too old and had seen too much to want to carry out such a punishment.

They waited and waited before the guards ordered them back into the carriages and they went on their way. That evening they stopped at a goods siding in Hanover, arriving in the middle of an air raid on the town. One bomb landed so close that the explosion lifted their wagon 6 inches into the air. The raid lasted for half an hour, during which it seemed there was a continuous cacophony of anti-aircraft fire, the whistling of falling bombs and explosion after explosion that merged into one thunderous roar. The smell of smoke filled the wagons. The city was burning.

They stayed there overnight, cramped and hungry. In the morning, the doors of the wagons were opened so that the toilet pails could be slopped out, and they were given some acorn tea and a small piece of fatty roast pork with crackling on it. It tasted delicious, and Ron continued to suck his for hours. While they were waiting there, looking out over the smoking city, with labour crews already starting to fill in bomb craters and repair the rails, a locomotive steamed slowly past them. It was pulling several wagons with anti-aircraft guns mounted on them. On each wagon was a small hut where the gun's crew could shelter and rest. On the last wagon, spreadeagled across the roof of the crew hut, was the dead body of the subaltern. The prisoners were shocked into silence as the grim spectacle clanked slowly past.

After Hanover, the train didn't stop again until it reached Fallingbostel, the location of Stalag XIB where Tom Carpenter had arrived some days earlier. Ron's reception was much more civilized than Tom's. When the prisoners were unloaded, the wounded were taken up to the camp by a horse-drawn cart. The horse was killed later at Christmas to provide some meat for their soup, but while Ron was waiting for its return to make the next trip, the chaplain, Rev. Albert Harlow, gave him 200 American cigarettes.

Arriving in the camp, he was pleased to find that his old comrades from the REME and some glider pilots who had been captured at the same time as him had already been allocated a hut and that Lance Corporal Jack Grafham had saved a bunk for him. It was a top one, so Ron had a great deal of trouble climbing in and out of it, but as he quickly found out, the camp was very crowded and he was grateful to his old comrades. The influx of prisoners from Arnhem changed the atmosphere, and at times it became very tense. The airborne troops were confident and aggressive, despite being captured, believing that the Germans were losing the war and that it would be over quickly. Rations were poor; this and the routine of roll calls each morning were both flash points. The men would often react if they thought the food was particularly poor or the guards were being deliberately bureaucratic.

Ron quickly found out how dangerous their situation might become. There were regular air raids both night and day, but there were no air-raid shelters for the prisoners. If a daytime raid took place, their orders were to return immediately to their huts and stay there until the all clear. Shortly after Ron arrived the sirens sounded for a daylight raid. A force of B-17 Flying Fortresses flew overhead, their condensation trails gleaming in the sun. Many of the prisoners took their time getting back into the huts, wanting instead to watch this magnificent sight, but the guards became increasingly agitated, telling them to hurry. Suddenly a shot rang out from one of the guard towers. Sergeant Hollingsworth, the glider pilot who had commanded Ron's small unit on the perimeter at Oosterbeek, fell dead. His beret rolled on to Ron's feet. With their rifle butts, the guards forced them through the doors of the hut, leaving Sergeant Hollingsworth dead on the ground.

27

BEHIND THE WIRE

September–October 1944

It was the second time that Pat Gorman had been taken prisoner and marched, hands up, in front of a German bayonet. Dirty and hungry, his nerves stretched by days of shelling, he now felt crushed by the fear and uncertainty of captivity once more. With the rest of the troops from the slit trenches around the church, he was marched up the hill to the grounds of the Hartenstein Hotel. The tennis courts, which had been put to use to secure the German prisoners, were now full of those remnants of the 1st Airborne Division who had been unlucky or just abandoned. As Pat reached them, a friend from his platoon shouted out, 'Say you're a batman, Pat, say you're a batman!'

Pat couldn't work out why he had shouted this until later that night he discovered that officers and their batmen were allowed to sleep in the wooden changing huts in the courts while the other ranks had to sleep outside.

The next morning, cold, tired and stiff, he was picked out with twenty others by a detachment of German soldiers. There was little reason that Pat could see for his selection save that he was close to the entrance. Their guards ordered them on to the back of several horse-drawn carts and they were taken eastwards along the Utrechtsweg until they came to the crossroads. Here they were told to assemble into smaller groups, and Pat discovered why they had been separated. They were going to bury the dead. Two big pits had already been dug in the earth close to Oosterbeek's graveyard, north of the railway line. One pit was a mass grave for German dead, the other for the British. Pat and the rest of his party were now given a ruined house to sleep in and a good supply of rations. None of this made up for the dreadful task that lay ahead of them.

Pat toured the recent killing grounds of Oosterbeek and Arnhem, loading the dead of both sides on to the wagons and taking them to the burial ground. The smell was vile, and the wounds that Pat saw were sickening. The sight of piles of dead young men was almost too much for him to bear, but he despaired most when he found the bodies of his friends and comrades from the 11th Battalion. Pat's guards during the four days that he carried out this gruesome job were soldiers from the SS battalions that had fought against the 1st Airborne troops. They found the task as unpleasant as their prisoners, and Pat echoed the remarks of many other veterans who had been captured, that the front-line German soldiers treated them with respect and decency. He couldn't have been more thankful, however, when they had recovered the last of the bodies scattered over the area and he, with the rest of his small party of prisoners, was told to get on to the back of a lorry. They were driven out of Arnhem, through woods and farmland that seemed untouched by the fighting; the sight of it helped lighten Pat's mood.

A few miles outside Arnhem the lorry turned into a small army camp, surrounded by barbed wire, with a parade ground and a few low, single-storey barracks. There were armed guards at the gatehouse and several others dotted around. The small group of British airborne troops were lined up, and Pat was taken by two of the guards and brusquely told to move forward. He thought that there was something different about these men and, as they handed him over to another guard in a cell block, he guessed that they were not German, but members of a Dutch SS unit. He was shoved roughly into a cell and the door was slammed shut behind him. He heard the keys turn.

He turned around. It was a bare, narrow concrete cell, with nothing in it but a solid concrete bunk against one wall. The bunk had three bumps in it and it would be impossible to sleep on it. In the corner were a water tap and a hole in the floor, which was obviously meant to be used as a toilet. There was a small hatch in the bottom of the door.

After a few minutes Pat noticed something sinister. He could hear nothing. There were no sounds of guards walking, no shouted orders, no noise of any life in the camp outside. The cell was soundproof! All he could hear was his own breathing and the thumping of his heart. In his short life Pat had faced fear in many places, from climbing into a professional boxing ring at the age of fifteen, to making his first parachute jump a few years later. Even the awful anticipation of imminent death during a mortar barrage couldn't equal the sudden dread that he felt as he stared at the concrete walls that enclosed him.

He paced a few short steps back and forward. He longed for a cigarette. Questions circled in his mind. Why was he here? How long would it be before he got out? What was going to happen to him? The more the questions went unanswered, the more anxious he became. He tried to sit down on the concrete bunk, but every position became uncomfortable after a short time. He waited for a guard to come and get him, but no one came. He sat and walked, sat and walked. Time became immeasurable. The cell grew cold and he walked to warm himself up. His eyes grew heavy with fatigue, but the concrete bunk was too uncomfortable to lie on, so he lay curled on the floor until the cold woke him.

After an eternity the hatch in the door opened and a slice of bread with some sort of fruit jam was pushed through, on the floor – there wasn't even a plate. There was nothing to mark the passing of time but Pat's own pulse and he believed he would go mad if he started counting it. He felt he was near to madness anyway. He pictured his home in Workington and his mother, knowing that thoughts like that would lead to his breaking down, but try as he might he could not suppress them. Time shrank and expanded, and as it did, it seemed that so too did his physical surroundings, and he started to feel that his mind had lost contact with his body. Occasionally he would break out in a cold sweat.

Pat sat it out. Another slice of bread appeared through the hole in the door, and Pat sat and walked. Nobody answered his calls, nobody came for him. He summoned up the strength from somewhere to hold on when everything around him, and the black thoughts that filled his head, told him to despair. It might have been anger; thinking back on those days now, it might have been the thoughts of home and his mother that gave him strength, however much he tried to push them away at the time; but he didn't crack. Twice more the hatch opened and the measly slice of bread and jam was thrust through it. Four days he was kept in the cell, silent, alone, before the door opened and a guard dragged him out.

Pat knew that at that point, when he first set eyes on another person and saw the world outside his cell, he might collapse, start talking, crying even; but he was determined not to, and he didn't. He was marched, unsteadily, down a corridor where an SS officer sat. He offered Pat a cigarette, which he took, and a bar of chocolate, which he also took and ate. The officer – and Pat was sure that he was Dutch – started asking him a series of questions about British plans for pursuing the war that absolutely astounded him. The number of divisions, timetables for the next advance – how on earth could he, a private soldier, be expected to know anything of this sort? Pat replied with his name and his army paybook number, and reiterated that he was just an ordinary soldier. How could he answer any of their questions?

The interrogation continued, but Pat was obdurate. After an hour of increasingly impatient questioning the officer lost his temper, shouted at the guard and Pat was hauled back down the corridor and, with kicks and blows, thrown back into the cell. But he had had a cigarette and some chocolate, and the cell was no longer so intimidating. He was on top of it.

Pat was psyching himself up for another extended period of solitary confinement when, just two hours later, he was dragged out of his cell again by the guards and thrown out of the cell block on to the ground in the compound. Picking himself up, he saw that the other members of his group were assembled in two ranks. The guards kicked him over to join them. He looked around. There were two lorries parked in the centre of the compound. One was empty, while a yellowish tarpaulin obscured the back of the other. Ominously, at the end of the building where Pat had been imprisoned was a wall of railway sleepers and their surface was gouged with bullet holes. Seeing this, Pat thought that he had been pulled out of the frying pan into the fire. It seemed obvious to him that someone – perhaps him, perhaps all of them – was going to be put against the railway sleepers and machine-gunned. He looked up at the sky, released from the purgatory of a soundproof cell but now facing another ordeal. He could have been killed at any time in Arnhem and Oosterbeek, had watched while men in front of him had died from horrible wounds and known that it could easily have been him; but to stand, powerless, in front of a wooden wall and wait for the bullets to thud into him must be the worst form of torture.

Immersed in this foreboding, he was only faintly aware of a commotion at the gates, where a jeep had noisily pulled up and a black-uniformed SS officer had got out and was striding vigorously into the compound, while the gate guards and every other soldier in the place leaped to attention. He was a powerfully built man and clearly important. He marched into the building where Pat had been inter-rogated and the prisoners, standing outside, could hear him haranguing the Dutch SS men. This went on for ten minutes while their guards stood rigidly to attention. The officer came back out, holding in one hand a pair of black leather gloves, which he used to gesture at the lorries and then waved imperiously at the small bunch of prisoners, issuing orders in German to their guards as he strode to his jeep, where the driver still sat with the engine running. Then he turned and walked back to them. In an utterly different tone he said in English, 'I'm very sorry about what has happened to you. From now on you will be well looked after.' Then he left.

The prisoners were marched to the lorries and told to climb on the back. They were driven out of the gates and taken for a few more miles to a farmhouse, where they got out. Here they were led to an out-building and given a meal – a stew that Pat remembers to this day as being absolutely magnificent. It was certainly the first hot meal he had had for a fortnight and was the best he was going to get for the next six months. He was surprised to learn from his fellow prisoners that, while all of them had been questioned, he was the only one to have been put into solitary confinement. While he was struggling with his fears in a concrete cell, they had been sleeping in bunks in one of the wooden huts, where they had been given a lot more than a slice of bread and jam each day. He never understood why he had been picked on. He was shorter than most, and looked younger than his twenty years; perhaps his interrogators had thought that he was the most likely to break. In that they were mistaken.

Even while they were enjoying their meal, there was

an odd incident. Their guards – there were ten of them for just twenty prisoners – seemed extremely nervous, never taking their eyes off the men. He suspected that their reputation as tough paratroopers had created some tension amongst the guards, who, he saw, were armed with captured British Sten guns. They were aiming them directly at the prisoners and, what was worse, they had their safety catches off. It made him very nervous, because he knew how unreliable the weapons were. It would only take one accidental discharge and all of them would go down in a hail of bullets. That was how things worked.

Then Pat did something so stupid that even now he doesn't know what got into him. Had the events of the last few weeks given him a sense of invulnerability? He doesn't believe so, but for whatever reason he decided that he couldn't bear the tension any longer and he stood up. Several gun barrels swivelled in his direction. He slowly put his hands out, advanced to the nearest guard and pointed at the Sten gun, shaking his head to indicate that there was something wrong with it. The guard said, '*Was ist?*' and Pat put out his hand and moved the safety catch to on. He then smiled at the German soldier. There was a silence as the soldier, face frozen, stared back at Pat. Then he started laughing. The tension eased as everyone started to laugh, and Pat went back to his place.

There was one other incident that puzzled Pat, making him think that someone, somewhere, had decided that this small party of prisoners knew more than they really did. After their meal at the farmhouse they were taken by lorry to Apeldoorn, where they assembled by a railway siding. Curiously, there was no train available, so they sat down, still under guard, and waited. As they did so, two guards brought another prisoner to join them, an American airman in a pilot's uniform. Pat immediately approached him. He could only have recently been captured and he thought that the airman must have some cigarettes on him. All US servicemen did. As far as Pat was concerned, that was a law of nature. The newcomer had introduced himself as a prisoner, speaking in an American accent, so Pat asked him for a smoke, but the airman was reluctant to give him anything. Pat persisted, until finally the airman pulled out an unopened packet of Lucky Strike cigarettes, opened it and gave one to Pat. Pat tried to persuade him to part with some more, but the American was adamant that he needed them. Pat left him alone, but was sure that something was suspicious. Then he realized that the pilot's uniform was made of very poor-quality material. All the US uniforms he had seen had been well made and looked expensive. He was convinced then that the airman was a fake and he went around his mates muttering, 'He's a Jerry.' The rest of them cottoned on and asked several pointed questions about where he had been captured, where he was based and what he knew of England. The spy quickly realized that the game was up, and when the prisoners were moved along to get into a goods wagon he disappeared. Pat still finds it odd that such effort was spent on questioning ordinary private soldiers like himself, who had by this time been captive for over ten days. Anything they knew was surely by now also well known to the German Army.

After leaving Apeldoorn Pat's train stopped again and the wagons filled with more prisoners. The system for dealing with prisoners of war was clearly in crisis, because the first camp in Germany in which Pat was placed was severely overcrowded. It was Stalag XIIA, near the town of Limburg, and was a transit and processing centre, although some prisoners were kept there for several years. It housed thousands of men at any one time and so inadequate was the accommodation that large, circus-like tents were put up for shelter. It was raining heavily and the whole camp area was a sea of churned-up mud. Pat stayed in a marquee for almost a week. The camp organization had broken down under the pressure of the influx from Arnhem and none of the men in Pat's party was issued with any rations. Their protests at this treatment were in vain because there was nothing coming into the camp. Several days of this made them glad to be put on another train. Crammed once more into goods wagons, they all agreed that wherever they were going couldn't be worse than their present circumstances. Stalag IVB was their next destination, north of Dresden – another huge camp but better organized. They were fed and housed, and entertained by the long-term prisoners, who had organized a concert party.

The relative comfort of this camp didn't last, however, and Pat still felt that for some reason he had been singled out. With a mate from the original burial party at Arnhem and some others from the camp who were strangers to him, he was selected and put on another train. After a long journey they were finally disgorged and marched off. Pat was kept behind, however, and with his mate was driven in the back of a truck to a small town he later learned was called Eisleben, west of Leipzig. As a prisoner he was attached to Stalag XIB, at Fallingbostel, but he never saw it. Instead he was held in a small camp with eighty other British POWs. It was a labour camp and Pat was sent to work in the nearby copper mine, put on twelve-hour shifts and ordered to do the heaviest, dirtiest work at the seam face.

28

THREE MEN IN THE CAGE

October 1944–March 1945

All three men, Ron Jordan, Tom Carpenter and Pat Gorman, would now spend the next seven months in captivity. They were no longer held captive by members of the 9th SS Panzer Division, men who had fought against them and who in the majority of cases treated them with some respect. They were now far behind enemy lines, part of a camp system that was designed to humiliate and degrade, the product of a racist, totalitarian regime.

Tom saw this straight away when he was registered in the camp, in the theatre, although he says he only ever knew this building to be used for interrogations. All the new arrivals, however badly wounded, were forced to stand unaided for several hours until they were called forward in front of seven or eight of the camp's commanders, who were seated behind a desk.

Sometimes the questioning went on for over an hour, sometimes until the prisoner could no longer stand. Everything of value was taken from them, even rings and photographs of wives or girlfriends, and their dressings were searched in case they might be concealing something.

The condition of the Russian prisoners of war was a forceful reminder of how brutal the guards could be. In 1942 a typhus epidemic, coupled with severe malnutrition, had caused the deaths of thousands of Russians in the camp. These prisoners, in a separate compound inside the main camp, were treated like animals and often begged for some of the vile slops that the British prisoners wouldn't eat – a soup made from the green parts of various vegetables that was sometimes doled out. Ron observed that the guards wouldn't bother to enter the Russian barracks and rouse them for the roll call. They would just unleash their vicious guard dogs into the barracks and watch them chase the inmates out on to the parade ground.

In the first few days of their stay, the arbitrary system of food distribution threatened to reduce many of the more disabled British prisoners to starvation. Food was just dumped in dustbin-like containers in the compound to encourage a free-for-all; little effort was made to share it equally. Some of the men from smaller groups of soldiers like the REME tried to look out for each other, but Tom thought that many of the men that he saw were badly demoralized, in shock at their capture, and appeared lethargic and listless.

The situation changed a few days later at the early-morning roll call when, instead of the German guards shouting and hectoring, a penetrating English voice ordered them to 'Get fell in quickly.' Regimental Sergeant Major John Lord of the 3rd Battalion, who had acted as bodyguard to General Urquhart and Brigadier Lathbury during their incursion into Arnhem, was standing on the parade ground. He had been captured on the Thursday, the 21st, and was now in Fallingbostel. Tom didn't know how he had managed it, but he had placed himself in charge of the parade. The German guard commander stood behind him to one side. RSM Lord was ramrod-straight, his arm strapped in a sling with the sleeve of his uniform cut back above the elbow. He called the men to attention. Many mumbled their opposition, but he insisted, repeating the order until the assembled troops obeyed. Then he handed them over to the guard for the roll call. When the guards had finished their counting, he took control of the parade, once more ordering the men to dismiss.

Sergeant Major Lord then started organizing the men in the huts, setting up a more efficient and equitable way of getting the food distributed. They formed themselves into sections of eight, with two men from each section detailed to collect the rations. There was a bowl of meagre soup for everyone and a 1.5 kilo loaf of black bread between eight men.

Tom recalls that the process of dividing up the bread was acutely observed by everybody. Each member of the section would take it in turns to slice up the bread, and this man would be the last to receive his slice. The order in which the others picked out their slice was decided by lots, picking straws or, in Tom's case, drawing playing cards from a pack. Apart from the soup, the prisoners received about a third of a pint of acorn coffee in the morning and the same amount of mint tea in the evening. Tom says that men in a prison camp have to create a totally unique way of life. Everything was scarce and everything was shared, even razor blades or small pieces of soap.

After a while the British airborne troops were moved into a separate compound which had been used to house Polish civilian prisoners from the Warsaw Uprising, which had started in August. There were four huts surrounded by a fence of barbed wire, with guard towers dotted around the edge. Each hut was designed to house 200, but eventually 400 was the norm. Two huts were given over to the British forces, while the other two held American and Canadian prisoners, respectively. The compound had its own parade ground. Lord organized a committee of other non-commissoned officers and morale was gradually restored. The huts were swept with home-made brooms made out of twigs, but no attempts at cleanliness would remove the scourge of lice that infected every prisoner. They were particularly active at night, robbing the men of sleep.

THREE MEN IN THE CAGE

A bizarre black market operated in the camp, naturally, with everything able to be exchanged for anything else. The periodic appearance of Red Cross parcels gave an important boost to this barter system and revealed to Tom how desperate conditions were outside the camp. The first to arrive during his stay were from the US Red Cross and always contained 100 cigarettes. Tom was amazed when he realized the extent to which the guards also saw this as a magnificent opportunity. They smuggled in potatoes or bread – one guard even brought in a frying pan, so desperate was he for real coffee, Spam, chocolate or cigarettes. Tom's group managed to swap fifty cigarettes for a large loaf of civilian bread and some potatoes.

The REME prisoners were also a useful resource in improving conditions. The authorities realized that they were skilled electricians and mechanics, so they were often used to supplement the camp's inadequate maintenance team. Ron was detailed to look at a problem with an electrical circuit in one of the guards' barracks. He saw that it was a simple problem of some poor connections, but convinced the guard that he had to inspect the whole circuit. Over the next two days he managed to 'liberate' some copper wire, which he brought back into his hut wrapped around his body. He and his mates in the REME then used the wire to make some very primitive immersion heaters, with some pieces of metal wired up to the base of a light bulb. Tom thought they were potentially lethal, but they proved to be very effective and brought water to the boil very quickly. Before he had time to find more copper wire and start mass-producing them, the prototype they built in the REME hut had attracted a queue of prisoners and lookouts had to be posted to warn of any German guards approaching. There was one serious disadvantage to these primitive heaters. The prisoners would drop tea leaves or coffee into the boiling water with the element still in it, and the sudden change of resistance would cause the lights to dim. The German guards assumed that this was caused by an illicit radio and would make a raid on the hut searching for it. They never discovered the true cause.

The REME prisoners also came up with another way of heating water which utilized the tins in the Red Cross parcels. A small, four-bladed fan was made out of the bottom of a tin and was rotated with bootlaces. The jet of air it produced was funnelled through a tube, also made out of tin, and was directed at a small pan containing wood shavings or charcoal. It produced intense heat very quickly. The whole thing was mounted on a plank ripped from the bunk beds.

The ingenuity of the prisoners, however, couldn't make up for the poor diet and lack of medical care. The prison hospital housed several hundred badly wounded men who had been brought from Arnhem on a hospital train. Major Smith of the RAMC was in charge of these prisoners and struggling with the extremely poor conditions. There was neither heat nor light, except that provided by paraffin-fuelled hurricane lamps. The operating table was just a scrubbed white table, and there were no anaesthetic or painkillers.

Tom was allowed to visit the hospital every two weeks for treatment to his wound, which was growing worse. It caused him great pain and had become infected, constantly weeping and giving off a putrid smell. Walking was difficult and he had lost the use of his right arm. The medical orderlies in the hospital could do very little except try to clean the wound, then put on another paper bandage. The new dressing was soaked before Tom returned to his own compound.

On one of his visits to the hospital he was told that there were some members of his 9th Field Company in the hospital – Sapper Jack Everitt of 2 Platoon and Sapper Charlie Postans from 3 Platoon. On his next visit he managed to see them. Charlie Postans was covered in bandages and seemed in a very bad way; Tom was told that he had been caught by a flamethrower. Jack Everitt, by comparison, seemed to be fairly well. A few weeks later, however, Sergeant Major Lord announced at the morning roll call that Jack had died of his wounds. If there were any comrades wishing to go to his funeral, they should report to him.

Lord and his group of NCOs had waged a guerrilla war against the camp authorities and won minor concession after minor concession. Funerals of British soldiers were a regular occurrence and Lord had made a Union Jack that was used to cover the plain pine coffin. He had also managed to put together uniforms, which he kept well pressed and clean to issue to the pallbearers, and had battledress to give to a few other mourners.

Tom was far too ill to act as a pallbearer, but he walked painfully behind the coffin to the small cemetery about a mile away. The route passed the huge burial pits where thousands of Russian prisoners had been buried in 1942. There were fifty funerals like this in the seven months that Tom was a prisoner, and they had an effect on the whole camp. Prisoners of every nationality would stand to watch the funeral of a British soldier. Lord was well aware of the power of this ritual. After burying Jack Everitt, Tom was finding it too painful to stand upright. Lord noticed and, as they got to the camp gate, whispered to him, 'Come on, lad, march to attention. Show these people who we are.' The impact of these ceremonies wasn't lost on the Germans either. After a while the camp commandant issued orders that the Union Jack could not be displayed in the camp, but Lord insisted that it was draped over the coffin as soon as it left the main gates. The guards never interfered.

Winter added its own cruelties for the men in the camp. The guards were muffled up against the freezing winds with double topcoats, face protectors and ear muffs to prevent frostbite; the prisoners, however, had just one blanket per man. The nights were bitter, with sub-zero temperatures, and the protracted roll calls in the morning were agony for all of them.

There was a fresh influx of prisoners at this time and it added to the depression that Tom felt. The Germans had launched their offensive against the US front in the Ardennes, and the new American prisoners of war appeared to be evidence of a severe Allied reversal. The German propaganda radio station was kept blaring out in the camp, with its claims of sweeping the Allies back to the sea, and Tom found himself thinking that the war could drag on for years. He might die in captivity.

The pain in his back was now so bad that he was permanently hunched and it was an effort to walk. RSM Lord was still insisting that the men have a daily march around the camp ground. He knew it was good for morale, and the exercise helped keep the men warmer than they would have been lingering in the freezing huts. Tom could now barely manage to make one circuit. He knew he was seriously ill and was on the verge of despair. His one comfort in those times was his comrades, who stayed with him and kept up a steady banter, memories of beef dripping on toast, fish-and-chip suppers, jokes about the guards, and talk of their plans for life when the war was over. But their conversation was becoming more distant and remote, until one day Tom ceased to be aware of them.

He awoke to find himself in the hospital compound, with Major Smith and another medical officer discussing his case with a German officer. They persuaded the camp authorities to get Tom to a civilian hospital in Fallingbostel, where he was given an X-ray, which allowed Major Smith to pinpoint the location of the piece of shrapnel that had lodged deep in Tom's body. The prospect now facing him was alarming. It was remarkable that he had managed to survive this long without suffering from gangrene or some other fatal infection, but the chances that he would continue to do so were very slim. He had reached the end of the line. An operation in the prison hospital with its primitive facilities was equally dangerous, but it had to be endured.

The operating theatre was a room containing a couple of chairs, a cabinet and a white-wood trestle table. Tom had to lie face down on the table and one of the orderlies, nicknamed Butch because he was always carrying amputated limbs, held him down. There was no anaesthetic. Tom felt the scalpel going into his back and then the pain became so severe that for a moment he had a feeling that his mind had left his body, that he was observing himself and the doctors cutting into his back, before he passed out.

He recovered to find himself in a lower bunk, with several wounded US servicemen sharing the room. He was told not to move, because the wound in his back was still open and was being drained. In his hand he had the piece of shrapnel that had hit him with the force of a hurled house brick as he abandoned the deadly position at the road bridge. It was just 1½ inches long and ¾ inch wide.

Tom remained very ill for several weeks. The British medical staff had nothing to combat the infection that had started to spread through his body, and there was nothing they could do but wait as he endured a series of high temperatures that left him weaker and more debilitated each time. Butch fed him small amounts of gruel and drinks of Horlicks obtained from the Red Cross parcels that were sent to the hospital. The huts were smaller and warmer than the main compound, however, and slowly he started to recover.

At the same time as Tom was finally having his operation, Ron Jordan was completing a test to see if he was fit enough to go on an outside working party. He and the rest of a group of about forty had been given the job of digging out some tree roots near to the main camp. It wasn't easy for Ron because the wounds in his ankle and leg were still causing him pain, but he wanted to get sent outside. There were rumours that the rations were better than in the camp and there was much greater opportunity to obtain anything that was in short supply. Ron succeeded in getting selected and was sent to Ulzen, a small town with a railway junction and goods siding.

Their task was to repair the tracks that had been destroyed by Allied bombers. Ron had been put in charge of the group because on the first night they had arrived in the town he had managed to organize the forty hungry prisoners into an orderly queue for the pile of loaves that were thrown into their sleeping quarters. The German *Feldwebel*, or sergeant major, and his guards were almost overwhelmed in the scramble for food and he was happy to give Ron a bayonet to cut up the bread in exchange for holding the prisoners back. From then on they got on well, and the next day when they marched to the railway siding Ron was ordered to take control of a huge steam-powered crane that was used to lift upturned locomotives. He knew nothing about this piece of equipment, but the *Feldwebel* believed that being in the REME gave him the ability to use it. Ron stood there while the driver told him in sign language to keep the fire stoked up, then with a thumb showed Ron where the various needles on the dials needed to be. After this cursory instruction, the driver disappeared. For the next few hours Ron alternately shovelled coke into the boiler and tentatively tested the levers to operate the jib and pulleys. The *Feldwebel* told Ron that he would get a cigarette a day if he managed to work the crane without causing any damage or killing anyone. Ron found it a perfect job. It was warm and he quickly got the hang of keeping the boiler banked up.

The damage that the Allied bombing raids had caused was considerable. A locomotive had been hit and had to be shifted on to the embankment, and a whole section of new rails needed to be lifted into position and laid on the sleepers. Ron wondered what he was going to do when the work was finished, but he needn't have. After three days another air raid took place and the damage was repeated. The work fell into a pattern of bombing, patching up the line, bombing again.

Ron and the rest of the team were sleeping in the town's market hall, which had a stone floor and a badly damaged glass roof. The first raid that took place while they were there was a nighttime one by the RAF. Through the partly open glass roof the prisoners could see the coloured marker flares coming down, then the bombs started falling. More dangerous was shrapnel from the exploding anti-aircraft shells which fell on the roof, bringing shards of glass down on to the prisoners. There were also daylight raids by American B-17 bombers. These happened while they were at work, but they were not allowed into the air-raid shelters; instead they had to remain on top of them. A South Staffordshire rifle-man, Private Wright, was hit in the leg by shrapnel during one of these raids, but nobody was allowed to help him until the raid was over.

After every raid it was their job to sweep up the debris in the streets, but there was a Jewish forced labour group who were given the task of collecting any unexploded bombs on a cart and taking them for disposal. There were limited opportunities for fraternizing with the civilian population; in fact, the locals hated the prisoners. Children threw stones at them and the women spat at them. There wasn't much opportunity for Ron to exchange his extra cigarettes for more food. Even the population at large were taking extreme measures to deal with increasingly severe shortages.

During one particularly heavy raid the town's water main was blown up and Ron and a dozen other prisoners were ordered to take a horse-drawn water bowser to the next village to fill up for an emergency supply. Unfortunately, the villagers had killed the horse some time ago to supplement their meat rations, so the prisoners had the arduous task of manhandling the bowser to the village, then pulling it back to Ulzen full of water. While they were in the next village, Ron met some Polish prisoners who had two fish wrapped in newspapers. They were prepared to exchange them for a cigarette. Ron and his companion from the 156th Battalion were so hungry that they ate every single piece of the fish, including the head and tail.

Pat Gorman had also found that being in a satellite camp some miles from Stalag XIB didn't match up to the rumours, at least not for him. There were other prisoners employed in the mine, but they had all been there for some time. A few of them had been taken into captivity before the evacuation of Dunkirk. Their conditions were much better than that of Pat and his mate, but there was no RSM Lord to establish order and create a sense of solidarity. The long-established prisoners never offered to help Pat. Many of them worked in the mine's offices, or outside, and were able to acquire some extra cigarettes or morsels of food, but none of these were ever shared with Pat and his mate. Next to the camp where he was kept at night was a group of Russians who had been Nazi collaborators. They worked in the nearby fields, growing potatoes and other root crops, but there was almost no fraternization, and none of the vegetables ever found its way into the British compound. All that Pat saw of food was a bowl of very thin soup a day and a piece of bread. Pat started to lose weight quickly.

Their working day was spent down the mine with elderly German workers who hated them. During the months that he worked there, he cut his hand on some machinery and the wound became infected. The resultant swelling started to spread up his arm, so he was allowed to go to a clinic where the Russian workers were treated by local doctors. Held down on a bed, the swelling was immediately lanced by what Pat thought looked like an ordinary tin-opener. It was done so quickly that he had no time to protest or feel the full horror at what was happening. After his hand had been bandaged, he was taken to a small clinic in nearby Eisleben, where a sympathetic German doctor dressed the wound properly. On hearing that he worked down the mine, the doctor tried to keep Pat in the clinic, but the guards were indifferent, as Pat knew they would be. He had heard the slogan 'no work, no food' more times than he could remember. The next day he was back down the mine, his arm bandaged, manhandling skips full of copper ore from the face. Eventually his arm healed, but the back-breaking labour continued day after day.

29

HOME

March–April 1945

Pat Gorman's life behind the wire dramatically improved at the end of March. He had been hearing distant gunfire over the past few weeks, but it had started to come much closer. One morning a German officer paid a visit to the mine and called out all the names of those prisoners who had been sent to work in it. Apprehensive, they lined up and were taken to a different camp. It was clean, with decent blankets on the bunks. It looked as though it had never properly housed any prisoners at all. There were some guards on duty, but there was no roll call, nor any other formality. The German officer directed them to the huts and told them to choose a bunk. Pat believed that this was a model set of huts to be used if there were Red Cross inspections of POW conditions. Whether there was about to be an inspection

Pat didn't care, and neither did his companions. They luxuriated in the space, the decent bunks and the relief of not working down the mine, even if only briefly.

They were not allowed to spend long in the huts, however, but were asked to form up in the small parade ground. There stood a German civilian, badly disabled with the loss of half a leg and an arm. He spoke good English and it turned out that he had been wounded on the Russian front. Now he was dressed in his civilian clothes and asked the prisoners if any of them could cook. He showed them to the kitchens where there were piles of fresh vegetables and even some pieces of meat. He told them that because the war was approaching, he and most of the villagers were leaving. They had to look after themselves.

Pat took charge. He loaded the vegetables and meat into a big boiler and cooked up a stew – it was the best food they had eaten for almost seven months.

Three days later they noticed that the guards had also disappeared, and the sounds of gunfire were very close. Pat and two others went to the gates and opened them. They waited. Was it a trick? Nothing happened. Nobody stopped them, nor opened fire. They stepped into the road, which ran by the side of a small canal, then continued walking along it. The fields seemed deserted. They went on for a few hundred yards, tasting freedom again, well fed and rested for the first time in months, enjoying the sun and the birdsong. Then in the distance they saw a tank.

In the main camp of Stalag XIB at Fallingbostel the situation had been getting worse over the past few weeks. Long lines of prisoners had been arriving as the Germans fled the Russian advance. Subjected to forced marches, the new arrivals were in a bad way, some almost skeletal. There were no facilities in the camp for them. The huts already held 400 men each, so tents were pitched in the parade ground and they lived there as best they could. A group of RAF prisoners arrived early in April suffering from exhaustion and malnutrition. They slept on the ground outside, then the next morning the guards marched them onwards. Later this group was attacked by RAF Typhoons and fifty-six of them were killed along with many of their guards.

One day shortly after that, shells from an 88mm gun battery in the nearby hills passed over the camp. The prisoners hurriedly started ransacking the stores and painted the letters POW in white limewash on the roofs. The camp commandant had already had discussions with RSM Lord about the situation. Lord had demanded that a British prisoner be attached to the guards in case the SS men in the nearby training camp decided to take some last-minute retaliation against the prisoners. The camp commandant had readily agreed. He was more concerned that the Russian prisoners would become emboldened and seek vengeance on the guards. As the war moved closer, and Germany's defeat became clear, the commandant realized that the airborne troops were the most disciplined force in the camp.

A few days after the shells had been fired over Stalag XIB, Tom heard the sound of an aircraft flying low overhead. Looking up, he saw that it was an Army spotter plane. It circled and flew away. A few hours later two low-flying Typhoons roared overhead and fired a salvo of rockets at the battery of 88mm guns.

The number of German guards had gradually diminished as they saw the writing on the wall and deserted, to head west or make their way home if they could. Those that were left were now themselves escorted by two British soldiers, who accompanied them all the time they were in the camp.

On 16 April a British armoured scout car drove up to the camp. It was from the Desert Rats, the 7th Armoured Division. Within the next few hours other British troops arrived and Tom was no longer a prisoner of war.

Field Marshal Montgomery visited the camp the next day. In the theatre, which Tom remembered as the scene of humiliating interrogations, he addressed all those who had crammed into the building to hear him. The prisoners, he said, were to remain where they were while the army continued its advance.

Tom stayed in the camp for another ten days. Then decontamination units arrived and they were deloused before being driven with hundreds of other prisoners to a holding centre in Brunswick. They stayed overnight in a former aircraft factory, unpainted fuselages still hanging in gantries from the ceiling, like a ghostly reminder of the Blitz.

The next day he was shifted again, this time to a former Luftwaffe airbase where he was given a flight number. Dakota aircraft were landing throughout the day and unloading their cargo. The flight number would be called out and thirty men would climb aboard for the return flight to the UK. At seven in the evening, Tom finally boarded his plane. In a few hours he was at Blackbushe aerodrome at Camberley, from where he was taken at midnight to Great Missenden in Buckinghamshire to be debriefed, and given a cup of tea and a poached-egg sandwich.

The next day he started his journey to Birmingham.

Ron Jordan in Ulzen had seen more ominous signs of the impending German defeat. In the last days of the Reich the Nazi regime attempted to mobilize children and old people into militias. It was treasonable to avoid duty in these organizations, as treasonable as desertion, although there were many deserters trickling back from the front line too. The SS and young members of the Hitler Youth acted as vigilante squads, checking on the credentials of everyone they met. If the people questioned couldn't show the correct orders, they carried out instant judgement, and Ron saw their victims hanging from the lamp-posts in the town.

In late March, when the noise of battle sounded closer and closer, the *Feldwebel* in charge of their work party told Ron that it would be better if they moved away. The war would soon be upon them. He was leaving and so were the other guards. They left their uniforms and their weapons. Ron and a handful of the others decided to make a break for it. They took some of the guards' rifles and moved cautiously out of the town. No one stopped them. The population was too concerned with their own safety. The guards had melted away, and so too had the local Nazi Party officials and the SS.

Ron's group decided to move west and after some hours came to a farmhouse. Not only was there an old couple there, but so were their son and his friend, both of whom were deserters and in hiding. The mother was desperately frightened that her son would be discovered by the Gestapo and shot, but she welcomed the British prisoners, Ron believes because she thought they might be a safeguard. They slept in the stables and woke the next morning covered in fleas, which proved as impossible to get rid of as lice. There was almost no food on the farm, as all the animals had been eaten some time ago and no ploughing or sowing could be carried out. There was only some rough bread and stale cheese. They could hear the noise of battle quite close, but saw nothing.

The next day, however, as they looked out over the

fields, they saw a Bren-gun carrier moving towards them. Later a British Army truck arrived and delivered some rations. An officer told them that there was still fighting going on in the area, with armed Hitler Youth occupying a nearby forest, so it would be wiser to move to a village a couple of miles away.

They took his advice and found a small village which lay close to a forest. The main street had been used, in better times, to saw huge logs and there was still a hand-operated bandsaw to cut the logs down the middle. The prisoners decided that they would each occupy one of the houses in the street, so Ron took over the village post office. The postmaster and his wife were still in the building, as was a young Polish servant girl. It seemed to Ron that on his arrival the girl wanted to seek some sort of revenge on the German couple, and he had to hold her off with his rifle.

He made them heat some water and took his first bath for months. The Polish girl washed him, but he couldn't wash his hair because he had to keep her at gunpoint. He asked her to fetch him some of the man's shirts, but they were too small, so the girl cut up a nightdress for him to wear. It had a pattern of small rosebuds on it and frilly short sleeves, but it was the first clean clothing that he had worn since he took off from England. He cared nothing for how it looked.

Ron went with a member of the 156th Battalion on

a tour of the village to see if they could find any food to supplement the army rations they had been given, but there was nothing. Even in the butcher's shop all they could find were two fur coats. Germany, after six years of war, was a wasteland.

After a few days the British Army took them to Celle, where they were billeted in a factory canteen and fed a proper cooked stew. That same day they boarded some Stirling bombers and, sitting uncomfortably on the metal airframe, they were flown to England.

Pat had continued to approach the tank that he and his companions had seen in the distance. Its turret was trained on them as they approached, but Pat could see that it was a US Sherman. As they got closer, the hatch opened and the tank commander appeared. 'Hey,' he said, 'we were gonna shoot you but we figured you were Limeys. You walk like Limeys.' Pat didn't care what he walked like. The crew all climbed out and started to cook up a lunch. They had white bread and steaks which they were frying over a camp stove. Pat couldn't believe his eyes. They were given coffee and a share of the steak, but it was impossible for him to eat it – his body rebelled at the rich food. Later he was taken back to the US HQ and offered some eggs, which he was able to eat, then given a hot shower and shown to a bed with clean sheets. It was the ultimate in luxury.

It took several days for Pat to make contact with

the advancing British Army. He was first taken to a transit camp for displaced civilians – an enormous compound that housed some of the millions of people who had become the human flotsam of a massive, continent-wide war. There was almost nothing there, except rows and rows of tents, with soup kitchens and the most primitive facilities. To Pat it seemed no better than where he had been before. He spent three days in this sea of lost souls before being rescued by a British Army supply convoy. Eventually he was transported to Le Havre in France, where a huge US rest and recreation centre had been established. Here he spent three weeks eating and sleeping. He had lost an enormous amount of weight in the mine, and he believed that the army wanted him to recover from the ravages of slave labour before he went back home. They were fattening him up. He didn't complain.

Pat's composure had been severely tested in the months since he had dropped on to Ginkel Heath at Arnhem, both by the bloody house-to-house fighting and by the rigours of his imprisonment. On his journey to Le Havre he had come across something that was deeply unsettling – as disturbing an experience as anything that had gone before.

He had been picked up from the displaced persons camp in a British truck and the driver had to pass through Celle, where the British Army had set up an administration centre. Travelling along the road, Pat became aware of an awful smell, one that he hadn't experienced since Arnhem. It was the smell of death. He was passing Belsen, originally part of the Fallingbostel prisoner-of-war camp system and once officially known as Stalag XIC. It had been turned into a concentration camp, housing Russian prisoners and evacuees from Auschwitz. When it was liberated by the British Army, 16,000 people had recently died there and the camp was piled with unburied corpses, while thousands of inmates were close to death through starvation and disease. The driver gave Pat a face mask, but it could not block out the smell of putrefaction.

Huge burial pits were being dug, and stick-like figures in striped rags stood around the compound motionless, as though they were human scarecrows. Like the piles of British dead that Pat had helped to bury in Oosterbeek, such a sight could only strike fear into anyone who saw it. There was nothing good left in Pat's world.

His stay in Le Havre was enjoyable, but no amount of food or rest could remove the memories of what he had seen and gone through in the previous eight months.

Tom Carpenter wasn't fattened up before he went home. On the train from Euston he cursed every delay. He arrived at Snow Hill in Birmingham at one o'clock in the morning and was met by a sergeant. Tom had his arm in a sling with the tunic sleeve pinned up. There were taxis available for returning prisoners, but Tom chose to walk. Piles of rubble from bomb damage had been cleared away and wild flowers were growing in the empty bombsites. There was peace. He marvelled at the street lights being on and the shop signs lit up. A policeman stopped him and asked if he wanted any help. He was offered a cup of tea and a sandwich at the local station, and Tom accepted.

After half an hour he went on and knocked at the door of his old home. The lights went on and his father opened the door. His mouth fell open – and then he looked at his son's empty sleeve and his face fell.

'It's OK,' said Tom, 'it's still there.'

Then his mother was hugging him. For months his parents had not known whether he was alive or dead and they had only recently been informed, in a brief letter from the Red Cross who had been supplied with information from the camp hospital, that he was recovering from his injuries. This news had brought both great relief and enormous apprehension. But now at last their son was home.

Ron also got a train back to Birmingham. His departure from the reception centre was delayed because of his previous record of service with the Fleet Air Arm, and he had to wait two days before his membership of the REME and his capture at Arnhem could be explained. He wasn't offered a taxi at the station, though if he had been he would certainly have taken it. The new boots with which he had been issued were causing a problem. The high boot top on his left foot was aggravating his wounded ankle, and after a few hours he could barely walk. He had undone the boot on the train, caught a bus at the station and then had to walk for about a quarter of an hour to the family house. After a couple of hundred yards he was in agony, so he took the boot off. He arrived home in one boot and a sock.

Ron's mother had died when he was fourteen and his elder brother had cared for him in the family home. Most of his brothers and sisters had left to join the forces, but his brother Len, his wife and their young son had moved in after their own house was bombed. They had received a telegram just an hour or so before Ron's arrival saying that he was in the country and his sister-in-law was telling all the neighbours that he was expected back. He saw her standing on the pavement and she rushed to meet him. She offered him a cup of tea, but Ron realized how exhausted he was. He wanted nothing but to go and lie in his own bed, and sleep for as long as he wanted.

Pat flew from Le Havre in a Dakota, and when he landed in the UK he was deloused again and given a medical to make sure that he wasn't carrying any infectious diseases. He was presented with a new uniform and a travel warrant, and a six-weeks' leave pass, as well as some of his nine months' back pay. He took a train to Workington. All the time that he was travelling from Germany to Le Havre and then on the train, he never felt at ease until he got to Workington station. Then at last he knew he was safe. He sat on a bench on the platform and for the first time he cried. Tears streamed down his face – in relief at being alive, at being back in England, and for all the horrors that he had seen and felt since the day he had landed at Arnhem. After ten minutes he stood up, slung his kitbag on his shoulder and went out of the station.

His parents had received only one telegram from the War Office since he had been captured in September. It said that he was missing in action. Pat can still quote the words: 'He may be a prisoner, or he may be elsewhere, but if after three months nothing more is heard, then you must assume that he has been killed.' His mother received no more letters or telegrams, but Pat's name had been mentioned in a broadcast from a German propaganda radio station known as Mary of Arnhem. This was all the indication she had that Pat was a prisoner, but it was enough to keep hope alive. Now, with stories in the newspapers and on the BBC about all the prisoners flying home, every day that passed without any further news of her son took a little bit of that hope away.

Pat stood at the front door and lifted the knocker. The door opened and his mother stood there, and Pat knew, as he saw her, knew instantly that deep down she had believed the worst. She could hardly believe now that all her hopes had come true. Her son was alive and he had come home.

AFTERWORD

Tom, Pat and Ron returned home, but despite their wounds and their poor physical condition they remained in the army. After his long leave Tom went to a camp in Hatfield, from where he was eventually discharged in 1946. Ron went to what he calls a 'quiet little billet' in an army camp near Nottingham. It was conveniently located close to a hospital, where he went every month for treatment to his badly damaged ankle. He was discharged in July 1946. Pat was ordered overseas once more, to serve in Palestine, until he too was discharged in 1947.

All three then went into jobs in the various engineering industries in Manchester and the Midlands. Ron enjoyed flying and parachuting too much to abandon it, however, and remained in the Territorial Army, attached first to the 16th Airborne Division and then to 23 SAS. Subsequently he took

over a pub – not the small country inn of some
people's retirement dreams, but the largest licensed
premises in Birmingham – and did very well. Their
lives have been marked indelibly by the fighting at
Arnhem, but they consider themselves lucky. They
survived.

The personal cost of Operation Market Garden is
obvious. The Airborne Corps as a whole had 11,000
casualties, as many as the British and American losses
on the first day of the Allied landings in Normandy.
At Arnhem, almost 6,000 British troops were taken
prisoner, and 1,485 men died. Around 400 Dutch
civilians were also killed in the fighting.

No sooner had the German troops moved into
Oosterbeek on that final day than they started
to round up all the civilians and ordered them to
evacuate the area. Ten thousand people were force
marched out of their towns and villages and prevented from returning to their homes until after the
war. Over 300 houses in Oosterbeek and Arnhem had
been destroyed in the fighting, but this wasn't the end
of it. The German Army removed 8,000 doors to
create a network of defensive trenches along the
Rhine and the empty houses were left open to
the elements and looters. The area was turned into a
no-man's-land and the Dutch civilians, when they
came home, confronted utter desolation. The road
bridge, which Tom and others in John Frost's small
band had fought so bravely to hold on to, was
destroyed by Allied bombers at the start of another

offensive across the Rhine. The one that stands there now – rebuilt on the original pillars, which still bear the marks of bullets and shrapnel – is called the John Frost Bridge.

Arnhem today has become almost a byword for courage and determination, the dogged bravery of a small group of British troops against overwhelming odds. It has also become associated with the phrase 'a bridge too far', the title of the feature film about Operation Market Garden, with its implication that the operation was doomed from the start – a careless, madcap scheme akin to the charge of the Light Brigade. This is misleading. The lives that were lost in the combined airborne landings and the ground advance by the Second Army were not thrown away on a whim. The aim was to end the war quickly. The operation was designed to outflank the German defensive wall along their border, cut off the German Fifteenth Army in the west of Holland and encircle the Ruhr, isolating this massive industrial centre from the rest of Germany. Behind these strategic objectives was Montgomery's desire to maximize British influence before her contribution to the war effort was eclipsed by that of her Allies. The stakes, then, were very high.

Immediately after the end of Market Garden people tried to put the best possible gloss on it. Churchill claimed that the battle had been a decisive victory. Montgomery wrote that it had been 90 per cent successful, on the basis that his troops had advanced over 90 per cent of the terrain envisaged by the plan. This is as absurd as is the description of the plan being 'a bridge too far'. Brigadier Hackett pointed out that either the operation succeeded in all its aims or else it failed: 'If you did not get all the bridges, it was not worth going at all.' This is true. There was no room for half-measures in Operation Market Garden. It either succeeded in its objectives, or it didn't, and the strategic objectives were very clear cut.

The truth is that the operation was a failure. The German western defences were not outflanked. The Ruhr was not isolated, and the German Army in Holland was able to pass back into Germany. Instead, the Allies were left with a deep salient extending 60 miles into Holland, which it took several divisions to hold and secure during a bitter and debilitating winter. The failure to liberate the whole of Holland meant that the Dutch population in the western provinces were at the mercy of the German occupying forces. In response to a Dutch train drivers' strike, the Germans placed an embargo on the transport of food. This, combined with the frozen canals and the German tactic of flooding much of the low-lying land, meant that the population of Amsterdam and the western provinces of Holland experienced famine. The 'Hunger Winter', as it became known, saw 10,000 people die of malnutrition in the winter of 1944/5.

British influence did wane after Market Garden,

and at the Yalta Conference between Stalin, Roosevelt and Churchill, Roosevelt made many concessions to Stalin against Churchill's wishes. The failure of Operation Market Garden contributed to the shape of post-war Europe for a generation to come. This is not a gross exaggeration. Eisenhower wrote to his senior officer two days before the start of Market Garden, 'We shall soon I hope be in possession of the Ruhr, the Saar and the Frankfurt area. Clearly Berlin is the main prize.' A great deal was riding on Operation Market Garden, and it did not deliver.

The failure was nothing to do with the commitment of the men on the ground. What more could be asked of men like Tom, Pat and Ron, or the courageous men of the US 504th Regiment, who paddled across the Waal? The great failure lay in the planning and the absurdly short amount of time devoted to the preparation of an immensely complicated operation. Time, or its lack, was the one element that led to the cumulative errors and obstacles that contributed to the defeat at Arnhem. Unlike the D-Day landings, which were meticulously planned for months in advance, Market Garden was mounted in haste. Because of this, compromises were made which proved fatal. Nearly every error occurred because of a lack of time for proper planning. Market Garden was a gamble for a glittering prize, but it was hastily cobbled together from a plan, Operation Comet, which many believed would also have proved a disaster.

With proper planning, the lack of air support from the RAF and, more importantly, effective procedures for requesting it might have been solved. Mechanisms for direct communication between the soldiers fighting the battle and support aircraft and their bases did not exist. Lack of planning meant that reconnaissance was imperfect and intelligence was flawed. The existence of the Heveadorp ferry, a still functioning crossing, was unknown to Urquhart's staff at a time when it could have provided a crucial way to get troops across to the southern end of the road and rail bridges. Hasty staff work led to confusion over whose job it was to secure the rail bridge. The radios issued to the airborne troops and which failed were known to be unreliable, yet they were still used, even though the distances involved in the operation exceeded their range. The decision to make two separate airlifts, and to land the airborne troops so far from their objectives, was a key contribution to the destruction of the three brigades as they made their way to the bridge at Arnhem. Landing all three airborne divisions in a single drop, denying the Germans time to react and organize their defences, would have quickly secured the bridges at Nijmegen and Arnhem. More time would have created better coordination and a staff structure that would have urged more speed on XXX Corps as it advanced. Surely senior officers, experienced as they were, would, with more planning and more time, have ironed out the fatal flaws in Operation Market Garden.

This is the conventional view – but it overlooks the fact that there was no time. Winter was approaching, the supply lines from the D-Day ports were stretched to breaking, and Montgomery, the army and the empire had no more resources left to enlarge their role in the battle for Europe. It was now or never. There wasn't the luxury of time to plan Operation Market Garden properly, because lack of time was the operation's justification. Behind it all was the need to move quickly, while the Germans were on the run, while Montgomery had Eisenhower's agreement for this plan, and while the commitment of British forces was still sufficient to affect the balance of power between the Allies. Market Garden was ultimately an attempt to seize not bridges but time, before it ran out.

This begs the question of what would have happened had the operation succeeded in its aims. Would the world have been different if the bridge at Arnhem had been held, if XXX Corps' tanks had rumbled across it, if Ron, as he fully expected, had joined up with the rest of the REME units to set up a workshop in Apeldoorn? Could the breakthrough, if it had occurred, really have been exploited, in the way that Montgomery wanted, to bring the war to an end before Christmas?

The answer to that question lies in the failure of Operation Market Garden itself. The operation was based all along on the single belief that German resistance was crumbling; but sadly, even as the aircraft and gliders took off and assembled over southern England, that assessment was proving to be over-optimistic. German generals had already started, with great flexibility and urgency, to stop the collapse of their forces in the west. This was, of course, one of the reasons why the troops at Arnhem were unable to consolidate their hold on the bridges, and one of the reasons why XXX Corps took so long to advance through Eindhoven and Nijmegen to Arnhem.

The German Air Force and Navy, as well as numerous rear-echelon forces, were being drawn on to create new units, and even if the bridge at Arnhem had been taken and held, this process would not have stopped. Ad hoc German units under the direction of a professional corps of officers fought successfully at Arnhem and would have fought on to defend their fatherland. The British Second Army was at the very limits of its supply chain, and it is questionable how far it could have advanced beyond Arnhem without the freeing up of the ports at Rotterdam. The war might have been very different had Market Garden succeeded, but it is unlikely to have been finished by Christmas.

At this point, however, speculation has to end. The hindsight of almost seventy years is worthless, and at the memorials of Arnhem the urgent strategic imperatives of the time fade and are forgotten. What stays vibrant in the minds of those remembering, as well as the courage and fortitude, is the damage done, both physical and mental, to those who survived and the tragedy of those whose lives were cut short, who paid with their blood the price of a grand scheme that went wrong. These are the important things, these are the things that should not be forgotten.

BIBLIOGRAPHY

Clark, Lloyd. *Arnhem*, Headline Review, London, 2008.

Frost, Major General John, CB, DSO, MC. *A Drop Too Many*, Cassell, London, 1980.

Hackett, General Sir John. *I Was a Stranger*, Chatto & Windus, London, 1977.

Kershaw, Robert. *It Never Snows in September*, Ian Allen, Hersham, Surrey, 1994.

Middlebrook, Martin. *Arnhem 1944*,Viking, London, 1994.

Piekalkiewicz, Janus, trans. H. A. and A. J. Baker. *Arnhem 1944*, Ian Allen, London, 1977.

Powell, Geoffrey. *The Devil's Birthda*y, Leo Cooper, Barnsley, 1992.

Pronk, Patrick. *Airborne Engineers*, RN Signal Publishing, Renkum NL, 2001.

Ryan, Cornelius. *A Bridge Too Far*, Hodder & Stoughton, London, 1974.

Urquhart, Major General R. E., CB, DSO. *Arnhem*, Cassell, London, 1958.

Waddy, John. *A Tour of the Arnhem Battlefields*, Leo Cooper, Barnsley, 1999.

Unit War Diaries *pegasusarchive.org*

Unpublished accounts

Major Jack Winchester, 9th Field Company

Colonel Eric O'Callaghan, 9th Field Company

Picture Acknowledgements

IWM = Imperial War Museum
Credits run from top left clockwise.

Section one

Tom Carpenter in uniform: courtesy Tom Carpenter; Pat
Gorman in uniform: courtesy Pat Gorman; Ron Jordan in
parachute gear: courtesy Ron Jordan; portraits of the men
in 2010: all Rod Shone

Loading a jeep onto a Horsa glider, 22 April 1944:
IWM/37692; troops of the 1st Airborne Division
emplaning, 17 September 1944: IWM/K 7588; paratroopers are dropped near Grave, 17 September 1944:
Lightroom Photos/US Army/Topfoto; US first two gliders
to touch down, 17 September 1944: IWM/BU1164: paratroopers inside a C-47, 17 September 1944; IWM/7570

Men of the 2nd Battalion South Staffordshire Regiment enter Oosterbeek, 18 September 1944: IWM/BU 1091; troops at Wolfheze, 18 September 1944: IWM/BU 1144; German soldiers taken prisoner, 18 September 1944: IWM/BU 1159; Major General Friedrich Kissin, killed in ambush, 17 September 1944: IWM BU 1155; German tank, St Annastraat, Nijmegen, 17 September 1944: Regionaal Archief Nijmegen/F67736; Loyd carrier explodes during XXX Corps' advance up the Eindhoven road, 17 September 1944: IWM/B 10122A

Aerial view of the bridge: © 2003 Topham Picturepoint/ Topfoto.co.uk; 75mm howitzer in Oosterbeek perimeter, 20 September 1944: IWM BU 1101; British soldiers on a Sherman tank, Nijmegen, 19 September 1944: Regionaal Archief Nijmegen/ F35244; passing through Eindhoven, 17–18 September 1944: IWM/BU 945; Pat Gorman: courtesy Pat Gorman; damaged German Renault tank on the Utrechtsweg, 19–20 September 1944: Bundesarchiv, Bild 101I-590-2331-06; German soldiers with an anti-aircraft gun, Arnhem, 17–25 September 1944: Bundesarchiv, Bild 101I-497-3508-12

German tank in a street, Arnhem, September 1944: Bundesarchiv, Bild 101I-497-3529-03; German troops, Arnhem, September 1944: Bundesarchiv Bild 101I-497-3531A-31; Arnhem street, September 1944: © 2004 Topfoto/AP/TopFoto.co.uk; wrecked German vehicles in front of St Elisabeth Hospital, Arnhem, 17–25 September

1944: © Interfoto/Alamy; road bridge, Arnhem, 17–25 September 1944: IWM/HU2127

Section two

General Horrocks, Field Marshall Montgomery and Prince Bernhard of the Netherlands, 8 September 1944: IWM/BU 000766: Major General R. E. Urquhart, September 1944: © 2004 Topfoto/ TopFoto.co.uk; Lt Col John Frost (centre), and Lt Col Johnny Goschen: IWM/H 17349; Generalfeldmarschall Walter Model, Generaloberst Kurt Student, Generalmajor Wilhelm Bittrich, Major Hans Peter Knaust, Generalmajor Heinz Harmel, September 1944: Bundesarchiv Bild 146-1971-033-49; General Model, September 1944: © Roger-Viollet/Topfoto

British airborne troops holding British HQ, 18 September 1944: IWM/BU 1143; German self-propelled gun, Arnhem, 19 September 1944: Bundesarchiv, Bild 101I-497-3530-34A; German troops pinned down on the Utrechtsweg, 20 September 1944: Bundesarchiv Bild 101I-497-3528-14A; paratroopers in action with 3-inch mortars, September 1944: © Topfoto/TopFoto.co.uk

3-inch mortar team in action, 21 September 1944: IWM/BU 1099; allied tanks cross the Nijmegen bridge, 24 September 1944: © Topham Picturepoint/TopFoto.co.uk; 6-pounder anti-tank gun, Arnhem, 20 September 1944:

INDEX

445

Target Basra

Mike Rossiter

IN THE DEAD of night on 20 March 2003, Royal Navy Marines from 40 and 42 Commando board a fleet of 20 helicopters, about to undertake an audacious night-time airborne assault against heavily defended enemy positions. They'll be the first troops on the ground, and the first men to suffer casualties in the war against Saddam Hussein.

Burdened with the task of capturing the oil pipelines and pumping stations of Iraq and sealing off the whole of the al-Faw peninsular, the marines endure the battle only to be thrust into conflict with tanks, Ba'ath Party Fedayeen and Republican Guards as they move north towards their ultimate goal: Basra.

Told from the perspective and with the co-operation of officers and men in the Royal Navy and the Royal Marines, *Target Basra* is a story of courage, fortitude and the harsh realities of modern war, set amidst the turmoil of the Middle East.

'Fast-paced with relentless battle action, this is the superb story of the unsung heroes of the war in Iraq'
NEWS OF THE WORLD

9780552157001

Bomber Flight Berlin

Mike Rossiter

FLYING LANCASTER BOMBERS was one of the most dangerous missions of the war. Yet night after night Flight Lieutenant Geoffrey King and the crew of C Charlie risked their lives in the skies over Germany. Together they faced incredible dangers, flak damage, close encounters with the fighter planes of the Luftwaffe, and crash landings.

Against this background a friendship was formed that bound the crew of C Charlie together against all odds.

Geoffrey King and the crew of C Charlie are unique in having flown together for fifty missions and in living to tell the tale. *Bomber Flight Berlin* is the story of a group of ordinary men, from different walks of life, thrown together by the forces of war. It is the story of those missions above Berlin, as they flew into what seemed certain death, and aircraft all around them were blasted out of the sky. It is also a testament to a remarkable friendship.

> *'A testimony to the lifelong bond often forged by the intensity of combat'*
>
> SPECTATOR

9780552162326

I Sank The Bismarck

Mike Rossiter and John Moffat

MAY 1941, THE pilots of fifteen canvas-covered biplanes struggled to hold their Swordfish aircraft steady as they aimed towards the German battle-ship *Bismarck*. They flew low over a wind-wracked ocean, aiming their torpedoes, totally vulnerable in their open cockpits. If they failed now *Bismarck* would escape to safety.

Among these brave flyers was a young Sub-Lieutenant in the Fleet Air Arm, John Moffat. Only years later was John told that it was his torpedo that had prevented the *Bismarck* from outrunning her Royal Navy pur-suers.

I Sank the Bismarck is a personal story of a carefree young boy, raised in the Borders, growing up to join a fledgling Fleet Air Arm. It's the story of a young pilot, living for the moment, facing war, and taking part in one of the most important battles at sea ever fought by Britain and the Royal Navy.

> 'Ranks among the very finest moments of Fleet Air Arm
> and Royal Navy history'
> NAVY NEWS

9780552159487